IMAGES
of America

BISHOPVILLE AND LEE COUNTY

On the Cover: Members of Bishopville's volunteer fire department prepare to ride in the dedication parade for the town's new post office in June 1940. From left to right are fire chief Rob McCutchen, Will Hearon, Jeff Stuckey, Melisha M. Levy, John O'Kelley, Vern Hearon, Carroll Reames, George O'Kelley, engineer Marshall Wilson, and Rob McCutchen Jr. The truck is parked in front of Aubrey Wilson's Main Street Texaco. (Bishopville Fire Department.)

IMAGES
of America

BISHOPVILLE AND LEE COUNTY

Rachael Bowman Bradbury
and William P. Baskin III

ARCADIA
PUBLISHING

ISBN 978-0-7385-8643-4

Published by Arcadia Publishing
Charleston SC, Chicago IL, Portsmouth NH, San Francisco CA

Printed in the United States of America

Library of Congress Control Number: 2010924655

For all general information contact Arcadia Publishing at:
Telephone 843-853-2070
Fax 843-853-0044
E-mail sales@arcadiapublishing.com
For customer service and orders:
Toll-Free 1-888-313-2665

Visit us on the Internet at www.arcadiapublishing.com

To the memory of my great-grandfather, the late Joseph F. Stuckey, whose tireless efforts at recording the history of his birthplace are not forgotten. And with love to my daughters, Rebekah and Sarah Martin.

—R. B. B.

Dedicated to the memory of my late father, Sen. William P. Baskin Jr., who continues to inspire my love of history.

—W. P. B.

Contents

ACKNOWLEDGMENTS

We did not write this book alone but depended on the assistance of many individuals. Whether they donated photographs or simply provided information, this help was invaluable.

First and foremost we thank Judith Austin Watkins, without whose help this would not have gotten off the ground. In addition, we are grateful for the assistance of the South Carolina Cotton Museum (SCCM) and its director, Janson Cox, and to Melissa Brundage, to the *Lee County Observer*, and to the Lee County Historical Society.

We express our gratitude to Barrie Cunningham Hardwick, who brought in an old box of "stuff" that turned out to be an absolute treasure chest, and to Betsy Redick of Florence who shared her wealth of Lynchburg photographs.

Our sincere thanks go to Dr. Dale Rosengarten, Alyssa Neely, and Dr. Joseph Rubin at the College of Charleston's Special Collections for sharing their knowledge, opinions, and photographs.

And to everyone else who was involved: Ella Levenson Schlosburg, Leonard Levenson, Carolyn Levenson, Retta Tindal, Jennie Krasnoff Caine, Louise McCutchen, Ralph DesChamps, Margery Jeffords, Frances Ginsberg, and Sally Ginsberg Waters, Carrie Gass, Bernice Bradley, Robert and June Jennings, Don Melton, Cile Stuckey, Susan and Don Mathis, Bruce and Dot Smith, Leo DuBose Jr., John Reames, Jack and Ruth Shuford, Christine Shirley, the Bishopville Fire Department, Laura Kirk at Lee State Natural Area, Billie Steele Caldwell, Charles Gallun, Fran Gallun, Wayne Davis, Karen Melton Stevens, Elizabeth Massey Booth, and Henry Pittman.

Rachael would like to thank her parents, C. W. and Ruthie (Stevenson) Bowman, for the hours of babysitting, room, and board while she traveled to and from Bishopville. Additional thanks to her mother for being an encyclopedia of Bishopville knowledge, always on-call. She also wishes to thank her husband, John Charles, and her daughters, Rebekah and Sarah Martin, for their love and support and most of all their patience over the last year.

Unless otherwise noted, all images appear courtesy of the authors.

INTRODUCTION

The origins of Lee County lie in Craven County, which once consisted of all the territory north of the Santee River and east of the Broad River down to the South Carolina coast. In 1785, the state created Claremont and Salem Counties, both of which are now a part of Lee County. In 1798, these two counties were consolidated along with Clarendon into the Sumter District.

On December 4, 1786, 465 acres of land was granted by the State of South Carolina to Jacob Chambers. Chambers sold the land to Daniel Carter, who sold it to Jonathan Newman, who sold it to William Singleton in 1793. This tract of land, which remained undivided and became known as Singleton's Crossroads, composes the heart of the present town of Bishopville.

A famous description of life at Singleton's Crossroads in 1814 was given by the Reverend James Jenkins, an early Methodist circuit preacher, who recalled the area's depravity in his 1842 memoirs, *The Experiences, Labours, and Sufferings of Rev. James Jenkins of the South Carolina Conference:*

> What is now called Bishopville was then called Cross Roads, owned by an old woman, whose name was Singleton. . . .The old woman above-named kept an establishment, for which it would be hard to find a name. Here they would get drunk, quarrel, fight, dance, and commit murder; and the most of these they kept up day and night, Sunday not excepted. . . . As I passed one Sunday morning, I saw the drunken men lying about like dead hogs; some in the road, and others on the piazza.

In 1821, after the death of Frances Singleton, Dr. Jacques Bishop purchased the original Chambers tract from her estate. At this location, he formed a partnership with Columbus C. Campbell and John M. Gilchrist. By 1824, a post office at Bishopville had been established, and by the early 1830s, the settlement was described as a "charming and flourishing place" with a population of more than 150. Perhaps the demise of the tavern resulted in the rise of civilization.

While Bishop's origins are unclear, it is generally assumed he came to South Carolina from Pennsylvania. Regardless of his provenance, his marriage to Penelope Benton Brockington on November 29, 1803, aligned him with the upper crust of Pee Dee gentility. Penelope Brockington's family had prominent roots in the district; her father, Lemuel, was a Revolutionary War patriot and the Pee Dee District's first representative to the U.S. House of Representatives.

C. C. Campbell and Company remained in business until 1838 when it was forced to make assignment of all its assets at a sheriff's sale. The company dealt largely in cotton and took heavy losses in 1836 and 1837, and these, combined with the bank panic of 1837, may have made bankruptcy inevitable. Bishop lost all of his property, which had become quite extensive.

It was not until the railroad arrived in 1887 that the town saw significant growth—so significant, in fact, that the Town of Bishopville was incorporated in 1888. In the August 15, 1888, edition of the *Bishopville Enterprise*, editor Shepard Nash remarked: "Every store in town unoccupied is being renovated and prepared for occupancy this fall—a big boom is beginning in Bishopville."

The Town of Lynchburg, incorporated in 1905, lay approximately 20 miles south of Bishopville on the Old Mecklenburg Road, which led from Georgetown to Charlotte. In 1781, a skirmish between the British and Gen. Francis Marion's army occurred in the area. The "Swamp Fox" overtook the enemy in a grove of willow trees, and the nearby settlement took on the name Willow Grove. In 1851, the village took the same name as the train depot, Lynchburg. Both Sen. Ellison DuRant "Cotton Ed" Smith and Gov. Thomas G. McLeod were Lynchburg natives.

Lucknow was established in 1889 when the Bridges and McKeithen Lumber Company started a large timber-cutting operation in the area. Legend has it that the abundance of timber led one of the men to exclaim, "We have hit luck, now!" It was partially thanks to the timber company that telephone service was established in Bishopville. The men employed Dr. J. E. McClure as their physician, and a telephone line was erected between his home and the lumber company office. McClure's telephone number remained "1" until 1959.

Families had settled the Elliott area by the late 1700s. In a 1902 campaign speech in Bishopville, Col. William Elliott thanked the crowd by saying he was proud that the town of Elliott was named after him. In the early part of the 20th century, Elliott was a thriving little town with a hotel, bank, drugstore, furniture store, and other businesses that served the farming community.

For years there had been talk of forming a new county in the Pee Dee, and on October 22, 1901, an election was held to determine whether or not a new county should be formed. On February 25, 1902, the South Carolina General Assembly passed an act to make the formation of the new county possible; later that year on December 1, the South Carolina Supreme Court ruled that all requirements for the formation of Lee County had been met.

Bishopville had become a major shipping point for cotton. The back lots of stores were full of horses and buggies, and Main Street was congested with folks who had come to town on a Saturday evening. If things got out of hand, it was nothing a night in the drunk tank could not cure.

Bishopville was also a regular stop for the Redpath Chautauquas. And the state fair had nothing on the Lee County Fair with its rides, displays, and famous sulky races. Bishopville, and even the small communities in the surrounding countryside, had restaurants, drugstores, department stores, and banks. Entertainment might consist of following the fire truck or riding to town perched atop a wagonload of cotton. Young people swam and danced at Denny's Pool or Doc Ackerman's. Children could escape into the dark cool of the Andrews Theatre on a Saturday and stop by McLeod's for a Pepsi. The rich smell of the oil mill blanketed the town on a warm fall evening. In 1923, Marie Elizabeth Tedder, favorite Bishopville High School English and history instructor, was moved to write the following verse, which appeared in that year's *The Bishop* annual:

You cannot boast of millions
That reside within your walls;

You're not a busy mart,
or even a sight for Wisdom's halls;

No Charter Oak your soil has grown,
No Lincoln can you claim;

No King of Commerce yet produced,
To glorify your name

You cannot boast a Plymouth Rock
a Washington or Lee

But, Bishopville, my own home town,
you're good enough for me.

Hopefully, the images on the following pages will bring back these memories and bring inspiration for renewal to those who see them.

One

Changing Main Street

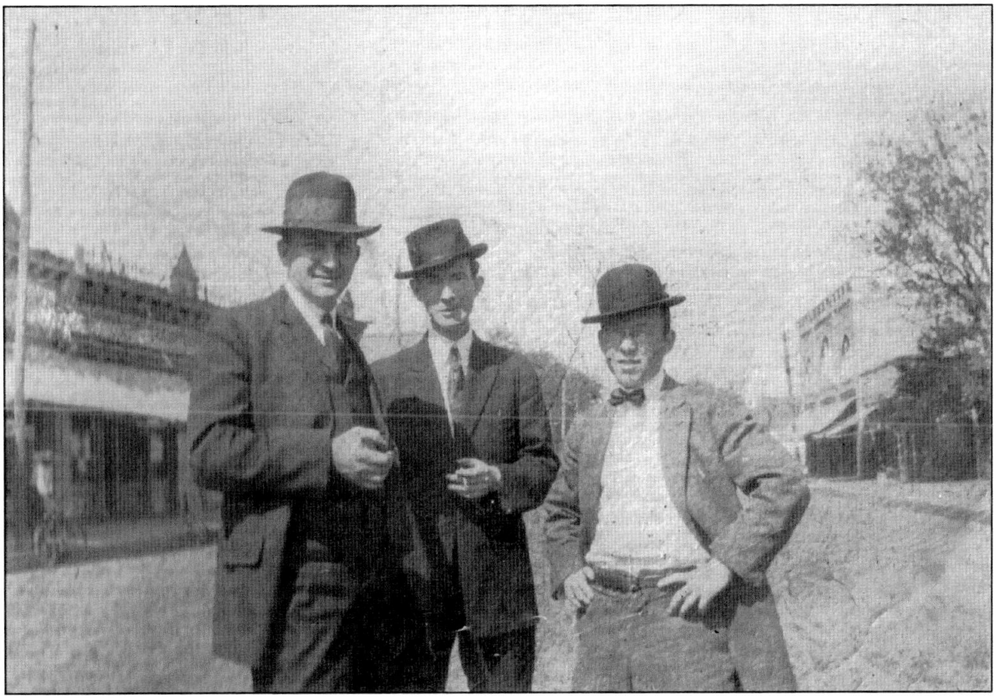

Downtown businessmen take a break from work in the middle of Main Street around 1913. From left to right, they are English McCutchen, J. F. (Joe) Stuckey Sr., and G. W. (Gus) Woodham Sr. The McLure Building, which once housed the infirmary of Dr. Harvey McLure, is visible to the far right. In 1918, Stuckey and Woodham began a business relationship as Stuckey and Woodham, Inc., dealing in real estate, insurance, and securities. Even though Woodham sold his shares to finance his own insurance agency, the name Stuckey and Woodham endured until the 1960s when the business became known as Stuckey and Alexander. (Ruthie Stevenson Bowman.)

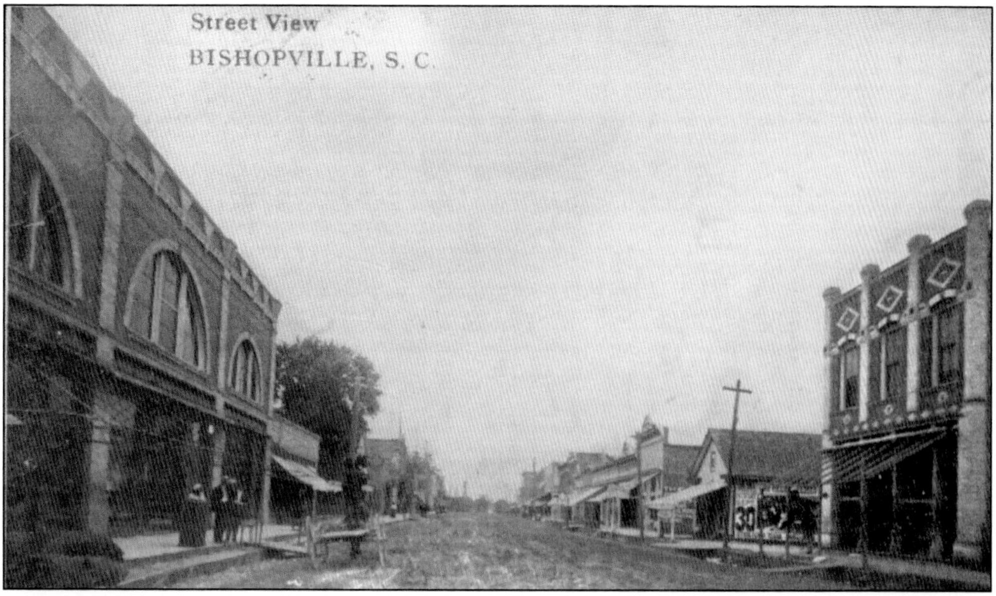

Wooden buildings and vacant lots are still prevalent in this *c.* 1902 photograph of Main Street. This view looks south from the railroad tracks, and the steeple of the old wooden Presbyterian church is faintly visible on the horizon. The building to the near left stands today as the Easy Living furniture store. In the early 1900s, it served as Dr. McLure's Infirmary. (Barrie Cunningham Hardwick.)

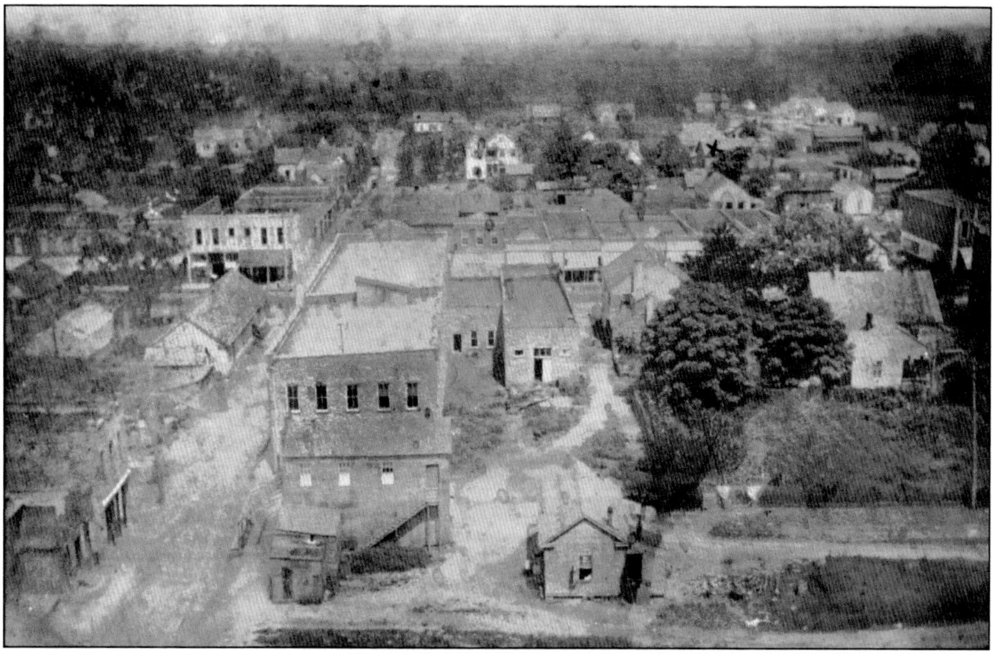

This aerial view of downtown Bishopville from the early 1900s was taken from the water tower and shows the intersection of Main and Council Streets. The brick building in the right foreground predates the former Lee Hotel and burned in 1915. It housed a grocery and a dry goods store. On the other corner sits a wooden clapboard general store that would soon be torn down to make way for the Bank of Bishopville building. On the opposite corner across Main Street is the building that would be known as Mack's in the 1950s. (*Lee County Observer.*)

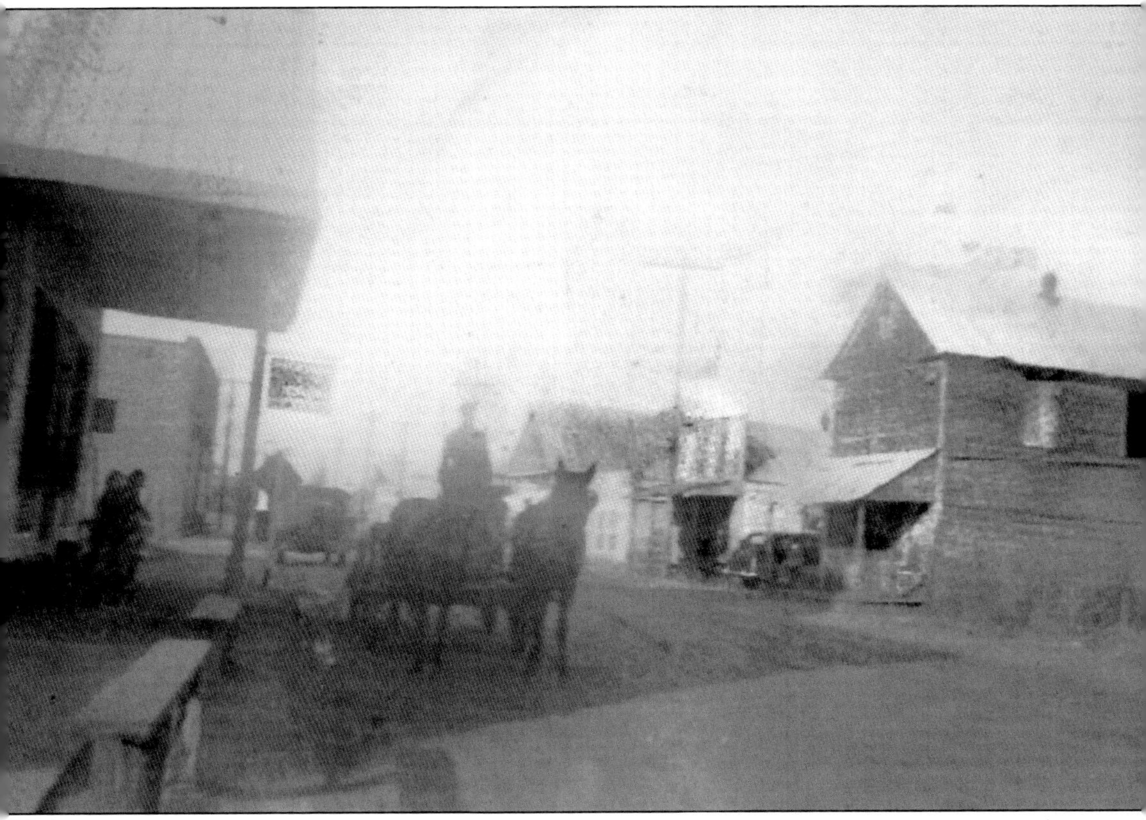

Horses pull a farmer and his cart through downtown Elliott around 1938. At one time, the community thrived under the farming industry and was home to general stores, a movie theater, a hotel, and its own schools. (Retta Dickinson Tindal.)

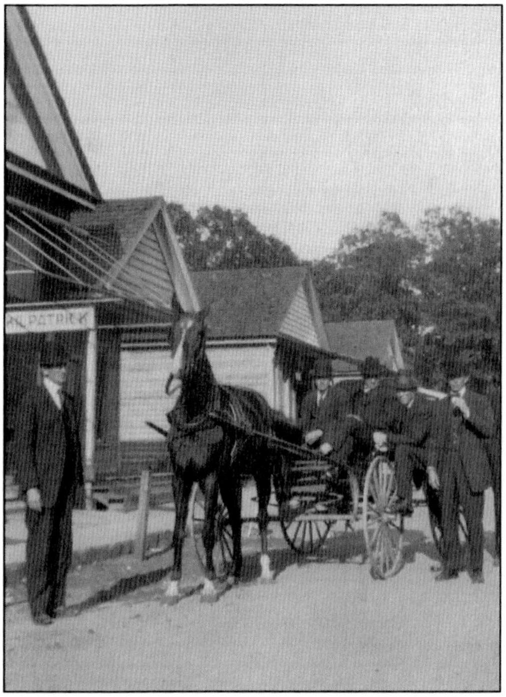

Seen here is a *c.* 1910 photograph of downtown Lynchburg. The State of South Carolina's original charter for the Lynchburg community was issued December 22, 1859. Railroad tracks had been laid through town a few years earlier, and the depot was named Lynchburg. Nearby settlements, formerly known as Willow Grove and Magnolia, were encompassed by the newly named community. By 1883, Lynchburg had six stores, and the nearby settlement of Magnolia had seven. (Betsy Redick.)

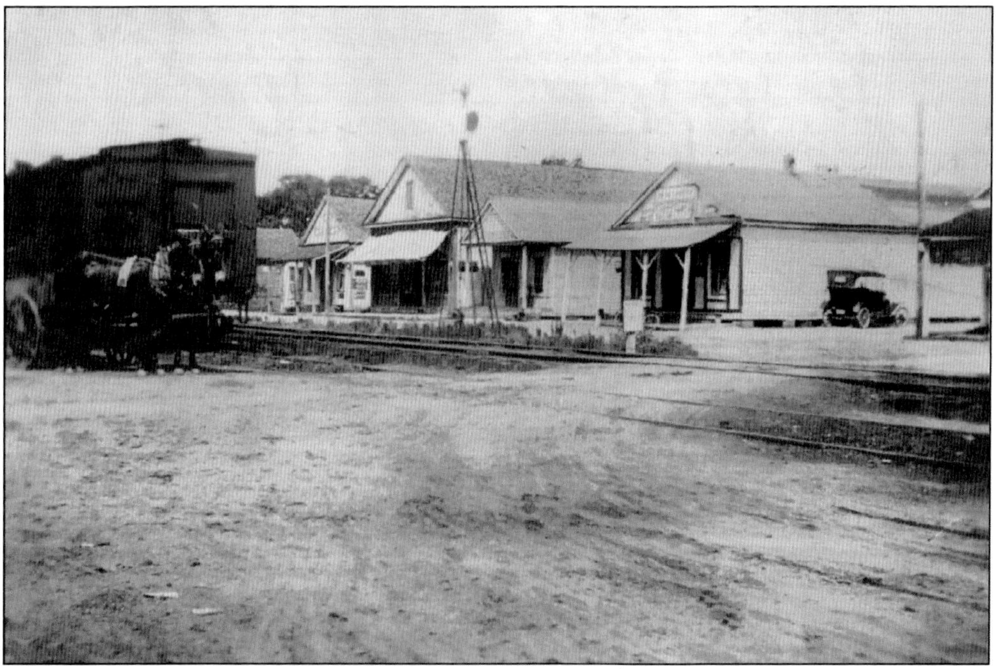

A pre-1920s photograph of downtown Lynchburg shows how Front Street was separated by the railroad tracks. In the 1850s, Elias McIntosh gave land for a railroad right-of-way and soon a passenger train made a daily stop in the village, excepting Sundays. As a result of the railroad, people who had been living in outlying settlements migrated to town. Wooden frame stores sprang up, and Lynchburg developed into a small but thriving community. Note the contrast between the mules pulling the wagon into town and the Model T parked across the street. (Betsy Redick.)

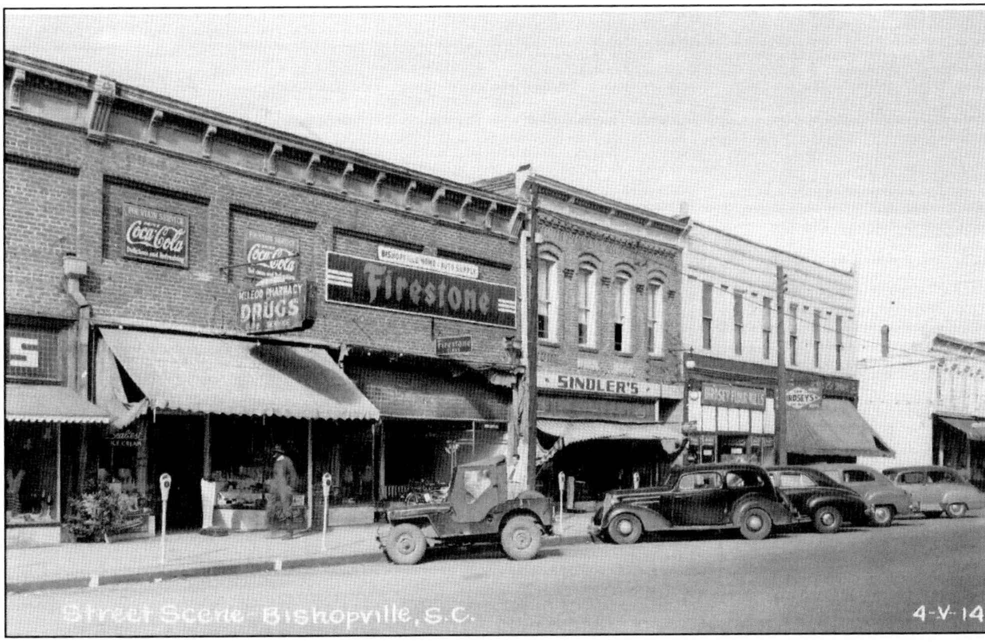

This classic c. 1940 view of Main Street between Church and West Council Streets brings back memories of when vacant storefronts in Bishopville were few. From the left are Sollie Krasnoff's, McLeod's Pharmacy, Bishopville Home and Auto Supply, Frank Sindler's Men's Store, an unidentified business, and Mack's 5¢, 10¢, 25¢ store. (South Caroliniana Library.)

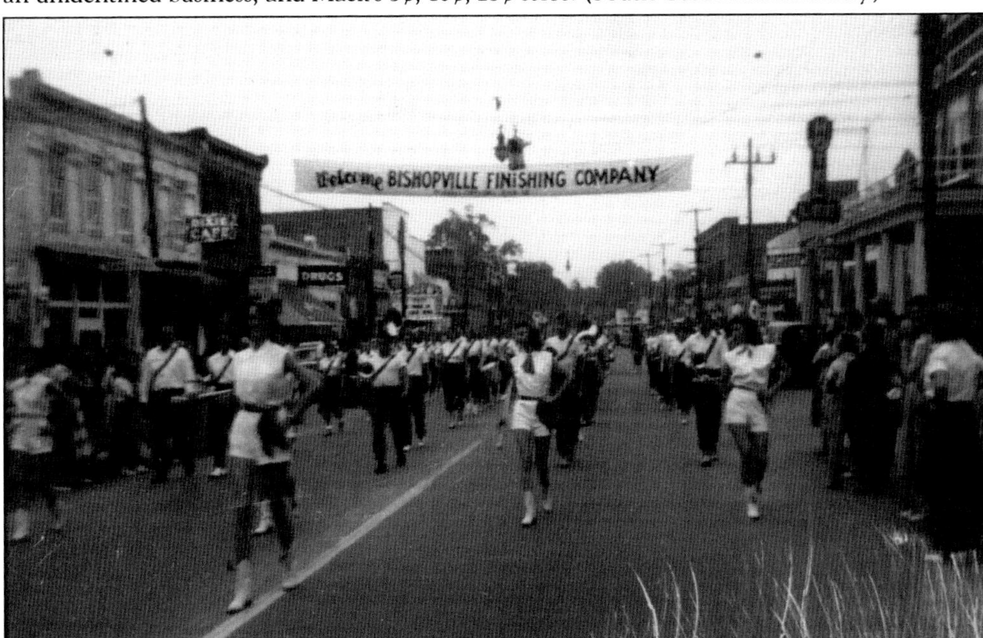

The Bishopville High School marching band, organized in the spring of 1950, performs in the 1952 end-of-school parade on Main Street. A banner welcoming the Bishopville Finishing Company to town hangs between the Dixie Café and the Lee Hotel. The Andrews Theatre can be seen on the left, past the drugstore and the liquor store. (Louise Hapeshis McCutchen.)

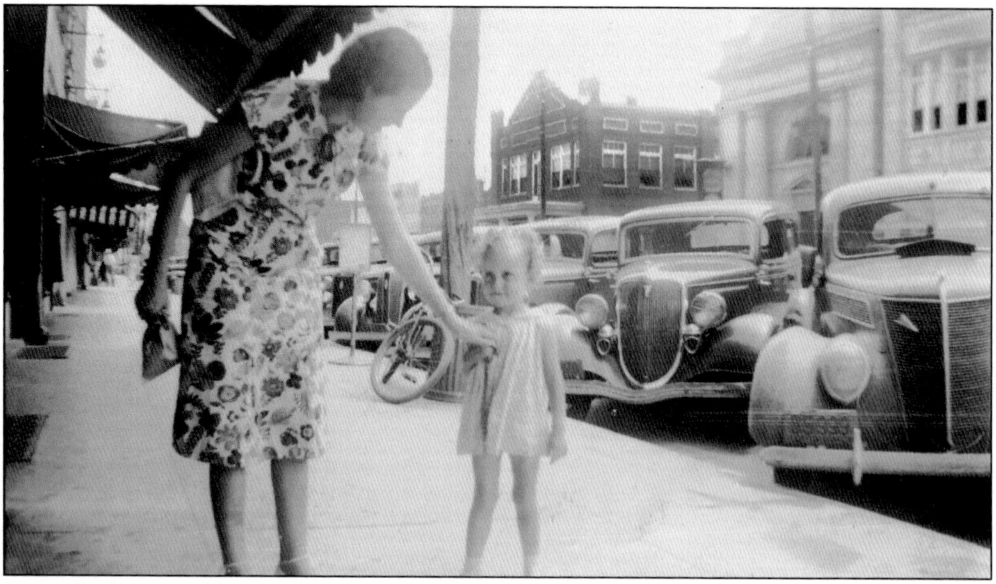

Peggy Andrews and her mother, Daisy, walk down Main Street in the summer of 1938. Daisy's father, Carl, owned the Lyric Theatre and later the Andrews Theatre. Every parking space is full and the Lee Hotel and Peoples Bank buildings can be seen in the background. The Lee Hotel is not the original building on this site. The first brick building located on the corner of Main and West Council Streets held the county offices prior to the completion of the courthouse in 1909. It burned in 1915.

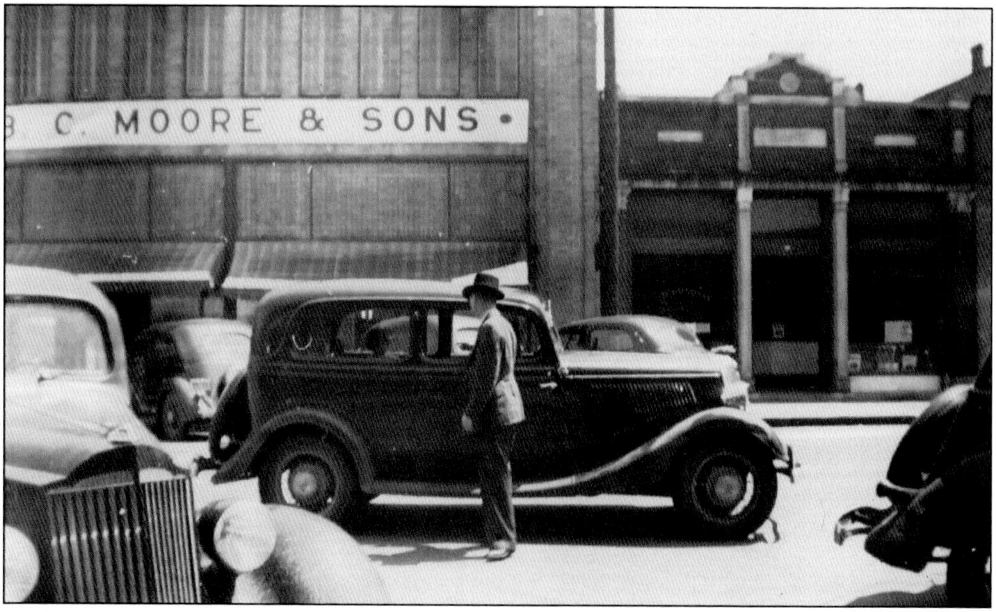

In the 1930s, life was still slow-paced enough that stopping a car on Main Street to chat was a common occurrence. In fact, Main Street could become so congested on the weekend that in the 1920s people who wanted to socialize had to stand behind a line painted in the street. In the background is B. C. Moore's department store. The smaller building on the right is the G. W. Woodham Insurance Agency. It occupied the building that was formerly home to the Bank of Bishopville.

Two gentlemen pose for a picture on the sidewalk in front of the Cliff Hickson store in downtown Lynchburg around 1940. Judging by the apron worn by the man on the right and the shoeshine box by the man on the left, they were likely employed by the grocery store. Even with its population of less than 1,000, downtown Lynchburg thrived for many years as a result of the county's farming industry. (Betsy Redick.)

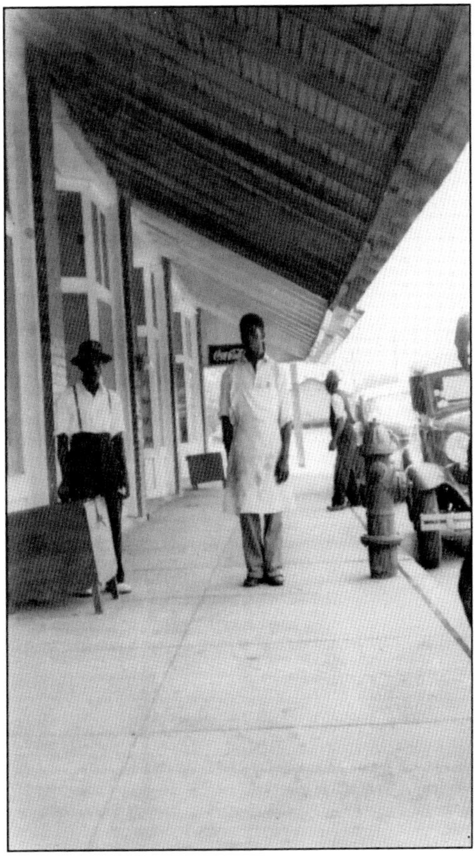

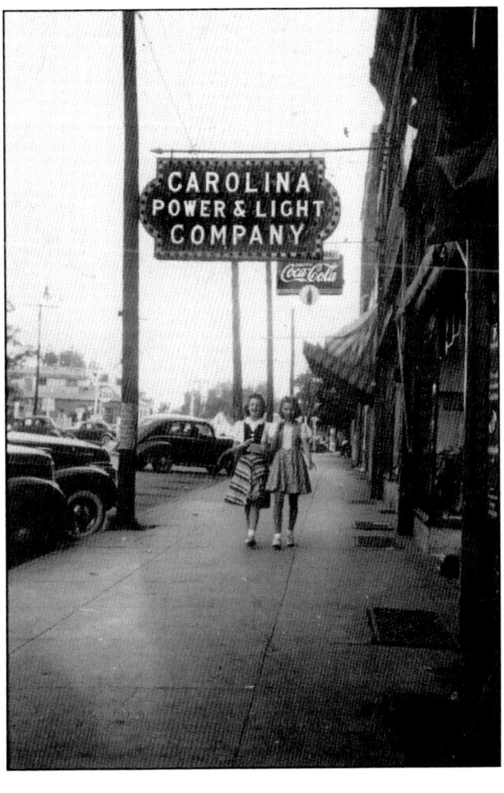

Two girls walk down North Main Street past the Carolina Power and Light office. Founded in 1908, CP&L served Bishopville since the early 1900s. The girls are walking towards the railroad tracks, and the courthouse can be seen at the back of the photograph. For many years, the CP&L office was staffed by Ruth Doris Saverance (Stephenson) and Helen Latimer (Lee). (Retta Dickinson Tindal.)

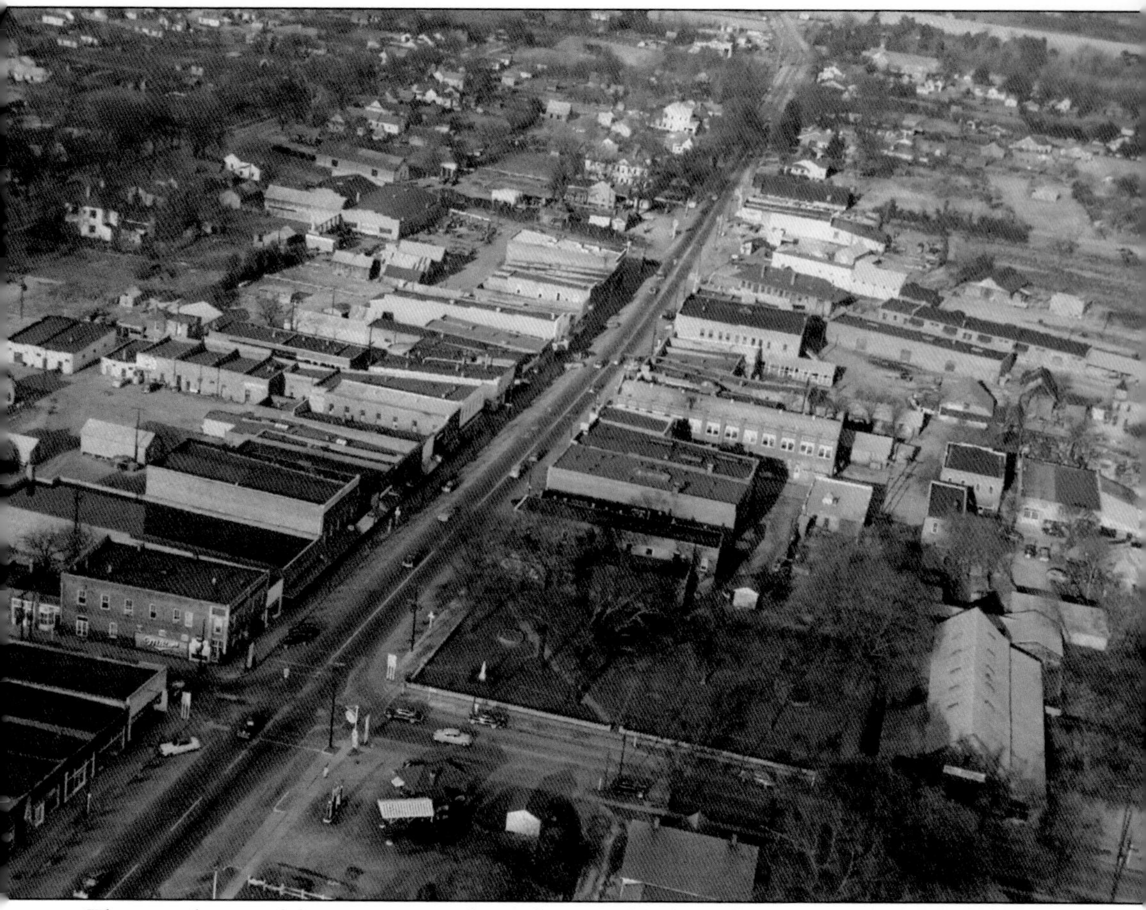

This aerial view of downtown provides a glimpse of Bishopville in the early 1950s. While the library has yet to be built on the site of Woodward Park, most of the buildings seen here are recognizable today. Alva Kelley's Esso station on the corner of Main and Church Streets is clearly visible as are Slesinger's Stables, Kirkley's and McLeod's Pharmacies, and the Lee Hotel. In the distance is the train station, and Bishopville High School is notable at the very back right of the photograph. (Bishopville Fire Department.)

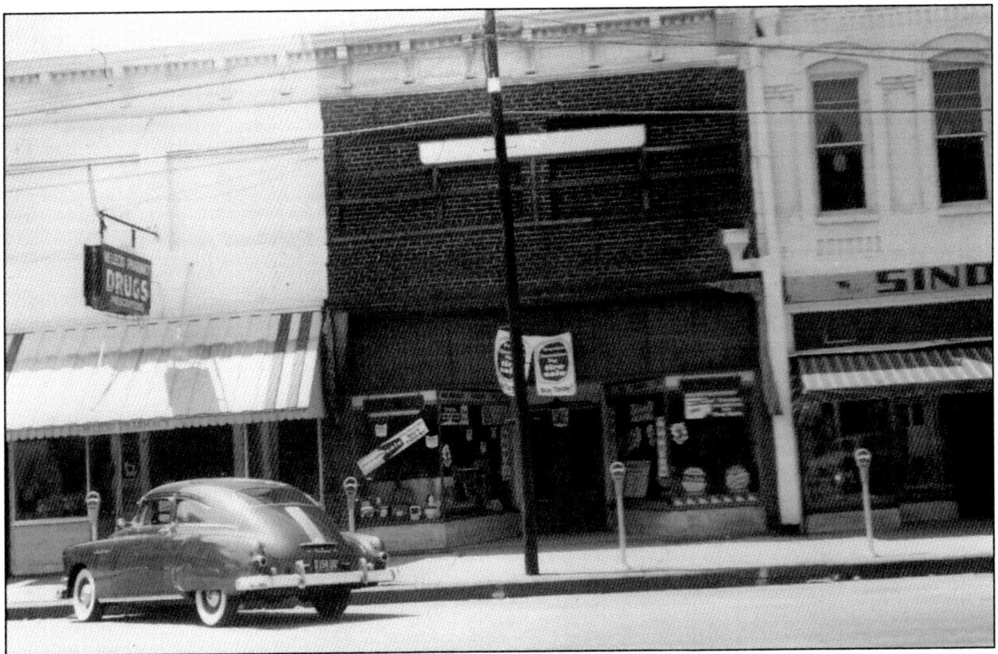

In 1954, Bishopville entered the "Finer Carolina" contest sponsored by Carolina Power and Light. Modernization and improvement of the business section was one of five goals set by the contest committee. One candidate for remodeling was Bishopville Home and Auto. Sandwiched between McLeod's Pharmacy and Sindler's, the business was a Firestone franchise owned by William Green DesChamps. The store carried a line of tires, batteries, electric appliances, and auto and bicycle parts. (Lee County Public Library.)

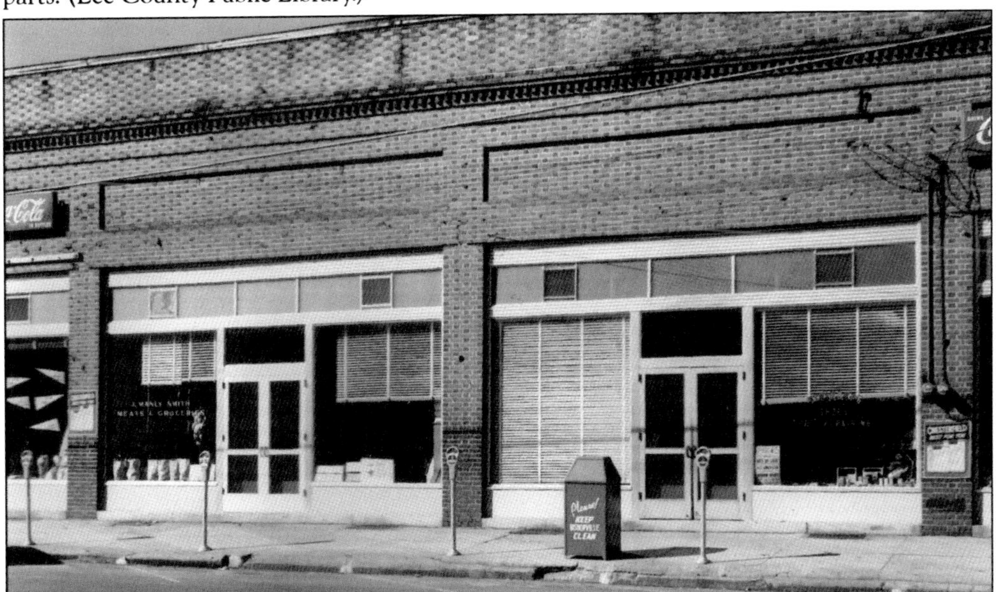

This 1954 image shows a portion of Main Street after storefront renovations were completed. On the left is J. Manley Smith grocery, one of the longest-operating businesses in Bishopville; to the right is Steinberg's Shoe Shop. Established by Howard Steinberg in the early part of the 20th century, the shop continued under Howard's son, David, for many years. (Lee County Public Library.)

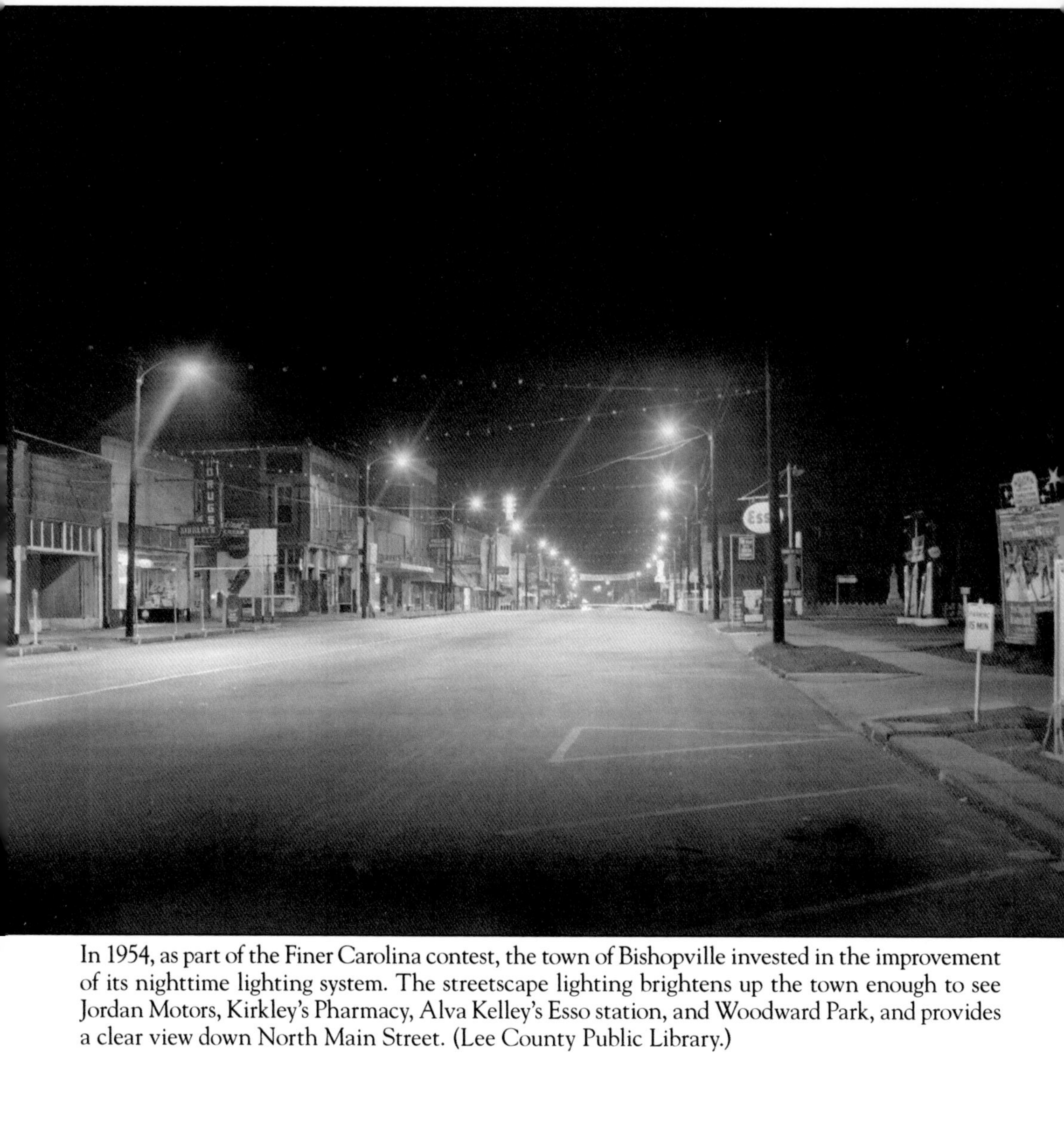

In 1954, as part of the Finer Carolina contest, the town of Bishopville invested in the improvement of its nighttime lighting system. The streetscape lighting brightens up the town enough to see Jordan Motors, Kirkley's Pharmacy, Alva Kelley's Esso station, and Woodward Park, and provides a clear view down North Main Street. (Lee County Public Library.)

Two

Business and Commerce

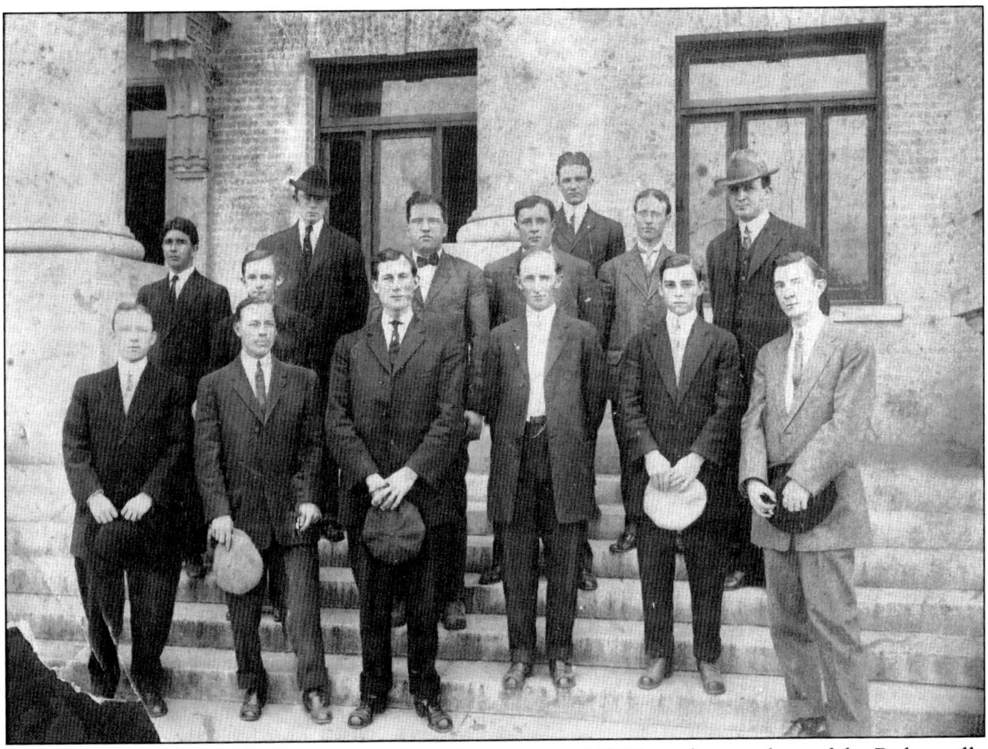

Pictured on the steps of the Lee County Courthouse around 1912 are the members of the Bishopville Business Men's Club, a forerunner of today's chamber of commerce. From left to right are (first row) Gus Woodham Sr., Edgar Woodward, Ed Ruffin, B. B. Epps, Marvin McLean, and Joe Stuckey Sr.; (second row) [Henry ?] Heriot, Jake Parrott, Collins Ruffin (wearing hat), Marion Wilson, Clinton Dixon, Carey Kilgore, future senator R. E. Dennis, and English McCutchen. Members not present were George Stuckey and H. W. Woodward. (Ruthie Stevenson Bowman.)

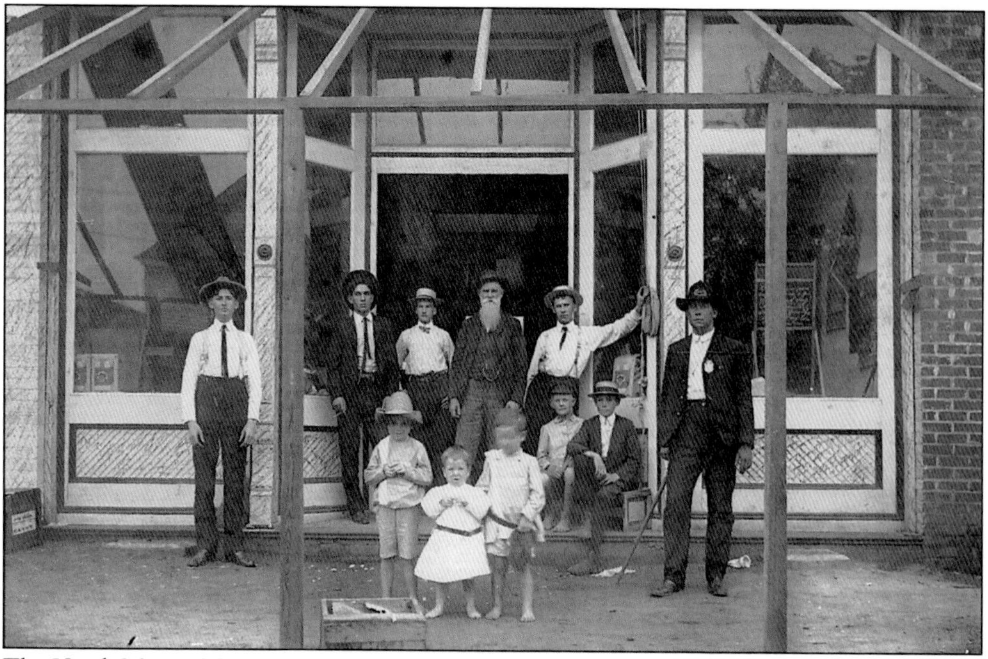

The Heath-Massey-Morrow Company was chartered in 1904 and was located on the west side of North Main Street across from what later became the Lyric Theatre. The post office subsequently occupied this building after Heath-Massey-Morrow moved to the two-story brick structure on the northeast corner of North Main and East Council Streets. In this c. 1904 photograph, the man in the foreground with the coat, hat, and badge is Bishopville police chief Folly Smith, who was 28 at the time. The three small boys are Henry, William, and Olin Massey. (Elizabeth Massey Booth.)

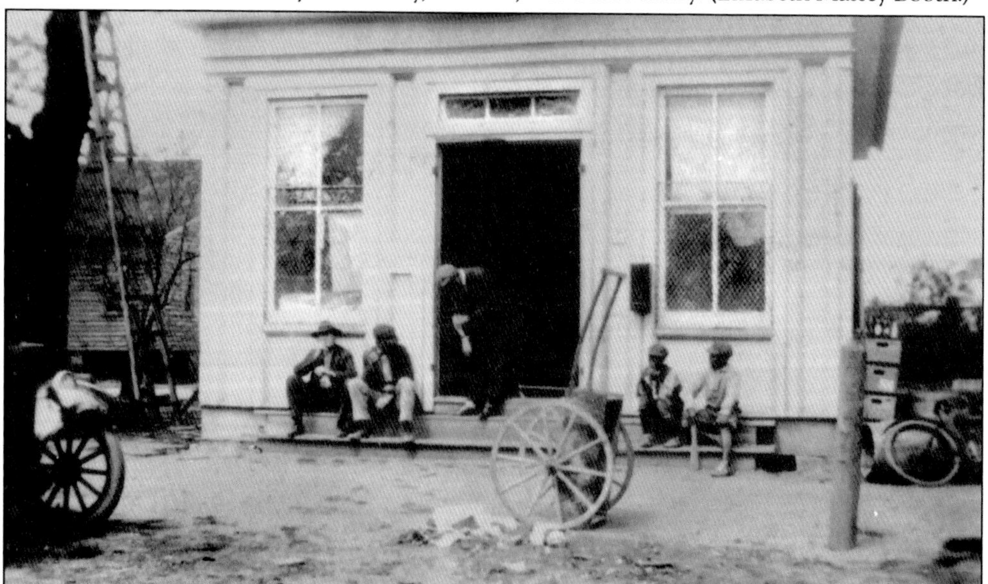

A photograph from around 1900 shows the Jefferson Hickson general store in downtown Lynchburg. Hickson was the father of both Herbert L. Hickson and Clifford Hickson, both of whom operated grocery stores in Lynchburg. Jefferson Hickson's store was directly across the railroad tracks from the cotton platform. (Betsy Redick.)

By 1902, Dr. R. Y. McLeod had already been practicing medicine and pharmacy for 25 years. McLeod had formerly shared a practice with Dr. J. E. McClure, but the partnership was dissolved around 1892. In 1903, R. Y. McLeod and H. A. McLeod incorporated the McLeod Drug Company, which is known today as McLeod's Pharmacy. In 1902, McLeod advertised fancy and toilet articles, stationery, cigars, and tobacco, and noted that its prescriptions were "carefully compounded at all hours." (South Caroliniana Library.)

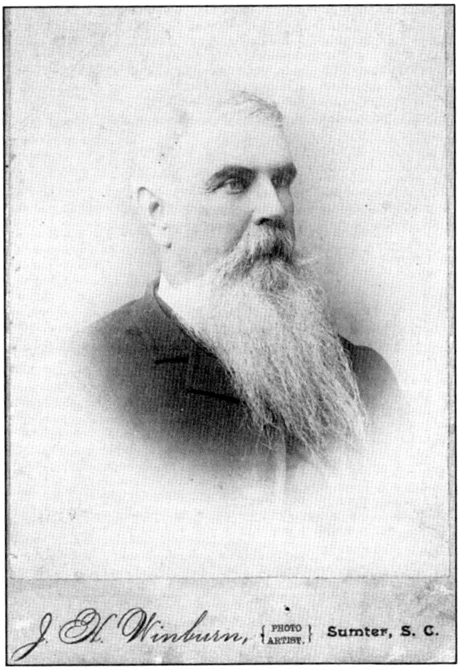

In the early part of the 20th century, downtown Bishopville experienced a boom in business, and competition was fierce. Growing from just a few stores around 1900, by 1910 Main Street boasted over 30 brick buildings full of purveyors of dry goods, general merchandise, farm equipment, and groceries. The advertisement below was placed in the March 28, 1902, *Lee County Vindicator*.

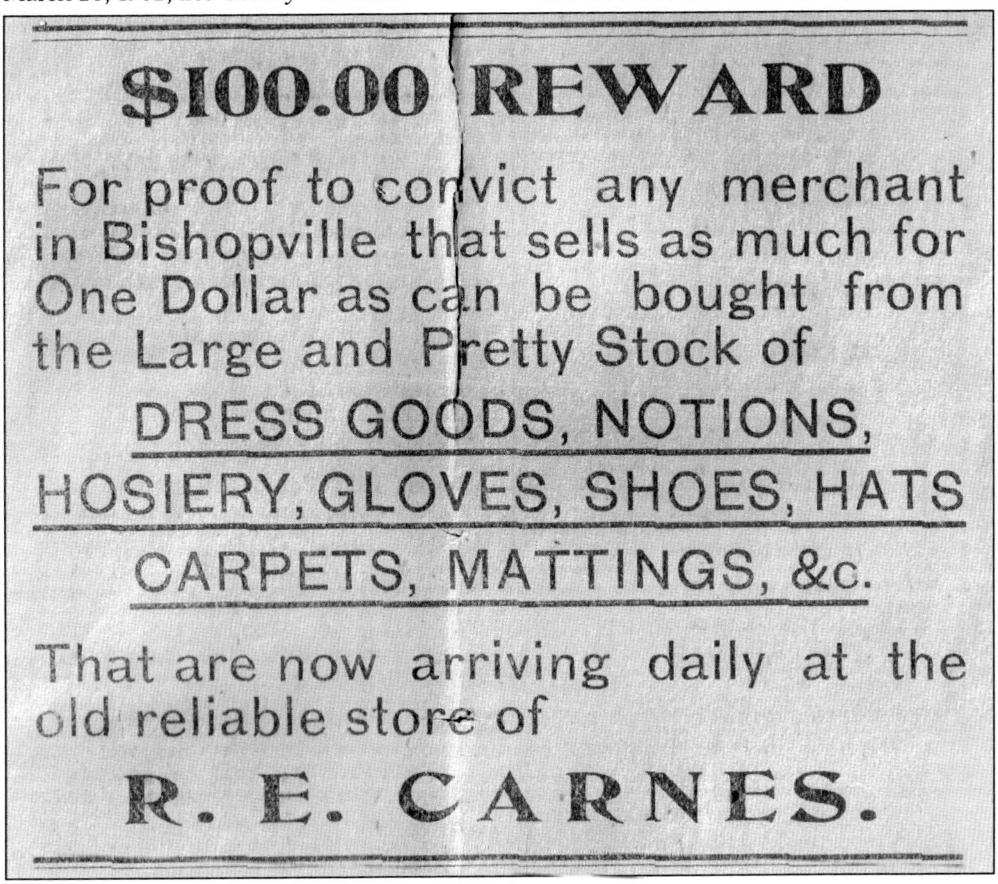

$100.00 REWARD

For proof to convict any merchant in Bishopville that sells as much for One Dollar as can be bought from the Large and Pretty Stock of

DRESS GOODS, NOTIONS,

HOSIERY, GLOVES, SHOES, HATS

CARPETS, MATTINGS, &c.

That are now arriving daily at the old reliable store of

R. E. CARNES.

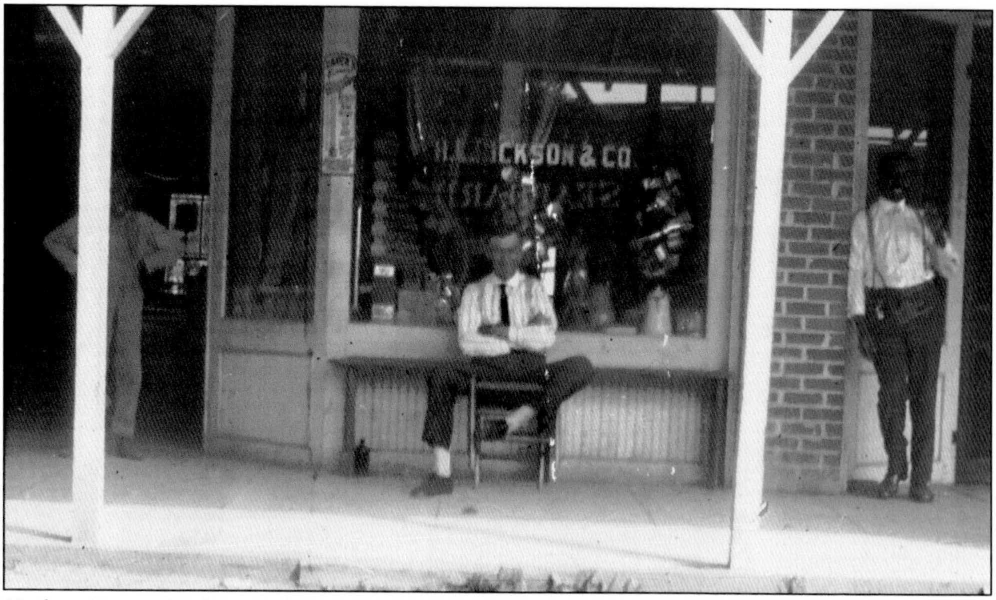

Herbert Lester Hickson takes it easy and greets customers outside his Lynchburg grocery in this early-1920s photograph. Located on Front Street, H. L. Hickson and Company can be seen painted on the plate glass. Hickson was married to the former Annie Cribbs, also of Lynchburg. (Betsy Redick.)

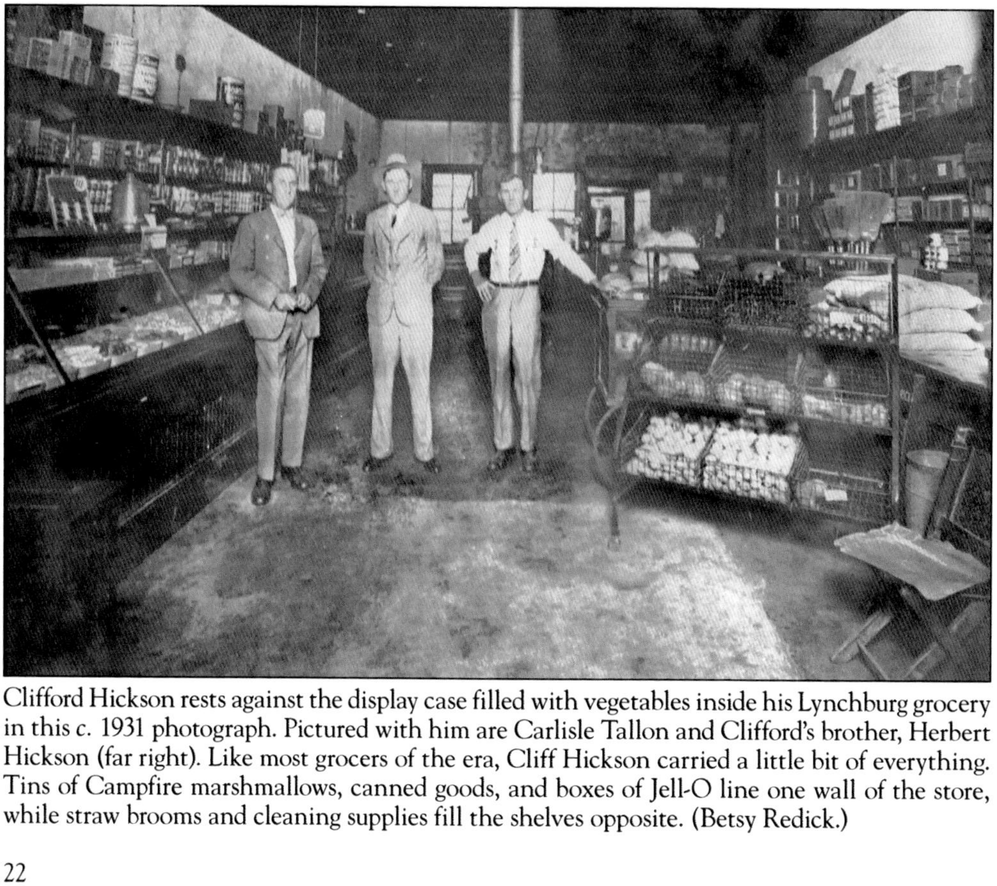

Clifford Hickson rests against the display case filled with vegetables inside his Lynchburg grocery in this *c.* 1931 photograph. Pictured with him are Carlisle Tallon and Clifford's brother, Herbert Hickson (far right). Like most grocers of the era, Cliff Hickson carried a little bit of everything. Tins of Campfire marshmallows, canned goods, and boxes of Jell-O line one wall of the store, while straw brooms and cleaning supplies fill the shelves opposite. (Betsy Redick.)

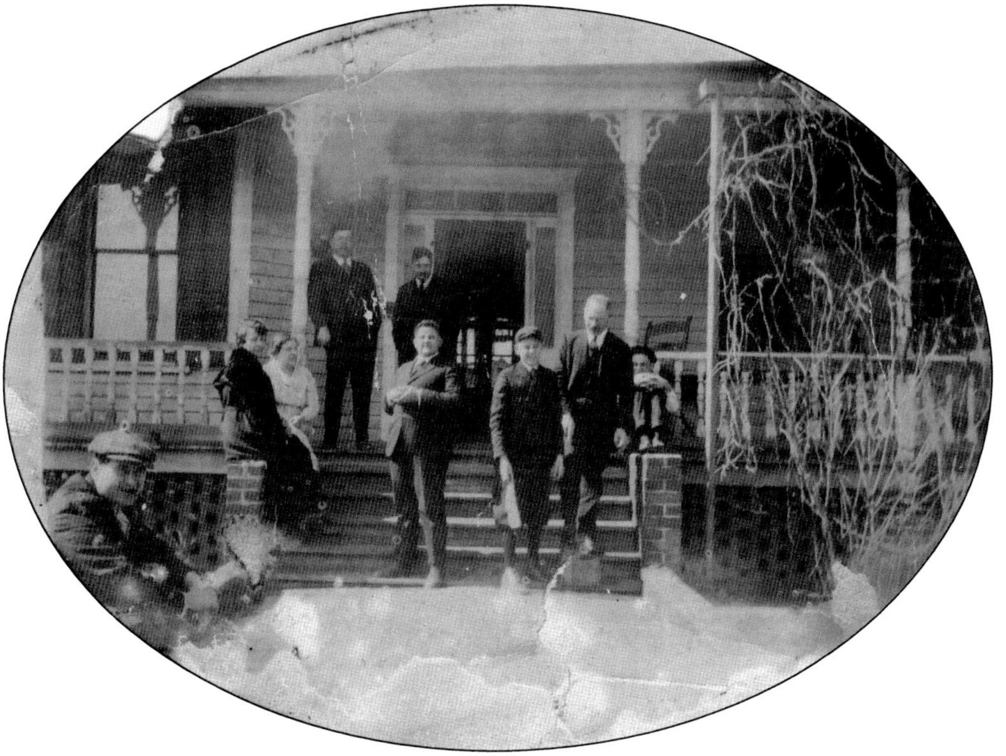

In the above photograph, Meyer Krasnoff (foreground) and family gather for a picture on the steps of his Lee Street home around 1917. The seated women are Meyer's sister, Fanny, and his wife, the former Jennie Levinson, who is wearing the white dress. Also pictured are his brothers, Augustus and Perry, as well as Fanny's husband, Morris Yoffee. The three young men are Meyer and Jennie's sons, Leo, Aaron, and Sollie. (Gift of Jennie Krasnoff Caine, Special Collections, College of Charleston.)

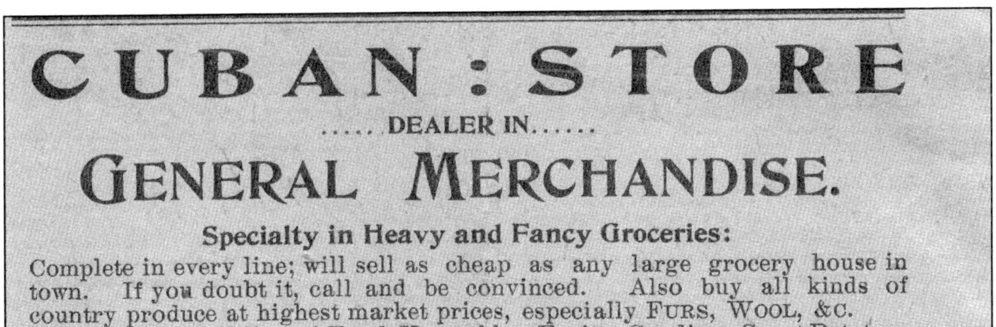

CUBAN : STORE

......DEALER IN......

GENERAL MERCHANDISE.

Specialty in Heavy and Fancy Groceries:

Complete in every line; will sell as cheap as any large grocery house in town. If you doubt it, call and be convinced. Also buy all kinds of country produce at highest market prices, especially FURS, WOOL, &C.

Keep also a full line of Fresh Vegetables, Fruits, Candies. Sweet Potatoes and Irish Potatoes always on hand.

A. M. KRASNOFF.

This advertisement for Meyer Krasnoff's store ran in the March 28, 1902, issue of the *Lee County Vindicator*. It was customary at Krasnoff's to give farmers charge accounts, allowing them to pay their bills when the crops came in. Meyer had an old coal stove to heat the store and the farmers would sit and chat around the fire on winter days. On one occasion during the Depression, Meyer reportedly tossed his ledgers into the flames and announced, "Let's all start over together."

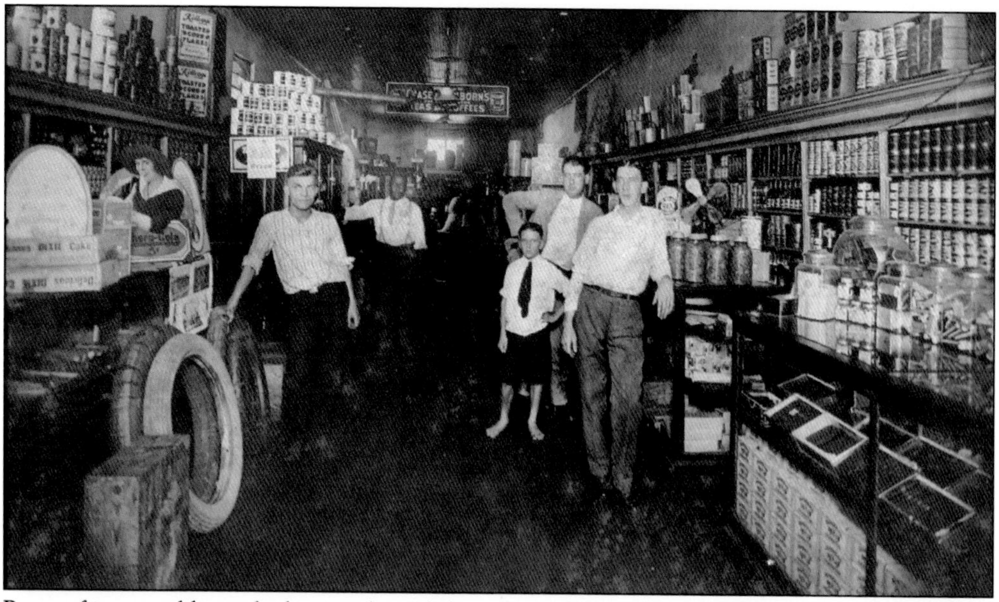

Rows of impeccably stacked canned goods line the shelves at McLeod Brothers Grocery in this c. 1920 photograph. The store was located on Main Street next to the Dixie Café. Standing in front on the left is Melvin Reames Sr., and at the rear of the store is a man identified only as Sam. Standing to the right, in front, is Norman McLeod. The young boy is J. Francis "Mac" McLeod, and behind him is Norman's brother, Thomas McLeod. (Lee County Historical Society.)

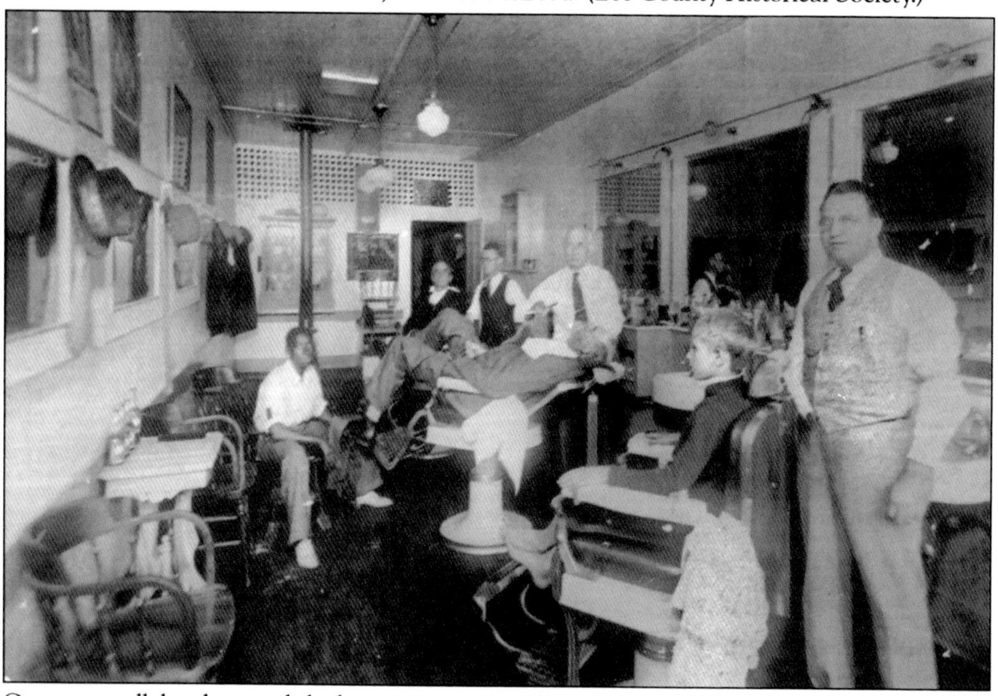

Customers talk local news while they await a turn in the barber's chair. Standing in the foreground is Julian Price, and in the process of giving a shave is W. T. Copeland. The shop was located two buildings north of the opera house; at one time it had been the offices of the Peoples Bank. (Liston and Betty Truesdale.)

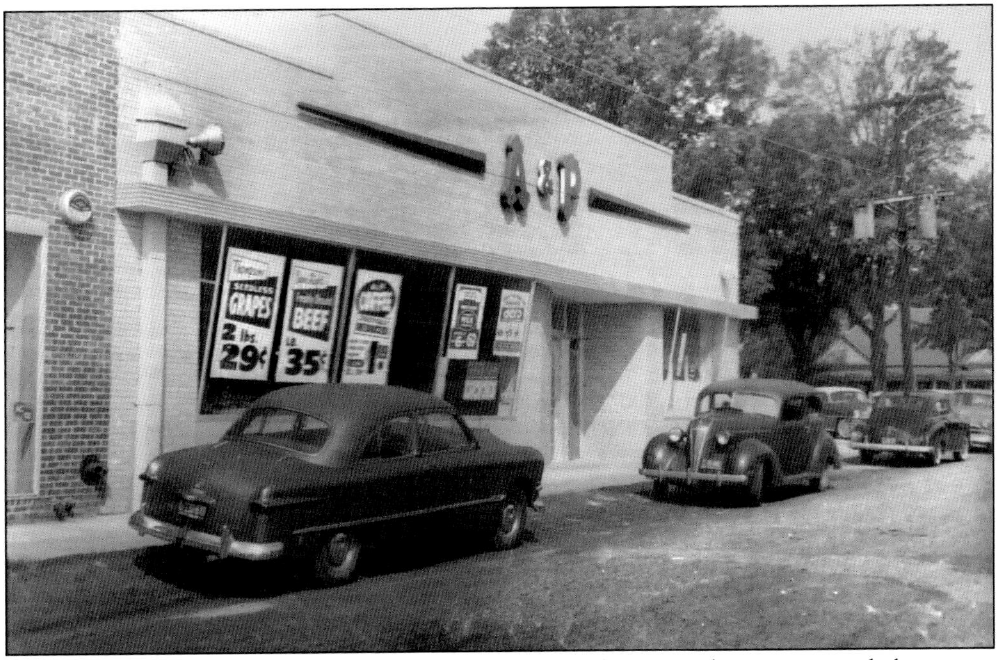

In 1954, the A&P grocery chain came to Bishopville. The original store, pictured above, was opened in what had at one time been part of Max and Irven Traub's stables. The A&P followed the lead of the Piggly Wiggly, which had come to town a few years earlier with the self-serve grocery concept. Years later, the store would relocate to the corner of Gregg and South Nettles Streets. (Lee County Public Library.)

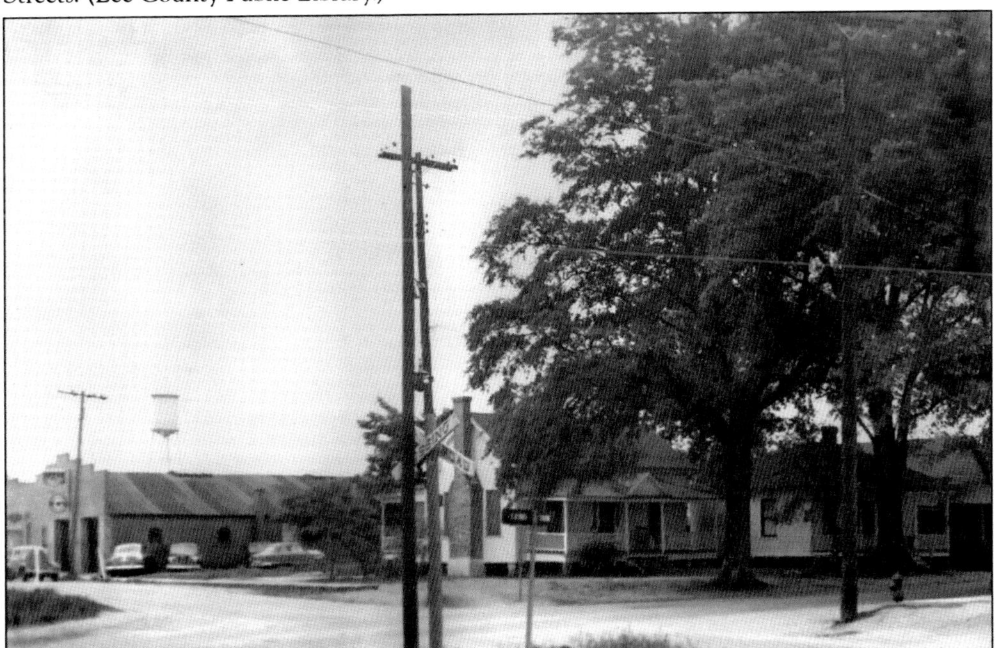

This 1953 view shows the intersection of Cedar Lane and Dennis Avenue prior to the construction of the A&P grocery store. The house on the corner was moved to make way for the parking lot. (Lee County Public Library.)

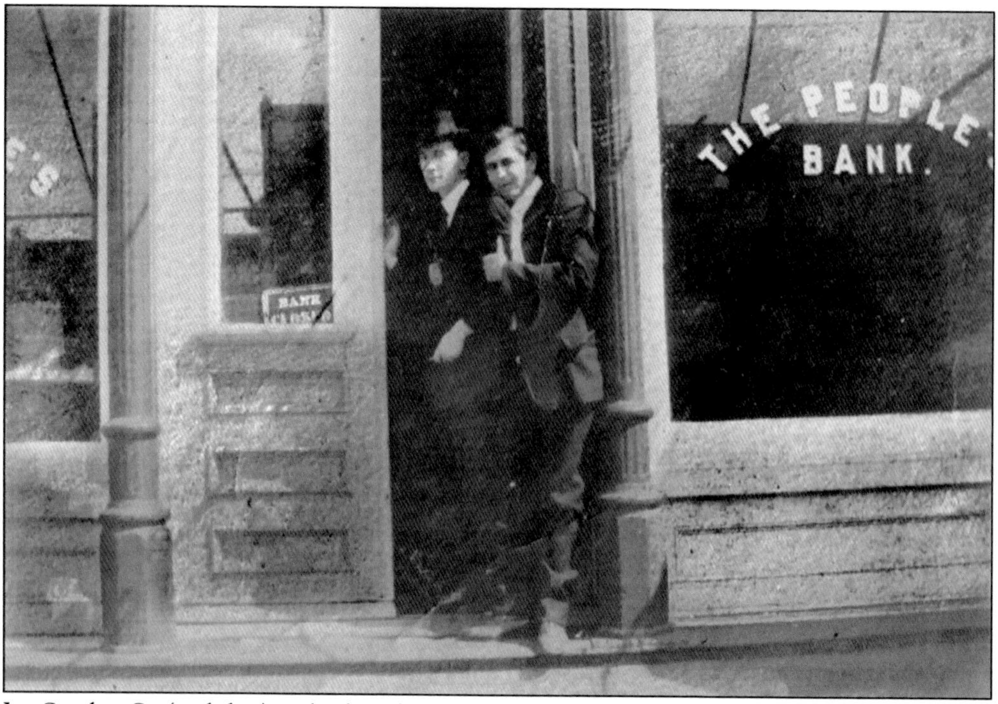

Joe Stuckey Sr. (with hat) and a friend take advantage of banker's hours and lock up for lunch. The Peoples Bank of Bishopville was incorporated on October 6, 1903. In 1915, Joe Stuckey was its assistant cashier. Bank president was George M. Stuckey, T. E. Davis was vice president, and Z. M. Skinner was cashier. The columns were once a prominent Main Street architectural feature. Today this building is home to the R. Travis Windham Insurance Agency, and much of the original architecture remains. (Ruthie Stevenson Bowman.)

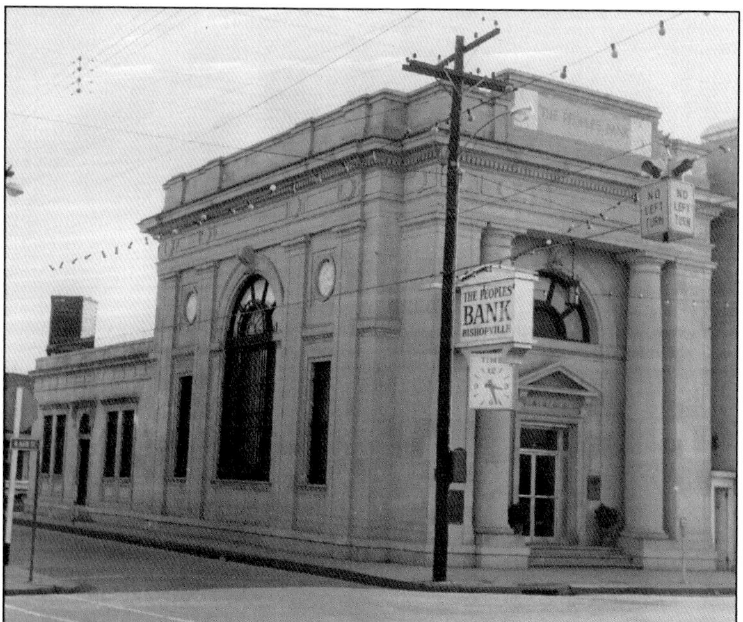

This late-1950s view of the Bishopville Peoples Bank shows the clock that had just been installed on the corner of Main and East Council Streets. The building was constructed about 1912 and was, for many years, home to the Bank of Bishopville. That bank did not survive the Depression. The building later became home to First Citizens Bank, and it is now vacant.

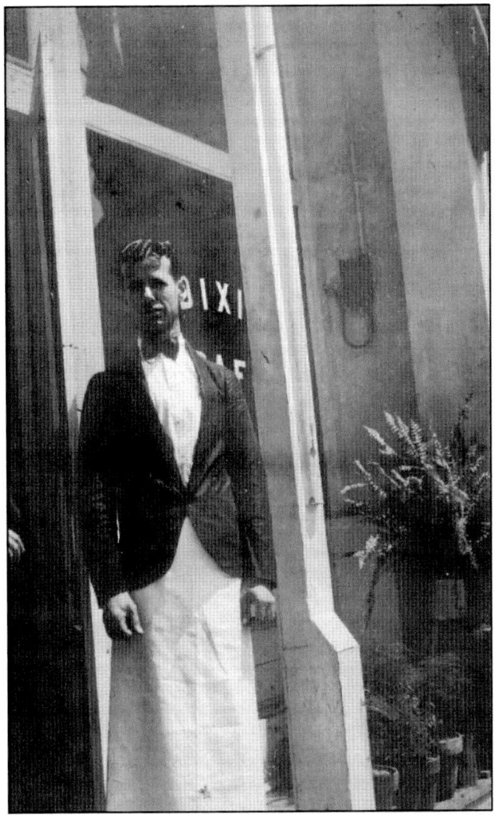

Louis Hapeshis stands outside the Dixie Café in his apron in this 1920s photograph. Hapeshis arrived in the United States in 1919, at age 19, from Cyprus, Greece. His parents were deceased, but he knew that family friend John A. Johnson (along with Christ Nicholson) owned and operated this popular Bishopville restaurant and coffee shop. Hapeshis spoke no English and made his way down the East Coast with a tag pinned to his jacket that read the name of his destination—Bishopville, South Carolina. After working for the Nicholsons, Hapeshis opened his own establishment, the New York Café, where he is pictured below with a customer. After he married, he and Margaret Hapeshis had three children, Louise (McCutchen), Harriet (Rhame), and George. (Louise Hapeshis McCutchen.)

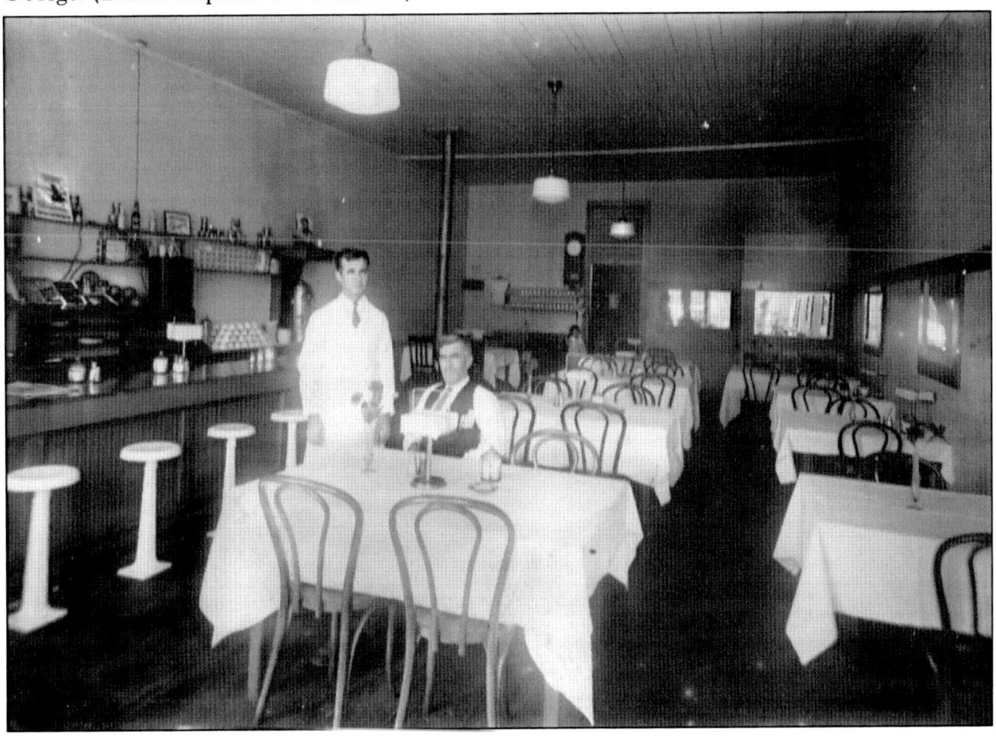

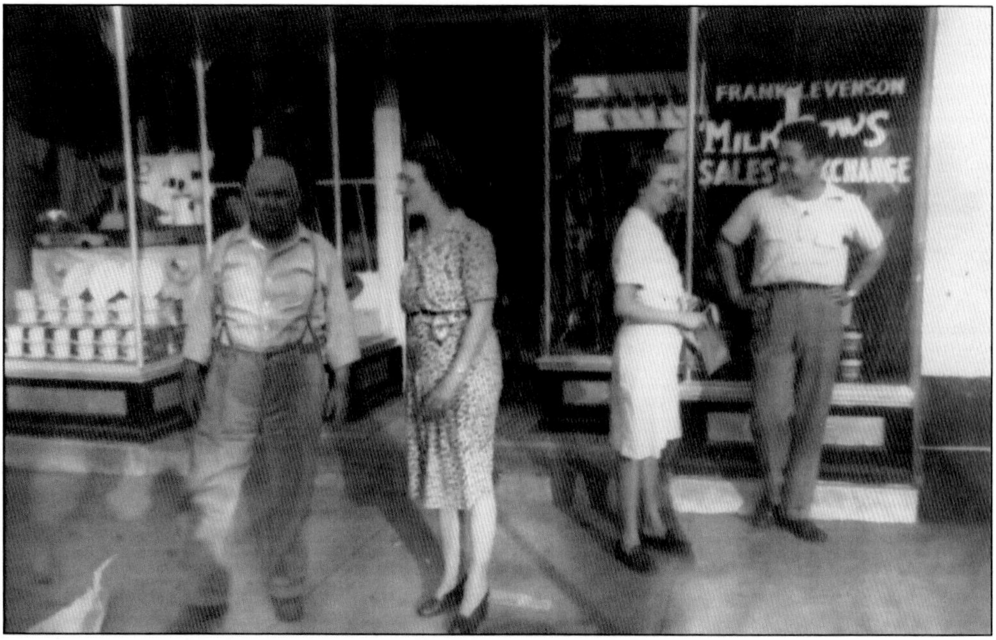

Frank Levenson greets customers outside his Main Street store. As a small child, he left Lithuania with his family. He and his father were traveling salesmen who eventually settled in Lee County. Levenson started a general store in Bishopville in 1910 where he carried a little bit of everything—fatback, harnesses, collars, plows, and groceries. The Levensons also operated livery stables behind the downtown store, one for cows and goats and another for horses and mules. In addition, they owned a liquor store, which would come to be run by his son, Sam (above, leaning on glass), and Sam's wife, Carolyn. (Carolyn Baruch Levenson.)

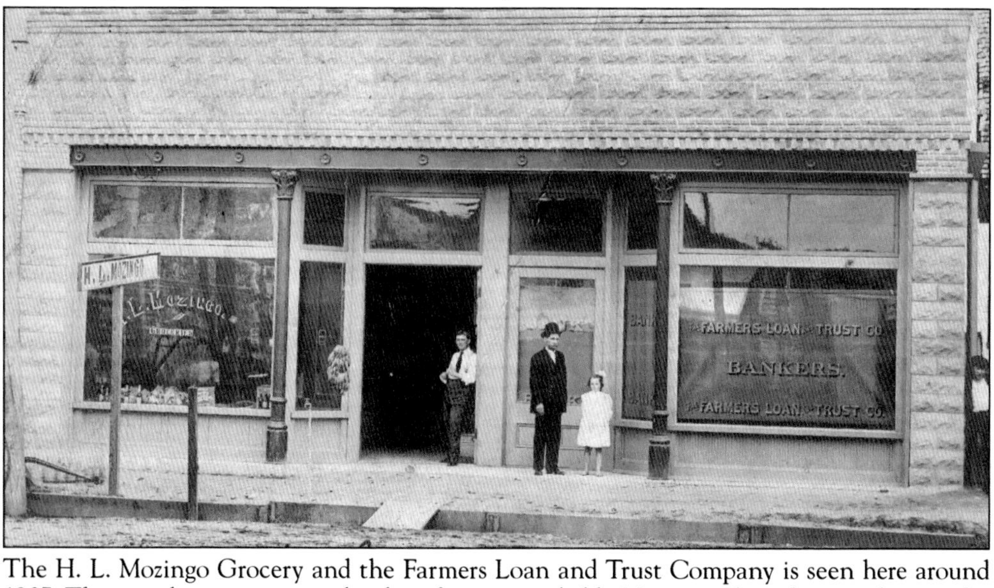

The H. L. Mozingo Grocery and the Farmers Loan and Trust Company is seen here around 1907. The man leaning against the door frame is probably Mozingo; the other gentleman, the little girl, and the boy peeking around the corner are unidentified. The Farmers Loan and Trust Company was incorporated January 1, 1906, with W. A. James as bank president. The building would become Frank Levenson's general mercantile store in 1910. (SCCM.)

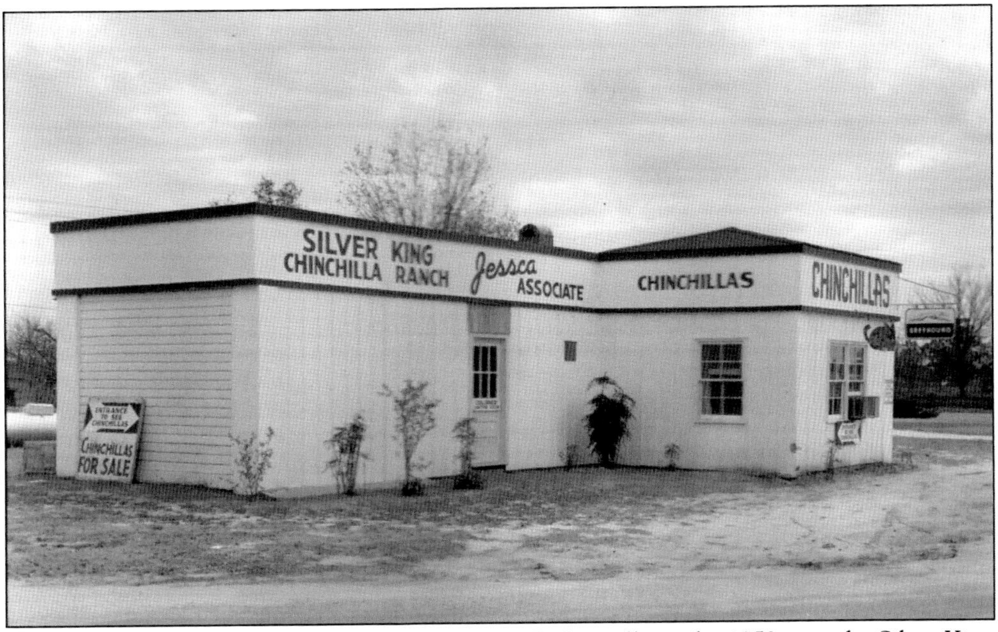

One of the more interesting businesses to open in Bishopville in the 1950s was the Silver King Chinchilla Ranch. Located on Highway 15 North, it also served as the Greyhound bus station. In this 1954 photograph, the door visible in this picture is labeled "Colored Waiting Room." The ranch was owned and operated by Fred Rogers and his sister, Mary Townsend. (Lee County Public Library.)

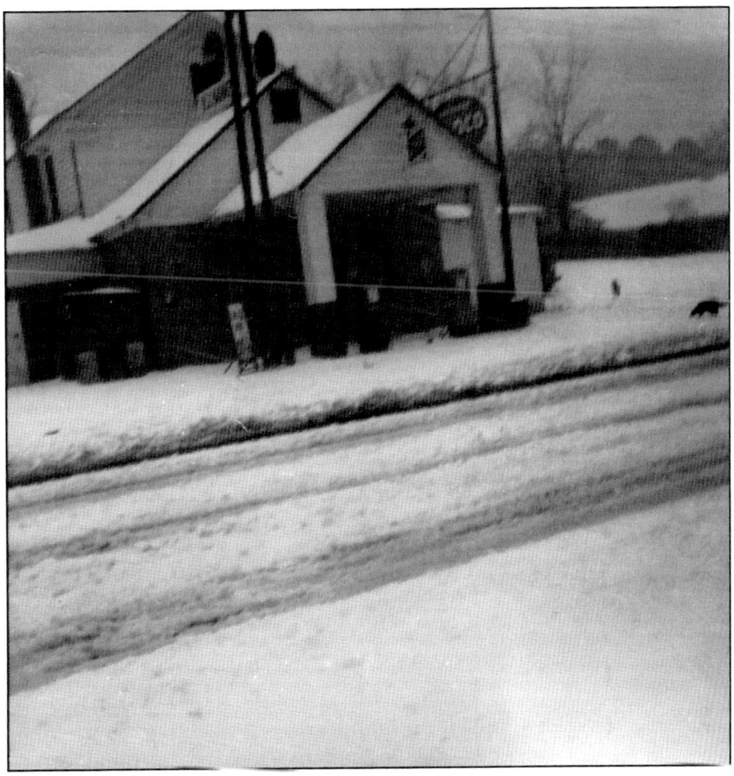

Pictured in the mid-1950s on Highway 15 South in Manville is the B. J. Barnett store. It provided a place to fill up and purchase necessities for those making the long journey south to Florida. It was said that Barnett's store was located exactly halfway between New York and Miami. In later years, the store was owned by Mac Fields. (*Lee County Observer.*)

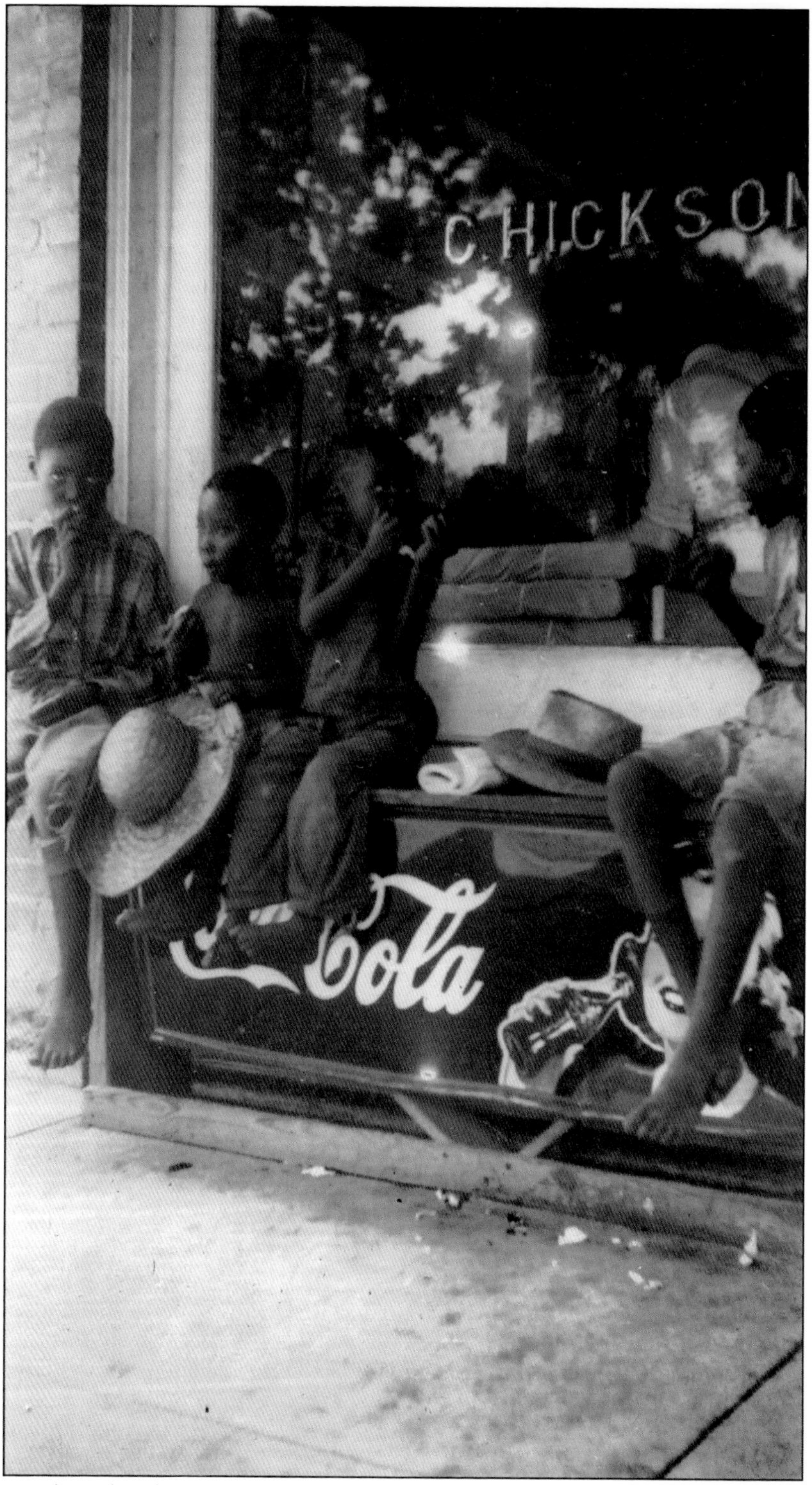

Young boys takes a break in the shade of the awning of Clifford Hickson's store in Lynchburg in this early-1940s Lynchburg photograph. (Betsy Redick.)

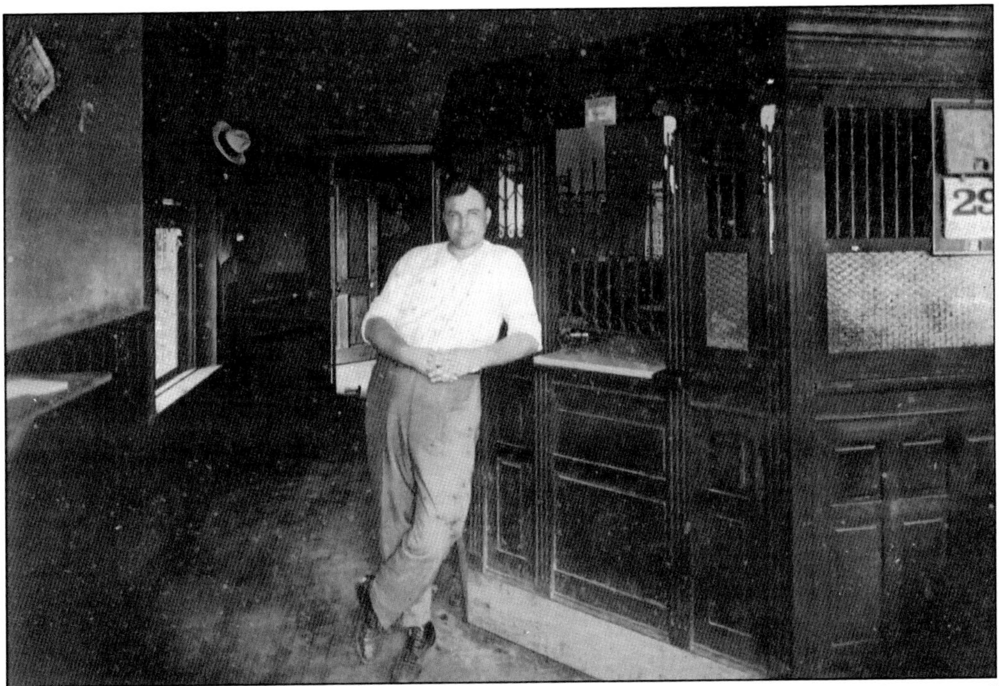

Cliff Hickson is pictured inside an unidentified Lynchburg bank. This is possibly the original cashier's window of the Lynchburg Peoples Bank, as Hickson served on its board of directors. It is also possible that he is inside the Bank of Lynchburg, which was chartered in 1907 with Charles A. Smith, president; J. W. Tarrant, vice president; and C. E. Timmons, cashier. (Betsy Redick.)

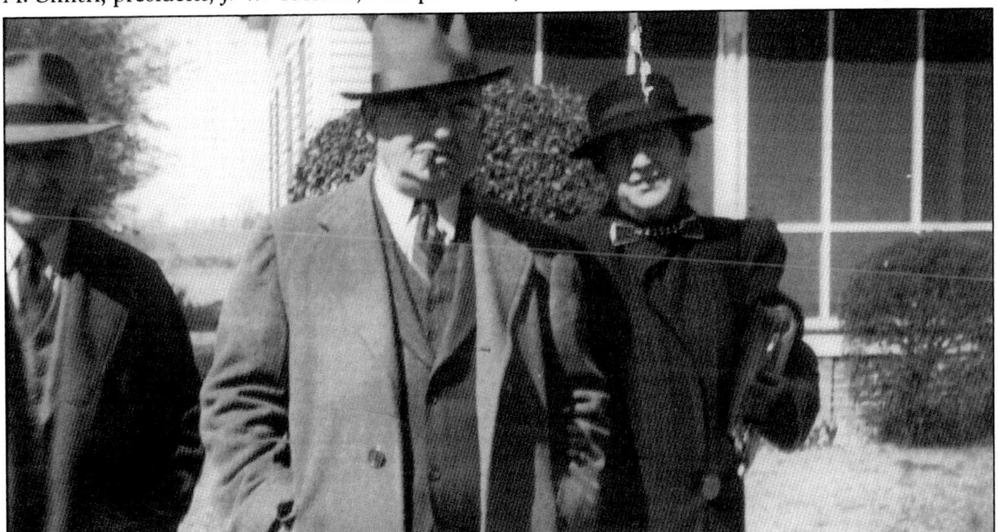

Sam (with cigar) and Fannie Ginsberg and Frank Sindler are seen in this late 1930s photograph. Frank owned Sindler's Men's Store, specializing in tailor-made clothes. Sam moved to Bishopville in 1925 to manage Snyder's department store and, in 1929, opened Ginsberg's. After his sudden death in a car accident in 1942, Fannie and their son, Howard, ran the shop. Later Howard's brother, Arthur, managed the business with his wife, Frances. From the beginning, Ginsberg's carried name-brand ladies' wear. When Ginsberg's closed its doors for the last time in February 2008, it was the second-oldest continuously operated business in Bishopville. (Frances Ginsberg.)

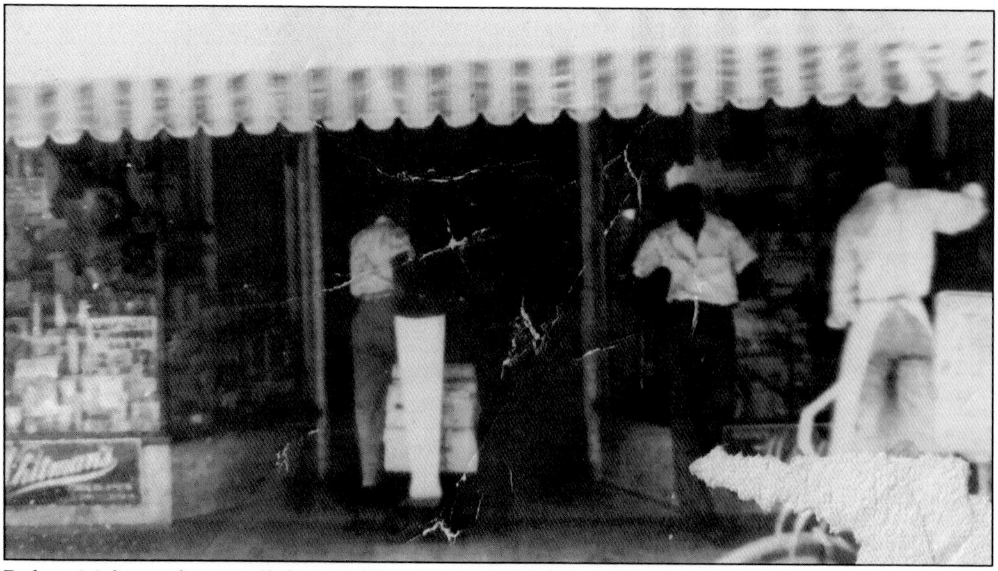

Robert Melton takes a well-deserved break outside McLeod's Pharmacy in this c. 1938 photograph. Affectionately known as "Mr. Sunshine" by his friends and customers, Robert went to work for McLeod's when the pharmacy was purchased from Dr. John Rhame by Leo DuBose Sr. in the late 1920s. He made home deliveries of prescriptions or even grilled cheese sandwiches on his bicycle for decades. In later years, he was elected to and served on the Bishopville Town Council. (Retta Dickinson Tindal.)

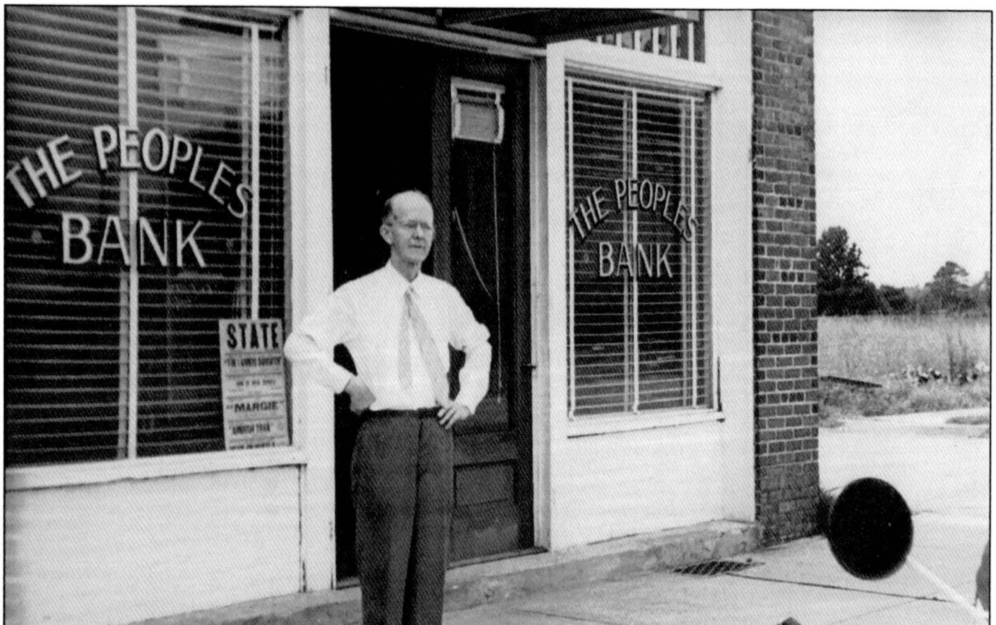

James D. "Jim" Dougherty Sr. is pictured in front of the Peoples Bank of Lynchburg in this 1955 photograph. Jim had been employed as cashier at the bank since 1927. He was elected mayor of Lynchburg in 1935 and was still filling that position at the time this picture was taken. Originally from North, South Carolina, he was married to the former Carrie Cribbs of Lynchburg. (Betsy Redick.)

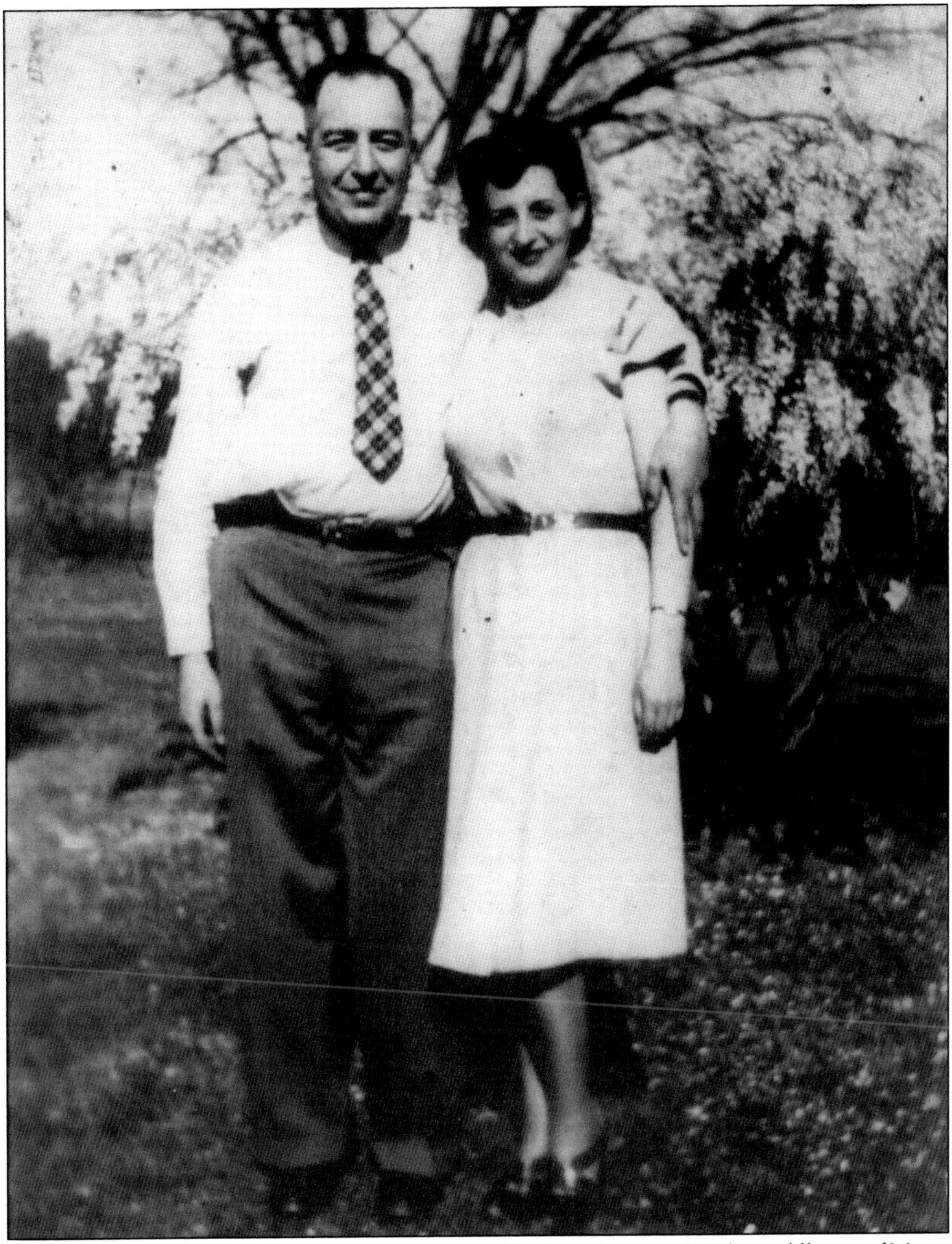

Sollie and Mildred Krasnoff are seen here in this mid-1940s photograph. The middle son of Meyer and Jennie Krasnoff, Sollie decided to go into business for himself after high school. His father gave him the dry goods from his store, Sollie cashed in an insurance policy for the rent, and took his pick of vacant bank-owned stores. He chose one to the left of McLeod's Pharmacy, and his name remains today, painted across the back entrance. At one time, Meyer, Sollie, and brother Leo all had shops downtown. Sollie and Mildred were the parents of Jennie and Dixie. (Gift of Jennie Krasnoff Caine, Special Collections, College of Charleston.)

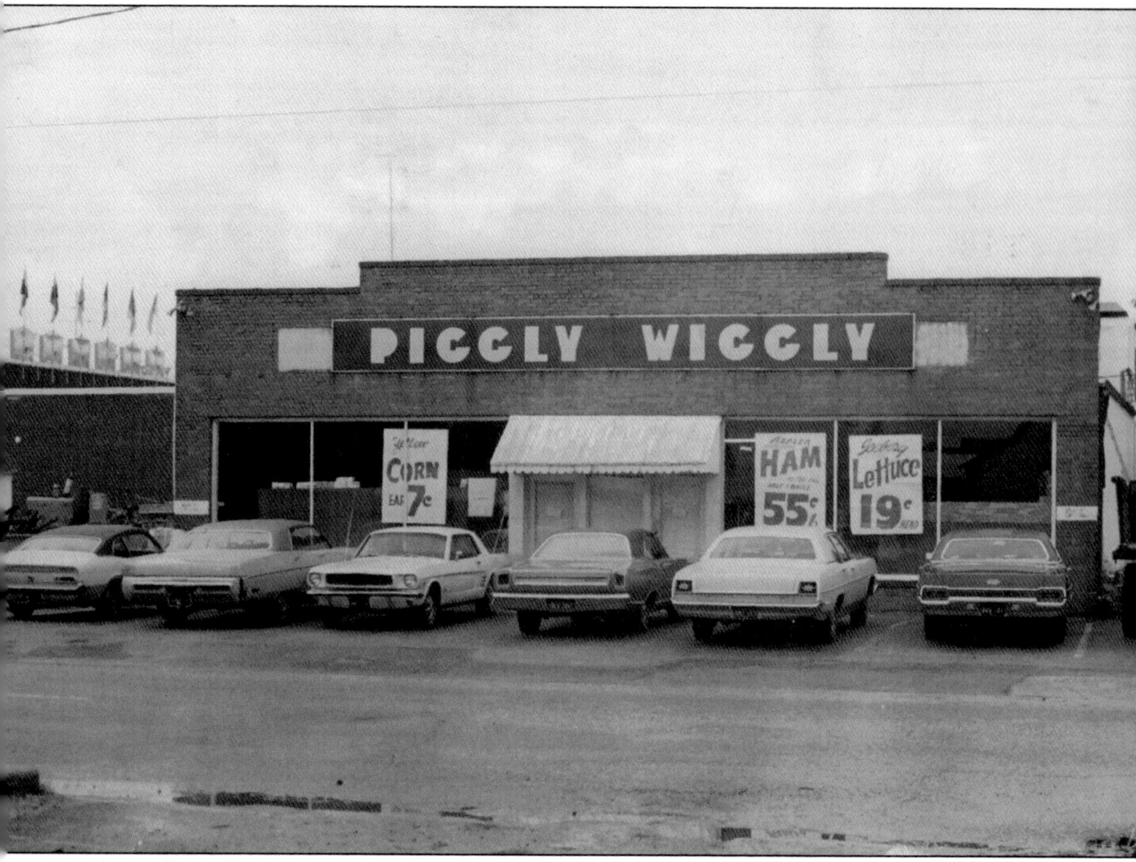

The Bishopville Piggly Wiggly evolved from Boulineau Grocery, which was owned by Frank and Helen (Smith) Boulineau. The store became a part of the Piggly Wiggly chain in the 1950s and was purchased by Don and Jeannette Melton in 1970. This 1972 photograph was taken just before the Meltons moved the grocery from its location on Church Street between Kirkley's Pharmacy and the Methodist Church to its current address on Main Street. The new building can be seen in the left background of the photograph. (Don and Jeannette Melton.)

Three

Cotton Fields Back Home

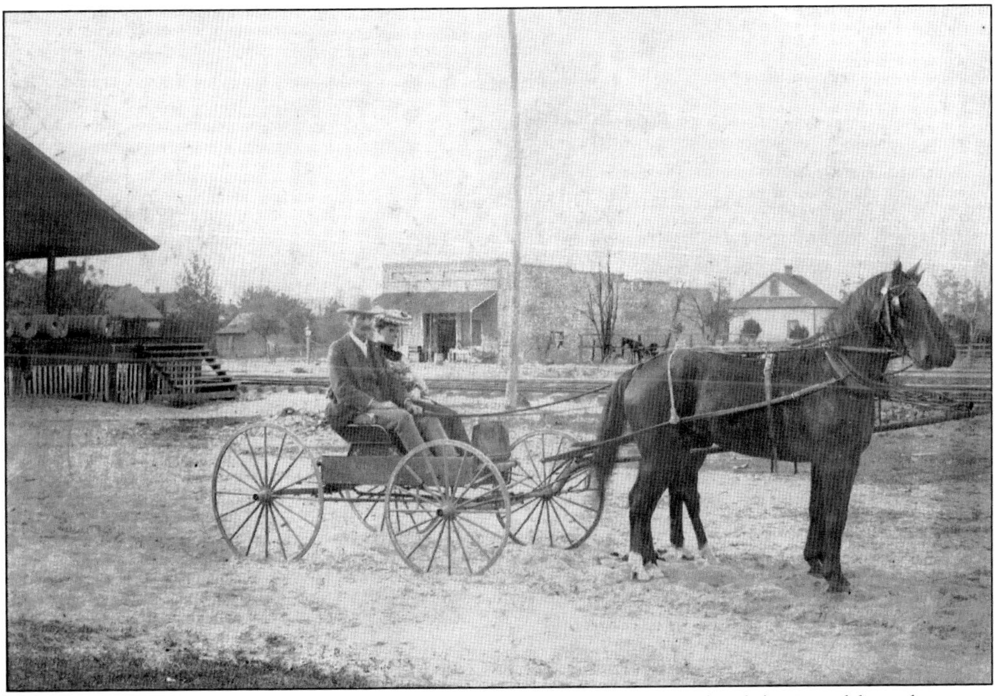

A couple rides their buckboard into town in this c. 1900 photograph of the Lynchburg business section. The general store of Jefferson Alexander Hickson stands on the other side of the train tracks that divide Front Street. Also seen is a well for watering the animals and another horse and buggy. Baled cotton rests on a platform in anticipation of the train. The mule, faintly visible coming around the rear of the depot, may be pulling in another wagonload of cotton for shipment. (Betsy Redick.)

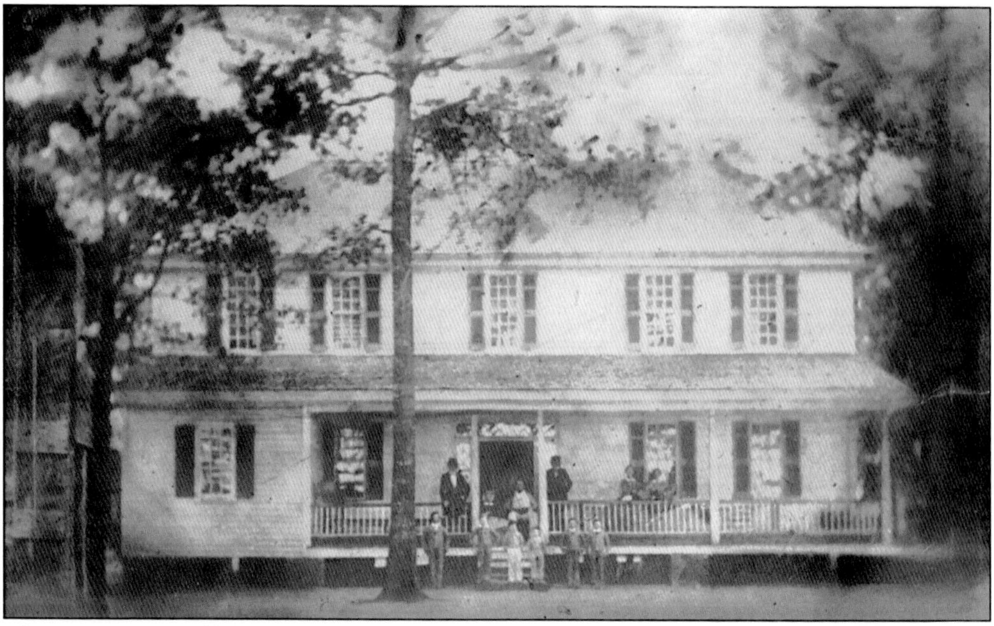

These two views of life at Stirrup Branch plantation were captured on June 8, 1857, the 75th birthday of Capt. James Rembert. The front view of the house shows the Rembert family and the rear view of the house depicts the slaves, who have been lined up according to rank. The home is a perfect example of the Plantation Plain style of architecture, quite popular in the antebellum South. Characteristics of this style include a house with two stories, one-room deep, with single-story shed rooms on the rear. The front of the home would feature a long one-story porch. The traveler's room, on the left of the porch, had a separate door and could be used by a passing traveler without disturbing the family. The wealth of this family is made plain by the many glass windows and especially by the glasswork around the door. (Barrie Cunningham Hardwick.)

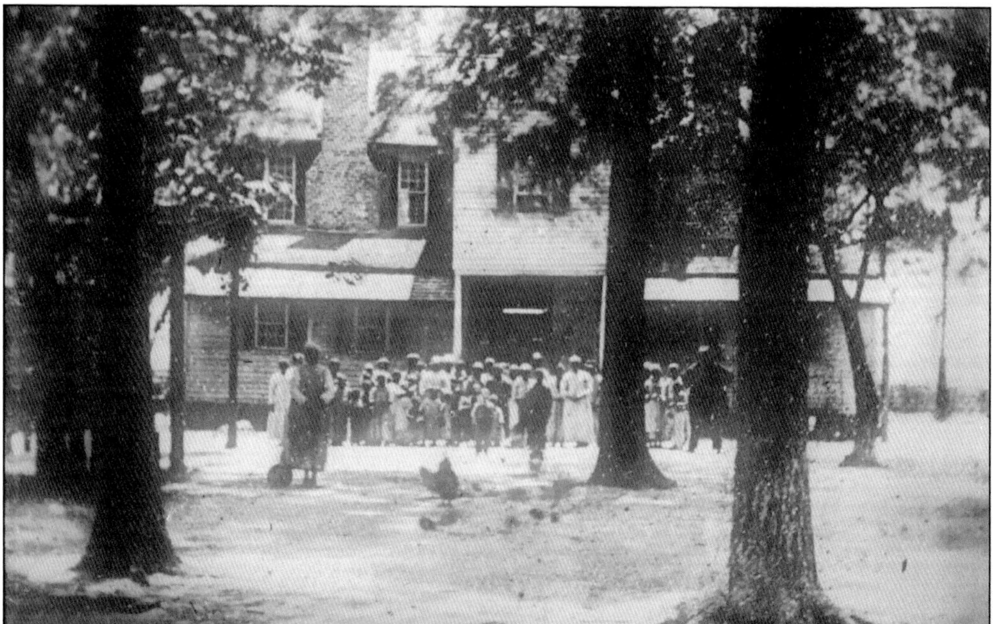

Bessie Cribbs Hickson stands beside a mile marker on the railroad tracks at Lynchburg. Rail service had been provided in the town since the mid-1850s. While most early settlements had been coastal or river towns, the advent of the railroad enabled folks to move inland, resulting in a population shift. The current town of Lynchburg was formed by this kind of migration toward the railroad. (Betsy Redick.)

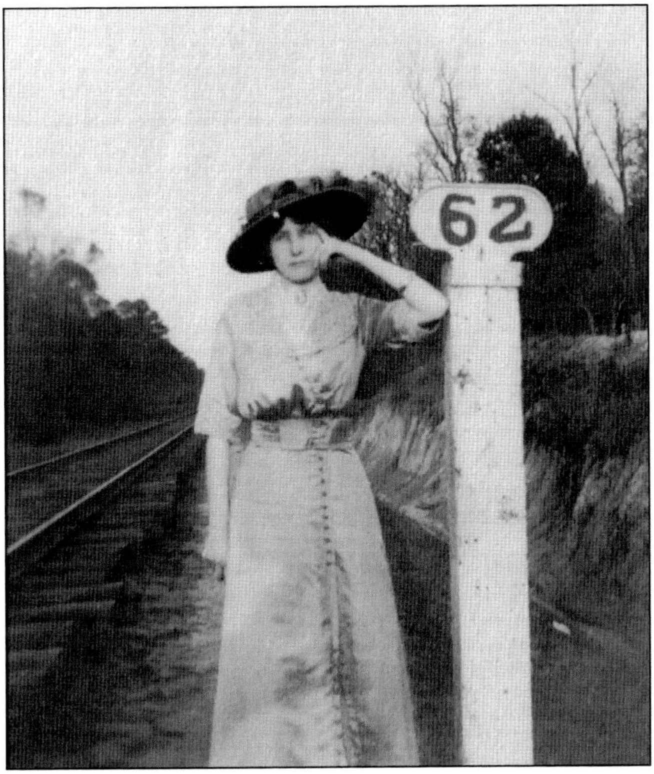

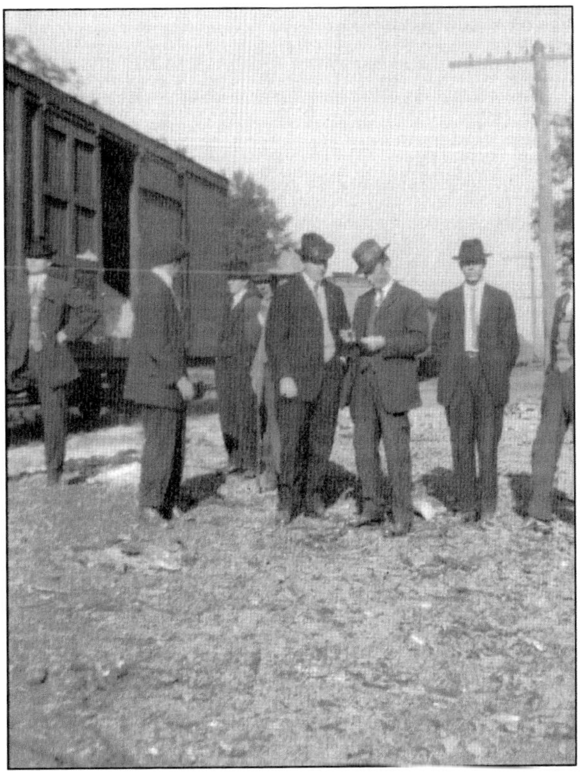

Cotton buyers inspect their purchases beside a railcar in this c. 1920 Lynchburg photograph. At harvest time, the buyers would converge upon Lee County, as well as other cotton-producing regions, with hopes of obtaining the highest grades of fiber possible. The cotton would then be shipped to such ports as Wilmington to be sold worldwide. (Betsy Redick.)

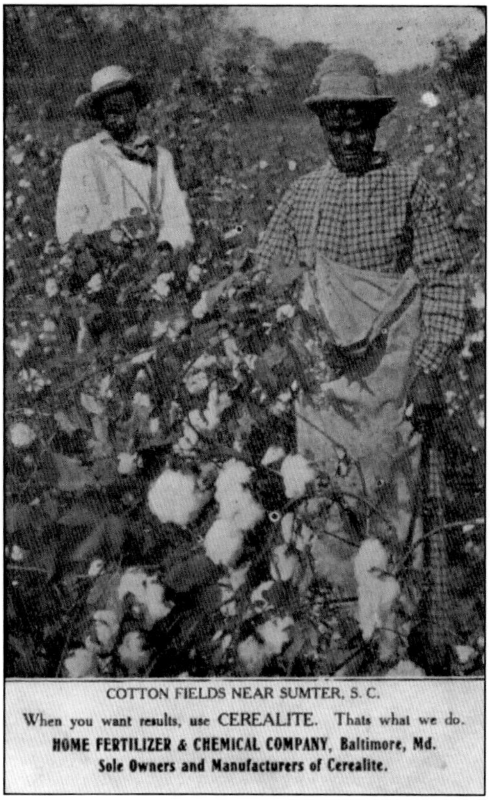

The caption "Cotton Fields Near Sumter, S. C." could easily place this photograph in the vicinity of Bishopville. Picking cotton was notoriously hard and painful work, and many farmers sharecropped their fields to get the job done in the years before tractors and combines. The backbreaking labor was not limited to men or even to adults. Note that the subject in the foreground of this photograph is actually wearing a dress. (Barrie Cunningham Hardwick.)

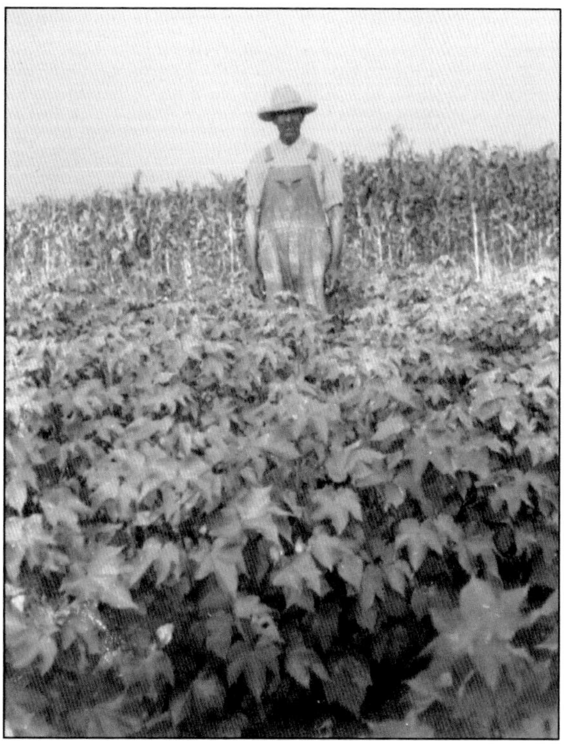

A sharecropper stands amongst cotton plants in a field outside Lynchburg. This tenant would have been given credit to buy his farming essentials—seed, tools, equipment—and living expenses. When the crop was harvested and sold, the sharecropper would receive a prearranged percentage of the profits minus expenses. Sometimes the landowners were not actually farmers themselves but simply investors. (Betsy Redick.)

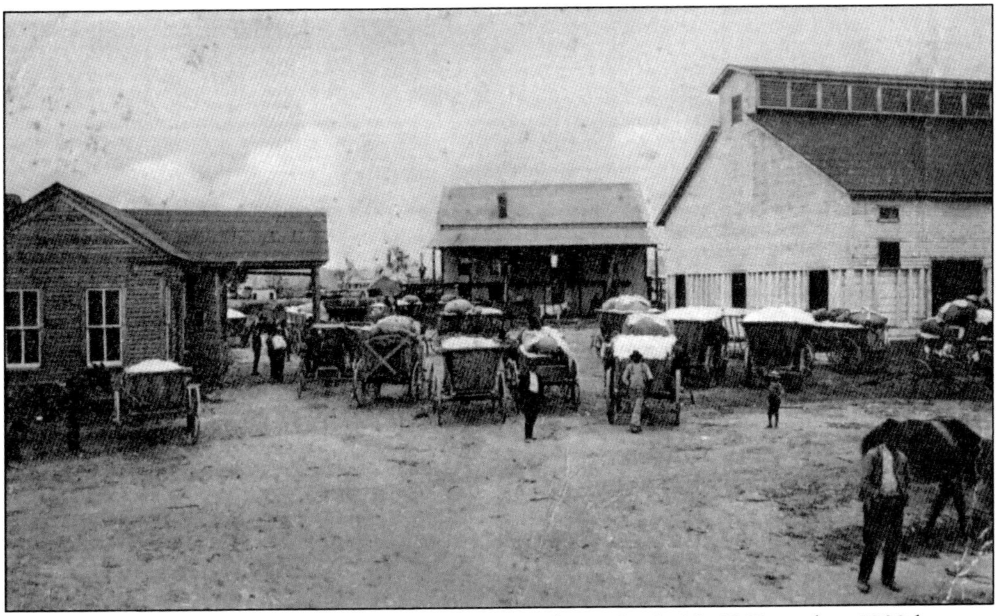

Lee County Manufacturing Company was chartered on March 25, 1903, and in 1908 became Palmetto Oil Company. By 1910, the elaborate operation consisted of a gin, seed house, a seed-milling building with a linter room, pressroom, meal room, and a building for meal and hull storage, all connected by a system of conveyor belts. The mill was located on the north side of the railroad tracks between Nettles and Lee Streets. Palmetto Oil was a state-of-the-art facility for its time, with seed cotton being fed simultaneously into multiple gins. (SCCM.)

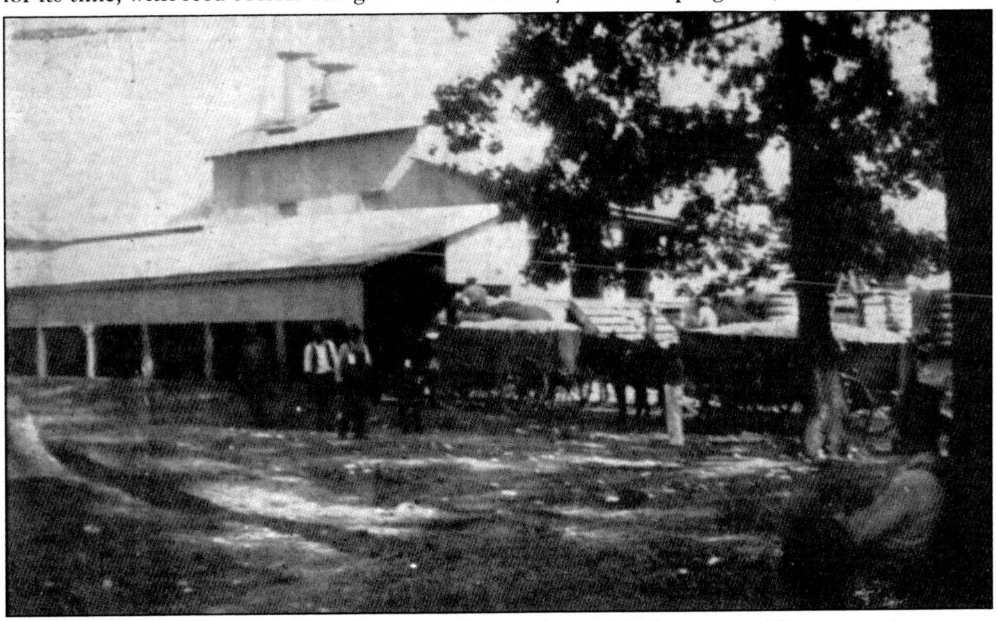

Cotton was the cash crop of Lee County well into the mid-19th century. Numerous gins sprang up in Bishopville, Elliott, Lynchburg, and other small communities to process the year's harvest. This photograph is of the Farmers Ginning and Trading Company on Lee Street operated by R. W. McCutchen. Formerly located on the vacant lot now owned by Palmetto Oil Company, a steam engine provided the power to run the gins and presses. (SCCM.)

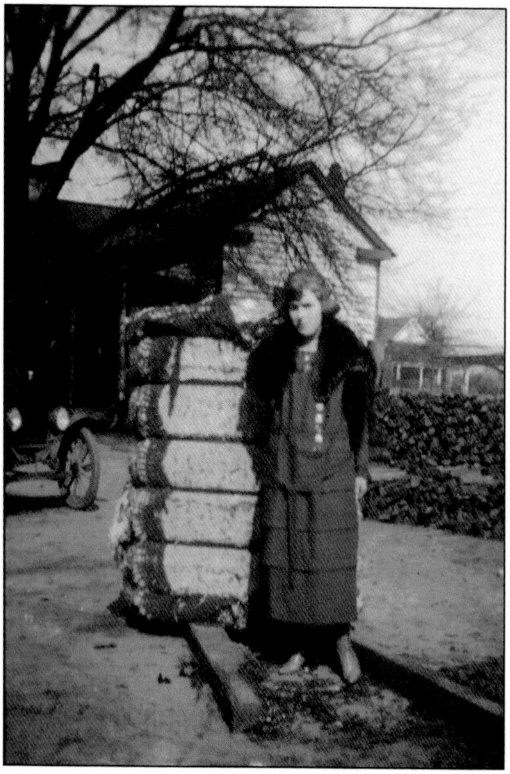

Carrie Cribbs of Lynchburg stands in front of a bale of cotton in this c. 1920 photograph. Although the Cribbs family lived in the town limits of Lynchburg, they likely owned acreage that they leased to sharecroppers. She would later marry Jim Dougherty, cashier of The Peoples Bank of Lynchburg and mayor of Lynchburg. (Betsy Redick.)

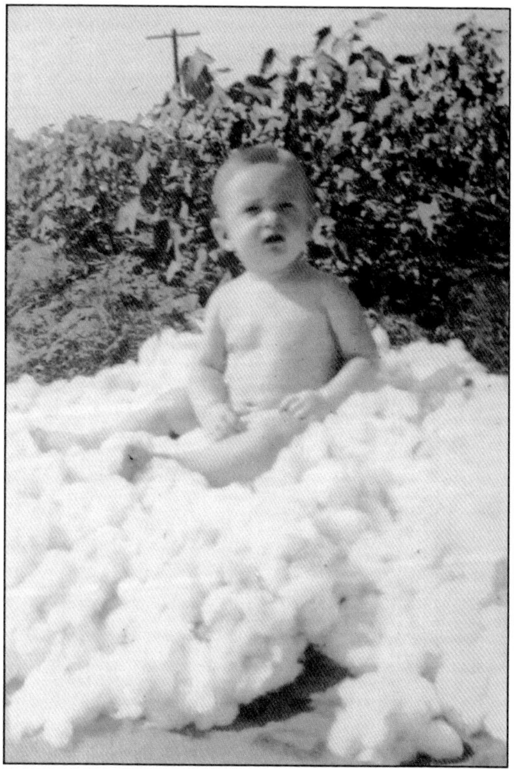

One-year-old Lee Stevenson sits high atop a pile of newly harvested cotton bolls against a backdrop of cotton plants in this 1944 photograph. Small-scale farming was not uncommon among city residents, and many vacant lots or backyards yielded a substantial cotton crop, as was the case for Lee's grandfather, a Bishopville businessman.

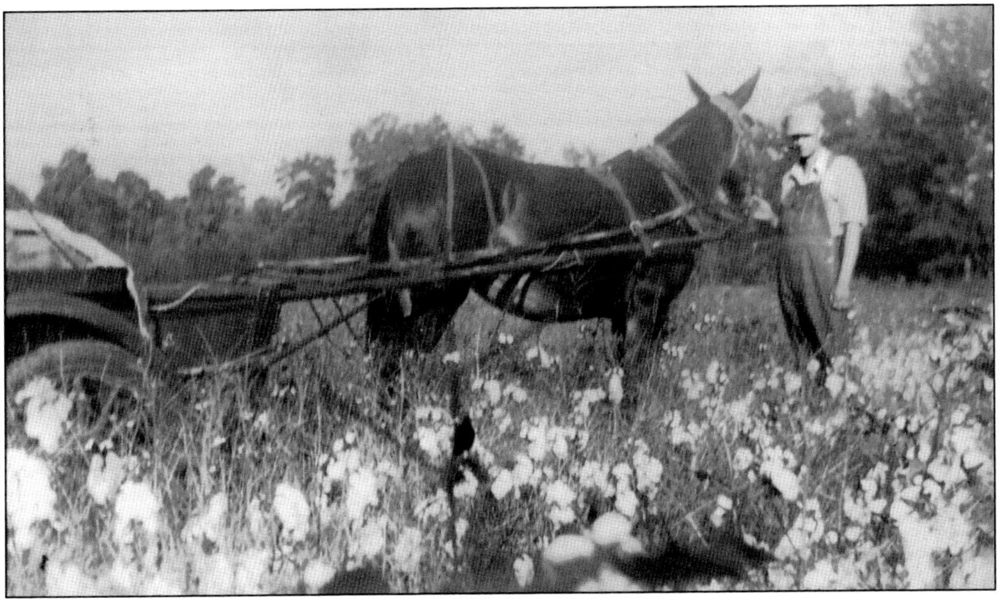

Even with the advent of the tractor, mules and other work animals remained quite common on the farm well into the 1950s and 1960s. Maude Harris of Lee County is shown here in the 1940s in his cotton field using his horse to pull a wagon. In the picture below, a mule is still doing the work in 1959. (SCCM.)

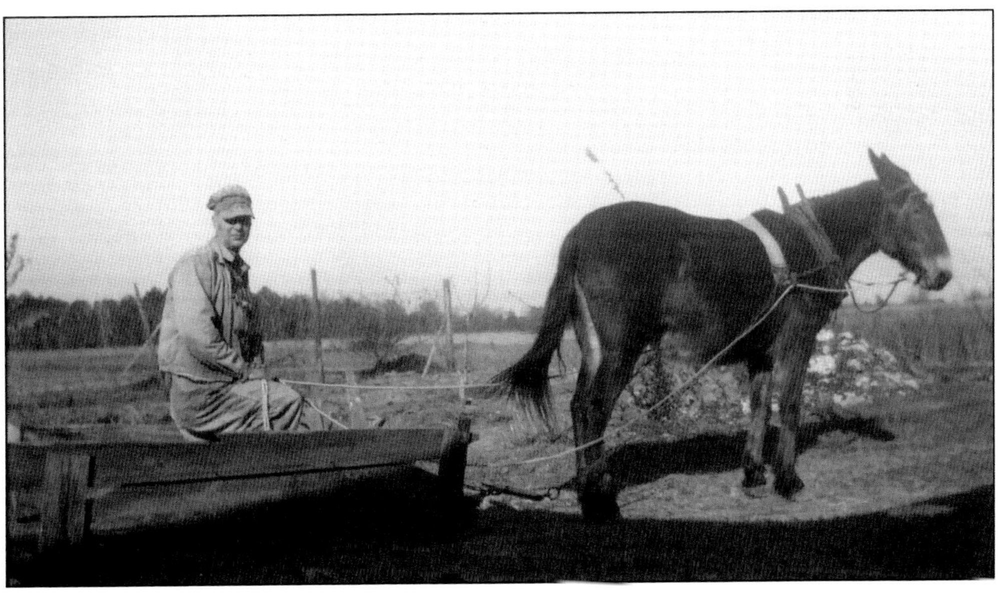

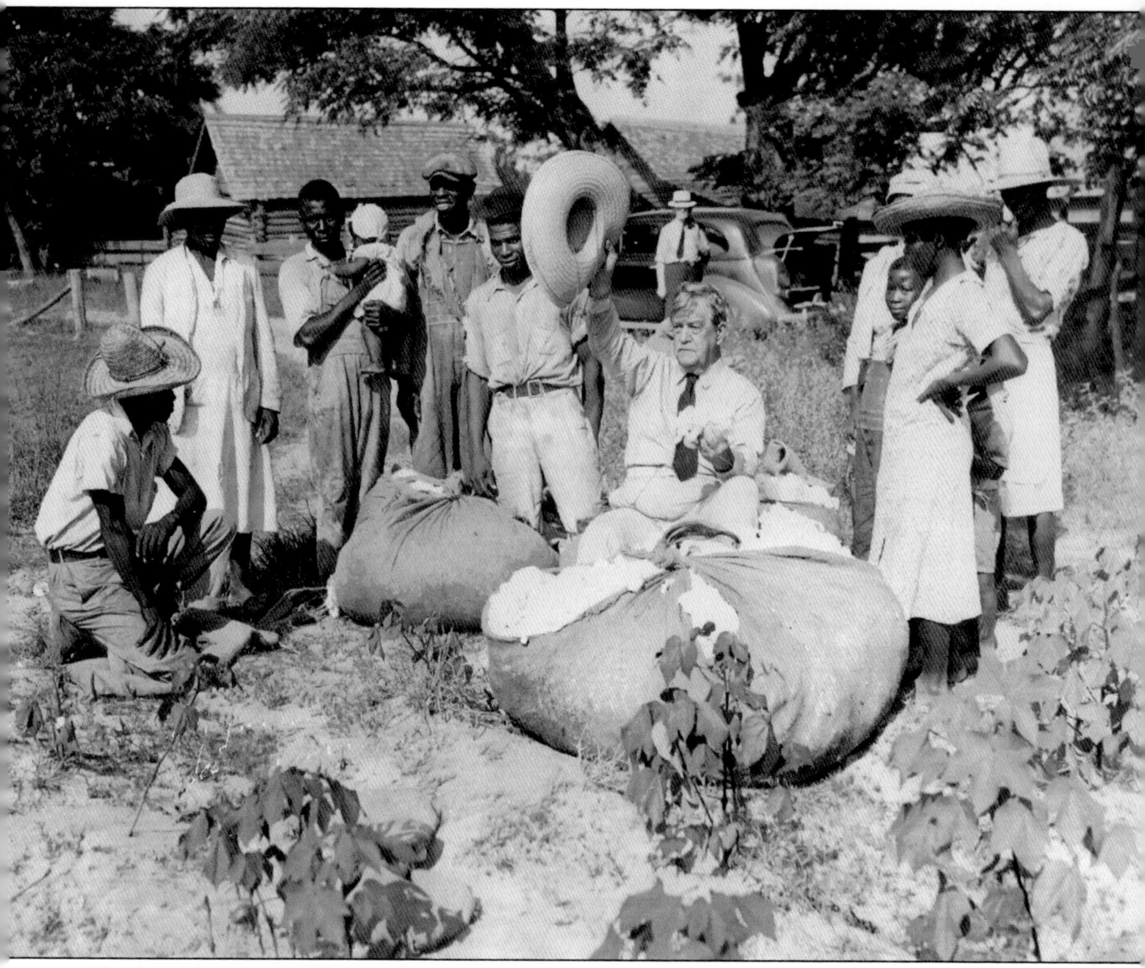

The best that many African Americans could hope for in the early 20th century was to be a sharecropper or a cotton picker. The sacks of cotton in this 1930s photograph represent hours of work under the hot sun with hands lacerated from the sharp cotton bolls. The labor was undoubtedly done by the men, women, and children in this picture. Surrounded by the workers is Sen. Ellison D. "Cotton Ed" Smith. He represented the state from 1909 until his defeat in 1944. A controversial figure who opposed President Roosevelt's New Deal policies, he dedicated his career to the support of legislation affecting cotton. (SCCM.)

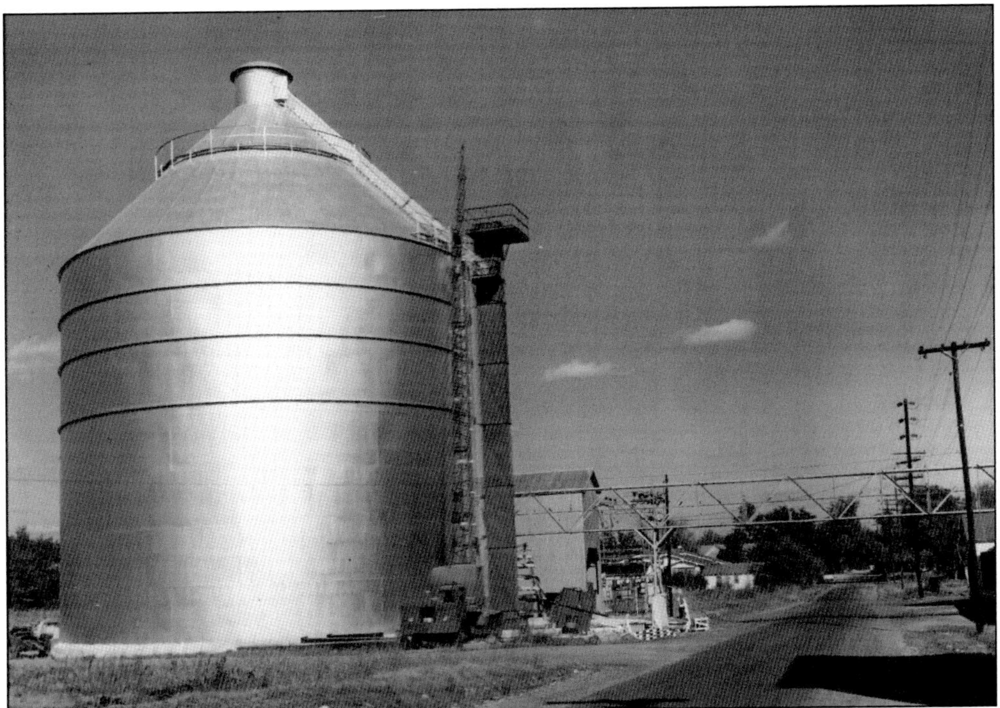

Pictured above is a 5,000-ton cottonseed silo, built in 1955 by Chicago Bridge and Iron. The photograph was taken at a time when the cottonseed bridged over and would not fall into the tank. The crane on the right was used to swing a large steel ball into the sides of the structure in an attempt to shake the seed loose. The ball was ineffective, and the cottonseed bridge had to be dynamited before the seed finally fell. To this day, dents from the ball are visible in the side of the tank. (Lee County Public Library.)

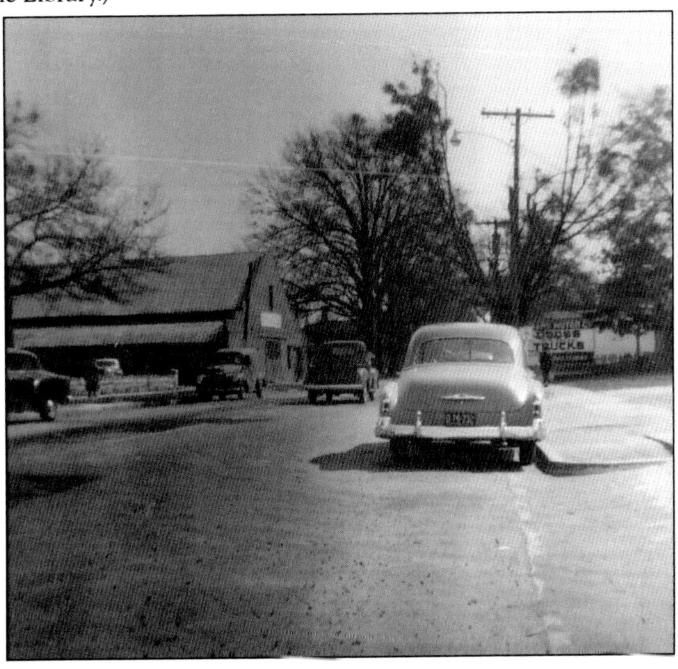

In this view looking north on Church Street just past the intersection with Main Street, a low stone wall around Woodward Park can be seen to the left. Just past the wall is Slesinger's Stables, which had been started many years before by Morris Slesinger. (Lee County Public Library.)

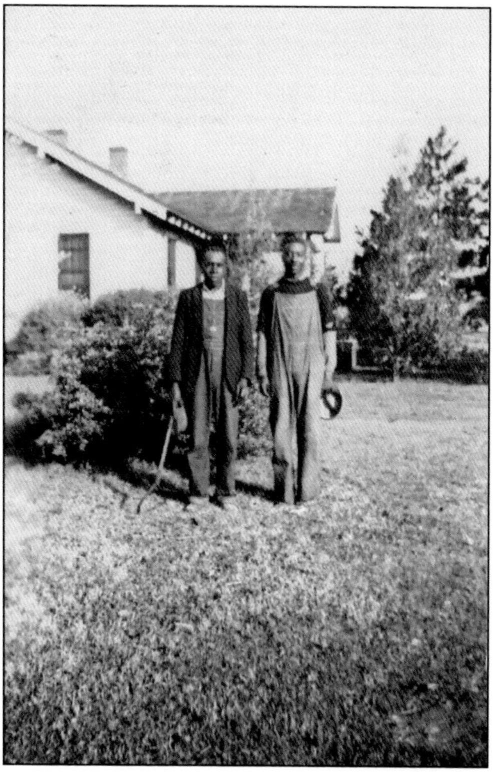

Prepared for a long, hard day in the cotton fields in 1941 are Link R? (left) and Johnson McDuffie. Johnson; his wife, Alice; and their children lived about three-quarters of a mile past where the railroad tracks intersect Bradley Avenue. After the harvest, Johnson would pile the cotton in his wagon, hitch up Minnie the mule, and drive the crop to the gin in town. In later years, Johnson worked at Laney Brothers Stables on Main Street.

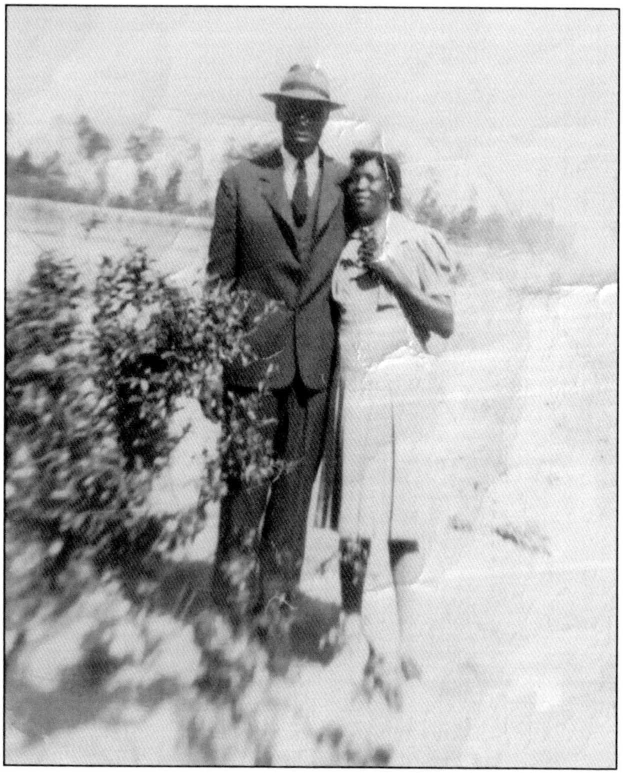

In 1949, after years of laboring as sharecroppers, Henry W. Isaac and his wife, Ethel Jackson Isaac, moved to Elliott where they had purchased farmland. Originally from Wisacky, Henry Isaac grew cotton, corn, sweet potatoes, rice, wheat, tobacco, and oats. Born in 1901, he recalled when there was "but one building from the train depot to Church Street with cotton fields in between." The Isaacs put all five of their children through college; four became schoolteachers. Politically active, Henry Isaac was instrumental in the construction of Mount Pleasant High School and served on the board of Allen University. The Isaacs were married for 71 years. (Bernice Isaac Bradley.)

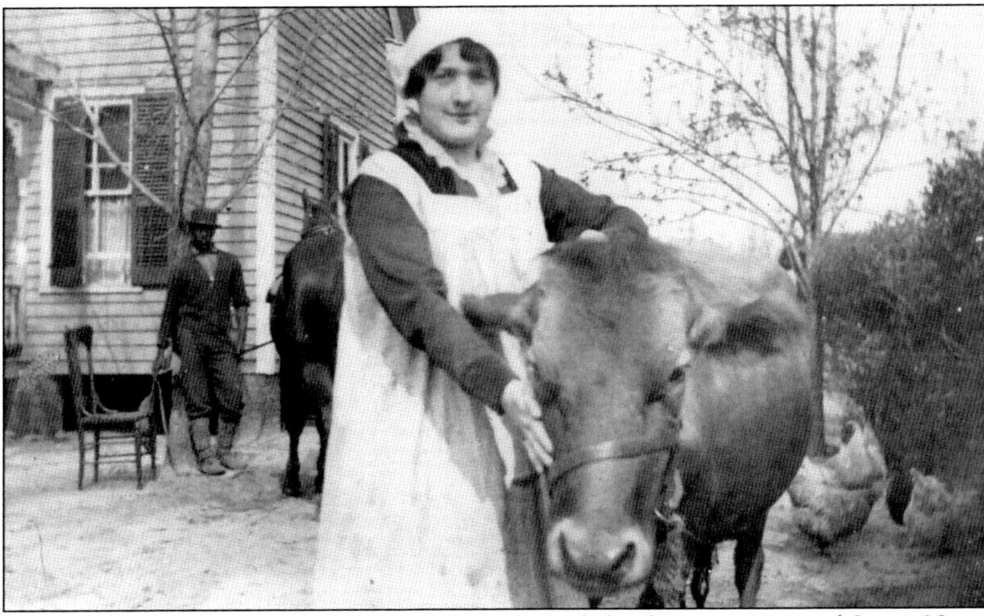

Nettie Cahn Levenson stands with her milk cow outside her home on Heyward Street. Nettie emigrated with her family from Lithuania to Baltimore at the age of 15. She would often come south to visit her brothers, Julius and Ellis Cahn, who lived in Bishopville. In 1915, she married Bishopville merchant Frank Levenson, who had a side business selling farm animals. Since the cows and goats for sale needed to be milked, Nettie always had buttermilk, cheese, and sour cream to share. In the background stands "Uncle Harrison." He was employed by the Levensons for many years and was dearly loved by their children. (Carolyn Baruch Levenson.)

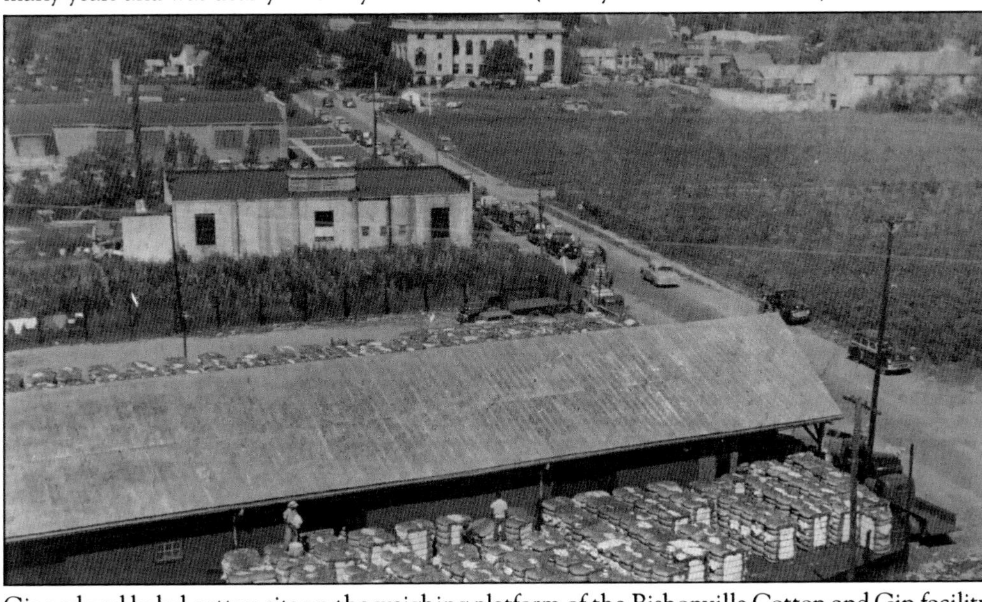

Ginned and baled cotton sits on the weighing platform of the Bishopville Cotton and Gin facility on Gregg Street. For many years, the job of county cotton-weigher was an elected position. This photograph was taken from the Bishopville Milling Company located next door. The line of trucks piled high with cotton stretches almost to the courthouse, and a field of cotton is planted where the jail stands today. (Lee County Historical Society.)

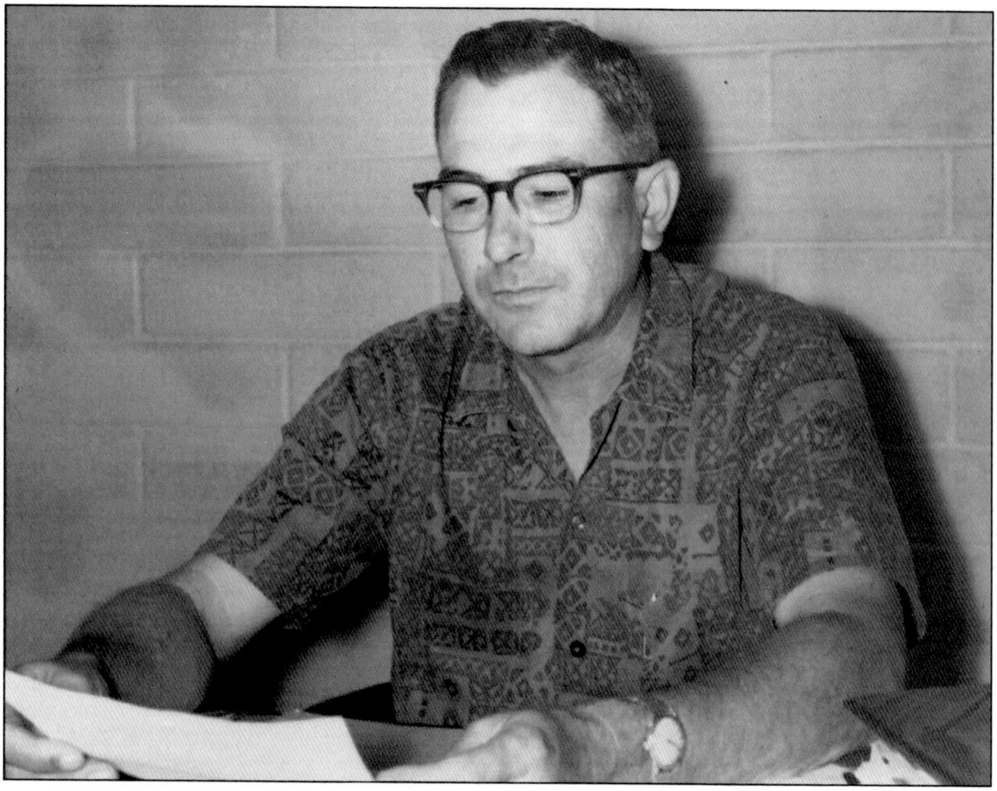

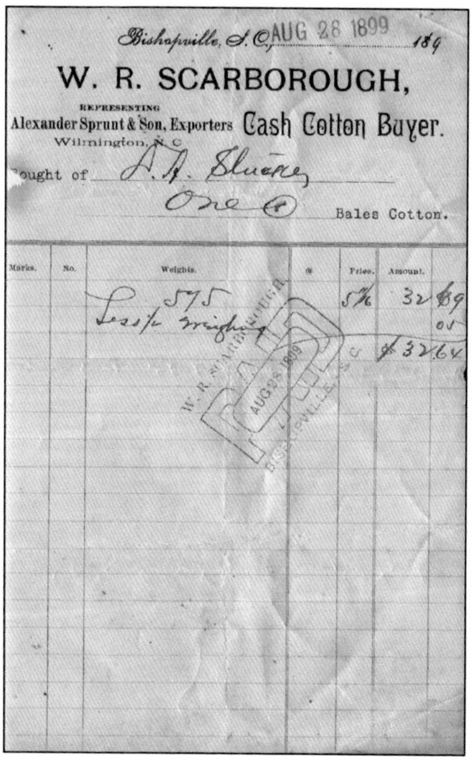

In 1913, brothers N. J. Laney Sr. and Rob Laney opened a livery stable that Lee County farmers would come to rely upon for over 70 years. N. J.'s sons, N. J. "Jay" Jr. (pictured), Dan, and Leopold Laney, later became part of the business known as Laney and Sons. Upon the death of N. J. Sr. in 1950, the business was renamed Laney Brothers. They sold mules, other farm animals, harnesses, collars, and farm machinery. When the business phased out livestock sales in the mid-1960s, it became an International Harvester dealership. (*Lee County Observer.*)

A receipt from W. R. Scarborough shows that on September 2, 1899, cotton was selling at roughly 5.67¢ per pound. Profit for the farmer on this transaction was $30.84 minus the half-cent charge for weighing the bale. One of the many cotton buyers in town, the receipt shows Scarborough to be an agent for the cotton-exporting giant, Alexander Sprunt and Son. Based in Wilmington, North Carolina, they pioneered the steam foreign trade with interests worldwide. Sprunt even had an overseas office in Liverpool, England, showing just how far Lee County's upland cotton traveled.

Four

NEIGHBORS

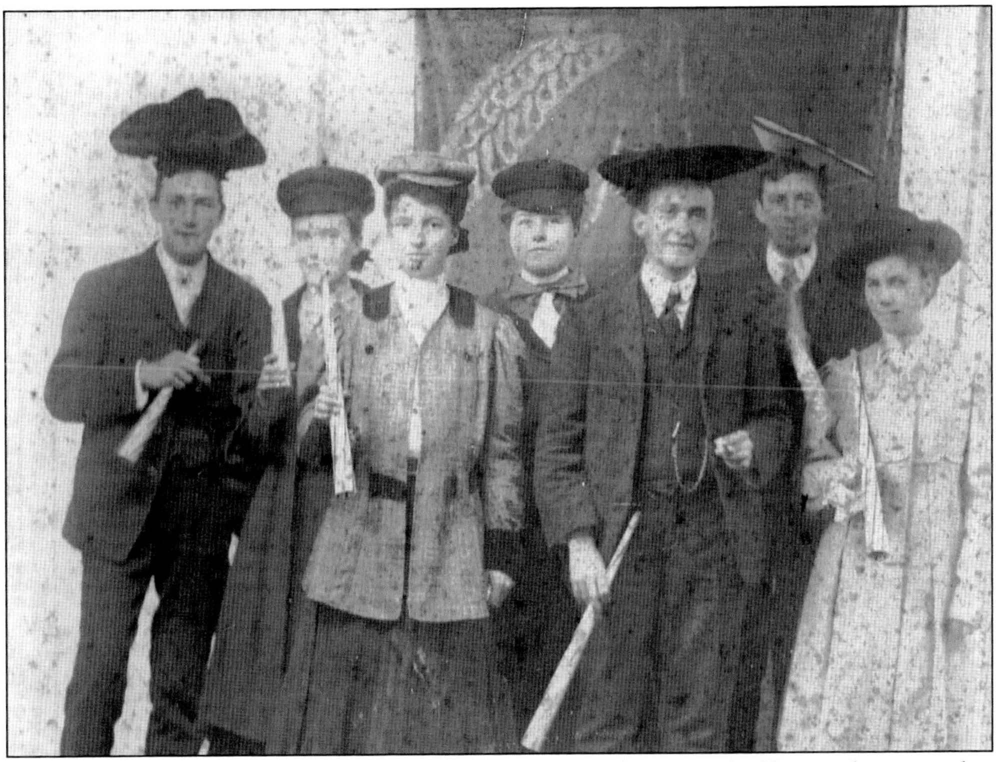

The young men and women at a Lynchburg Christmas party have switched hats with one another for this photograph taken December 25, 1905. From left to right, they are Herbert Hickson, Annie Cribbs, Sue Kirby, Bessie Cribbs, Walter S. Carter, Ellie Kilpatrick, and Viola McIntosh. (Betsy Redick.)

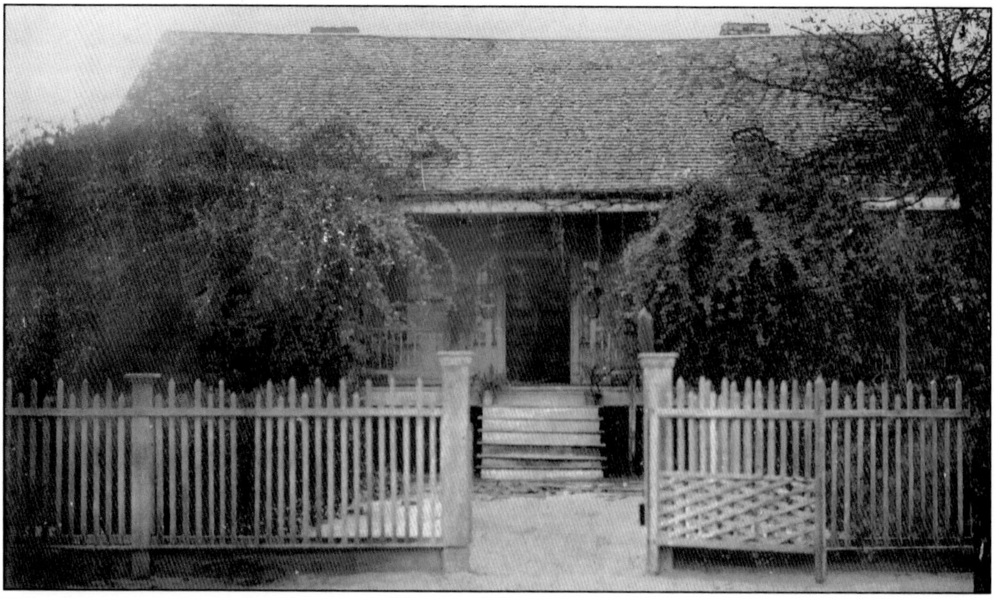

"The house now owned and occupied by our fellow townsman, Dr. R. E. Dennis, was the first house built and owned by Dr. Bishop," wrote H. S. Cunningham in the first edition of the *Lee County Vindicator* in 1902. The above picture, dating from the 1800s, bears almost no resemblance to the familiar West Church Street home of today. The structure has seen extensive renovation over the years; however, the four rooms on the first floor remain original to the house. Careful observation will show the glasswork above the door has not changed. Current owners Robert and June Jennings are the fourth generation of the Dennis family to call the West Church Street house their home. (Robert and June Jennings.)

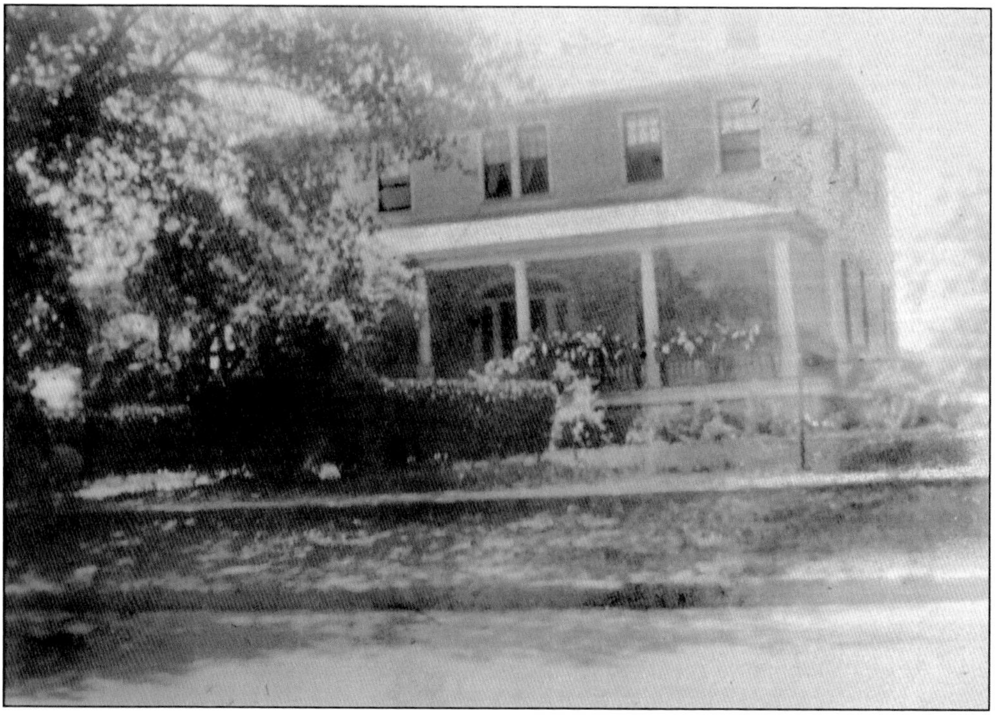

Dr. R. E. (Robert Ellison) Dennis served the Confederate army as a surgeon and was the primary physician in Bishopville for many years. His father, Dr. John Edward Dennis, was a native of Charlotte County, Virginia, who arrived in Bishopville about 1824. R. E. Dennis married the former Mary Green, a daughter of the Reverend Henry D. Green. Their children were Mary Green Dennis and Robert Ellison Dennis Jr., a Bishopville attorney who would later become a state senator. (Robert Jennings.)

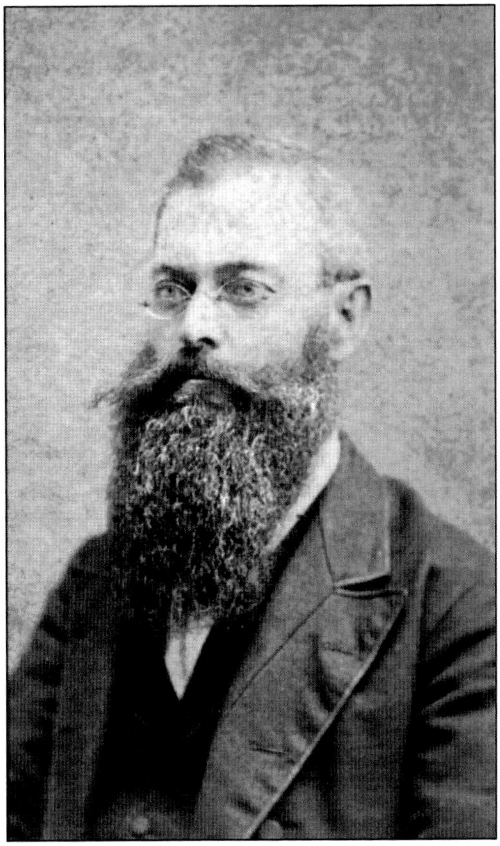

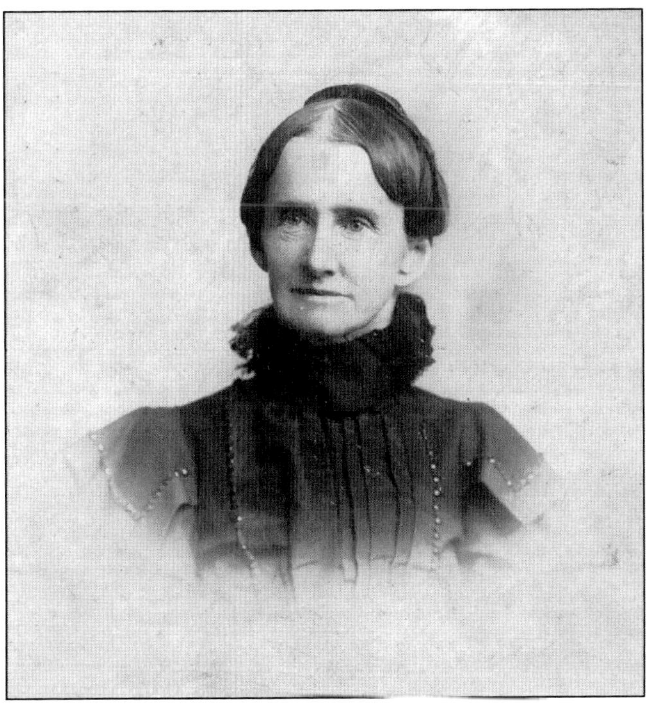

Mary Green Dennis was one of 10 children born to the Reverend Henry D. Green and his second wife, Rebecca Abbott, who lived near Rembert Church. Her father was a signer of the Ordinance of Secession for South Carolina. (Robert Jennings.)

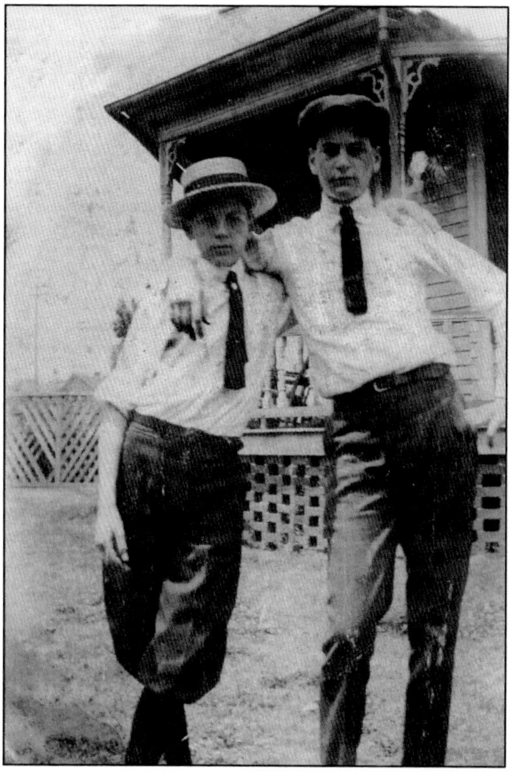

Brothers Aaron (left) and Leo Krasnoff stop for a picture outside their Lee Street home. Leo would marry Anne Pittle and raise two children, Bob and Arlene. Over the years, Leo operated several stores in town, including the L&S Department store, a liquor store, and a general store on Main Street. Aaron, a member of the Bishopville High School class of 1922, passed away in 1923 of complications from a ruptured appendix. (Gift of Jennie Krasnoff Caine, Special Collections, College of Charleston.)

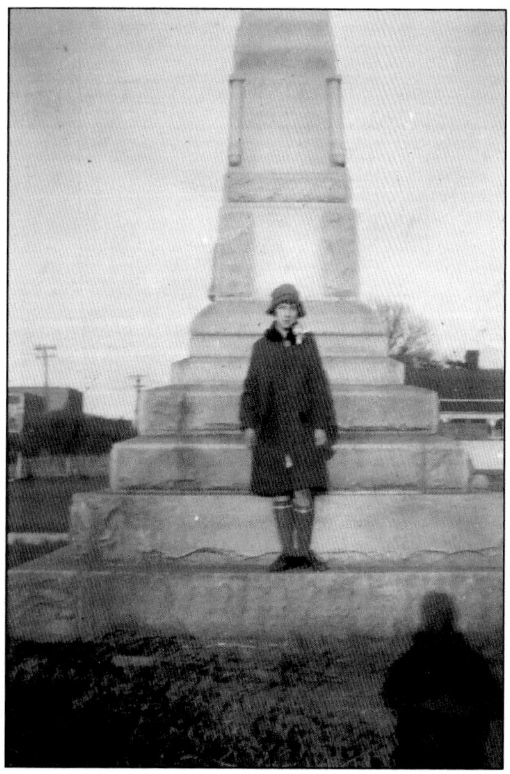

A young Betty McCutchen (Austin), a daughter of Dr. and Mrs. R. O. McCutchen, stands at the base of the Confederate Monument on the grounds of the Lee County Courthouse in the mid-1920s. In 1908, the Lee County Courthouse Commission passed a resolution to reserve a plot of land on the grounds to erect a memorial to the county's Confederate soldiers. After much fund-raising on the part of the Lottie Green Chapter of the United Daughters of the Confederacy, the monument was unveiled on Confederate Memorial Day, May 10, 1913. (Ruthie Stevenson Bowman.)

This portrait of William Robert Cunningham was made in 1901. In 1902, he married Annie Louise Witherspoon, described in the June 4, 1902, *Lee County Vindicator* as "one of Elliott's most popular young ladies." In 1902, Cunningham announced the opening of his printing business associated with the above newspaper. Cunningham's father, Herbert Shields Cunningham, had founded the *Vindicator* that same year. (Barrie Cunningham Hardwick.)

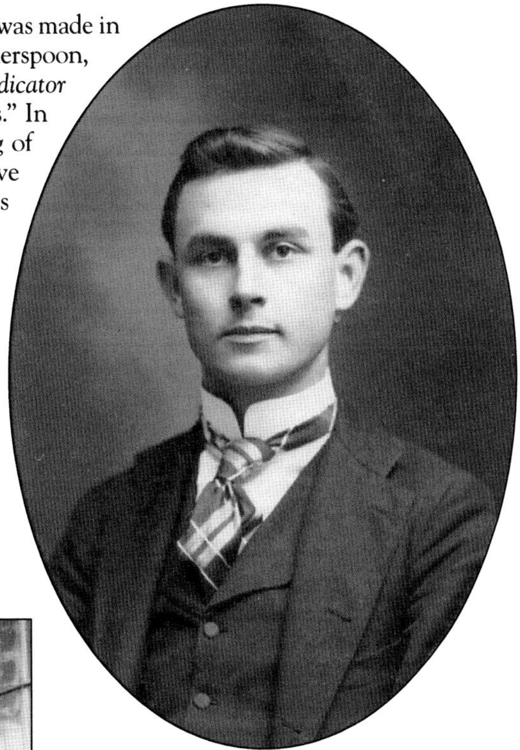

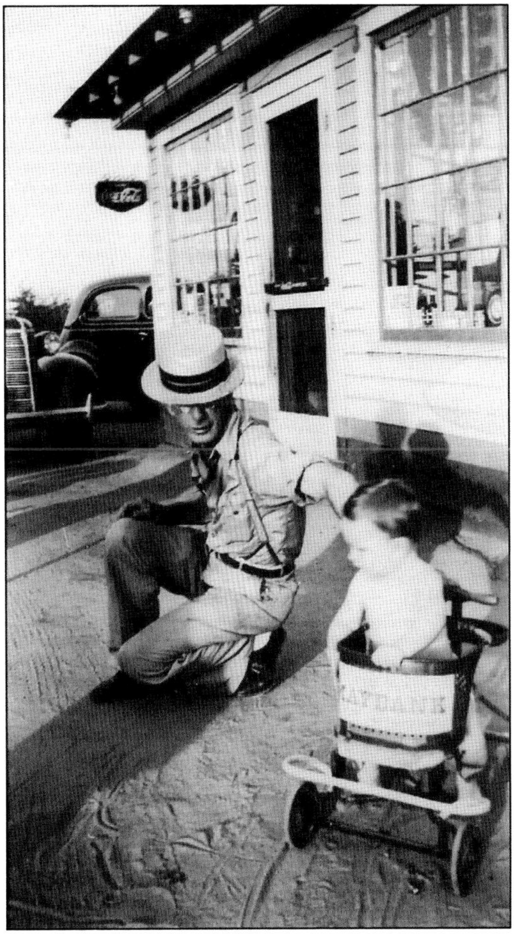

A young Wayne Davis campaigns for future South Carolina governor Burnet Maybank in this 1938 photograph. He is seen at left with his grandfather, "Doc" Ackerman, in front of Doc's service station at the corner of Highway 15 South and the St. Charles Road. Wayne's parents were J. W. and Roberta "Bobby" Ackerman Davis. (Wayne Davis.)

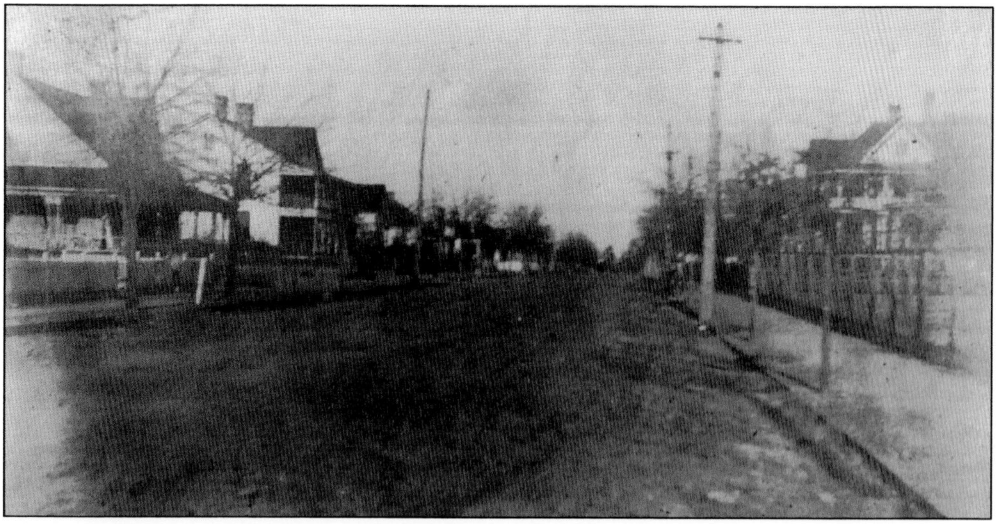

This *c.* 1900 photograph of Dennis Avenue was taken from the location of the Warley Parrott home. At one time, Dennis Avenue was Bishopville's main thoroughfare, boasting more traffic than Main Street. One would find the town's two principal hotels, the Durant and the Pioneer, located opposite one another on the packed-dirt street. The building on the immediate right in the photograph with the two visible chimneys is the Durant Hotel. The residence of William Apollos James and his family, now home to the Lee County Historical Society, is also on Dennis Avenue. (Barrie Cunningham Hardwick.)

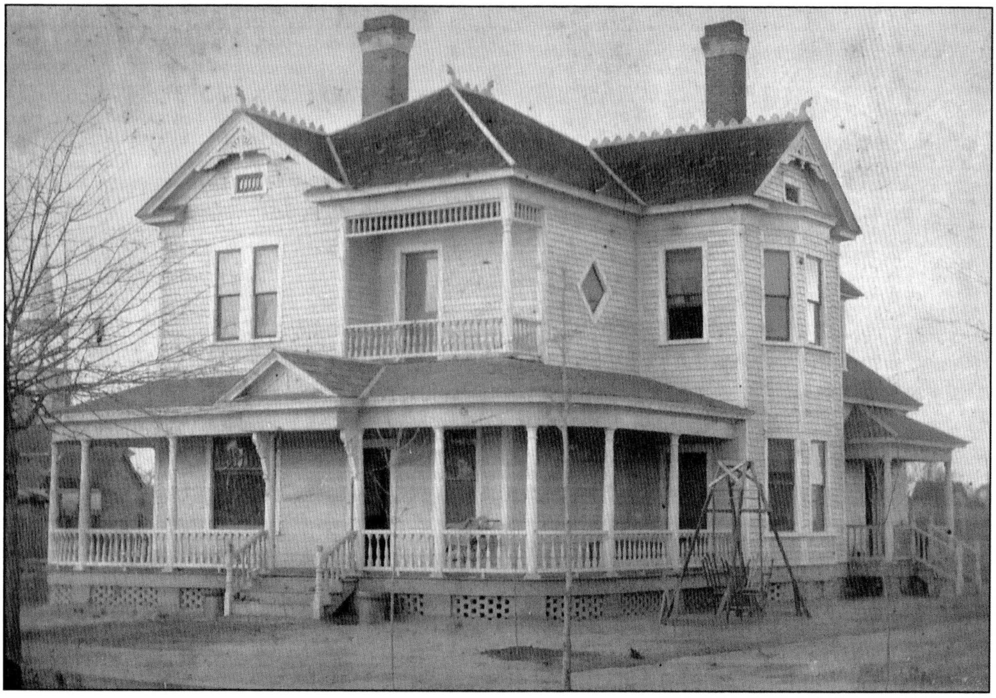

This stately home, which formerly stood on Dennis Avenue, was built in the late 1890s by Warley L. Parrott Sr. Fred and Alice Baroody owned the home in 1973 and sold the property to Hancock (now Hancock-Elmore) Funeral Home. The home was demolished that same year to provide parking space for the funeral home chapel. (Barrie Cunningham Hardwick.)

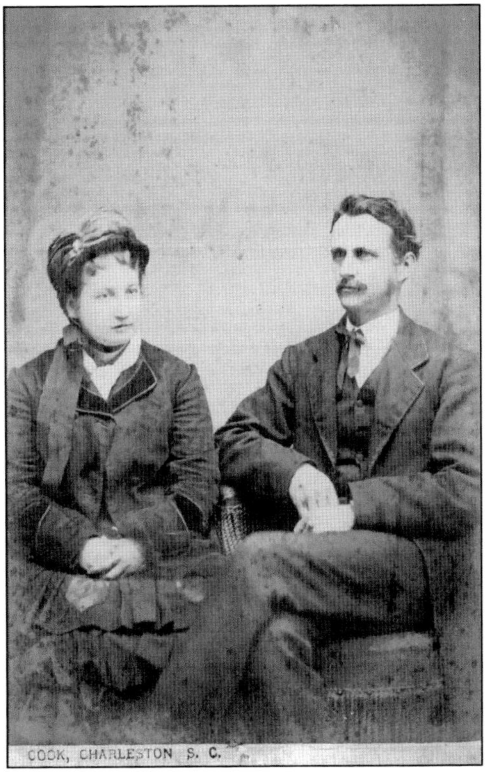

Warley and Florence Parrott likely sat for this photograph in the late 1880s. Parrott was cashier of the Farmers Loan and Trust Company and served as mayor of Bishopville for a number of years. He had recently been appointed postmaster at the time of his death in 1925. He married the former Florence Antoinette Barrett, and they resided in the home with their eight children: Warley Jr., Jewel, Annette, Grace, Florence, Mary, Inez, and Claire. (Barrie Cunningham Hardwick.)

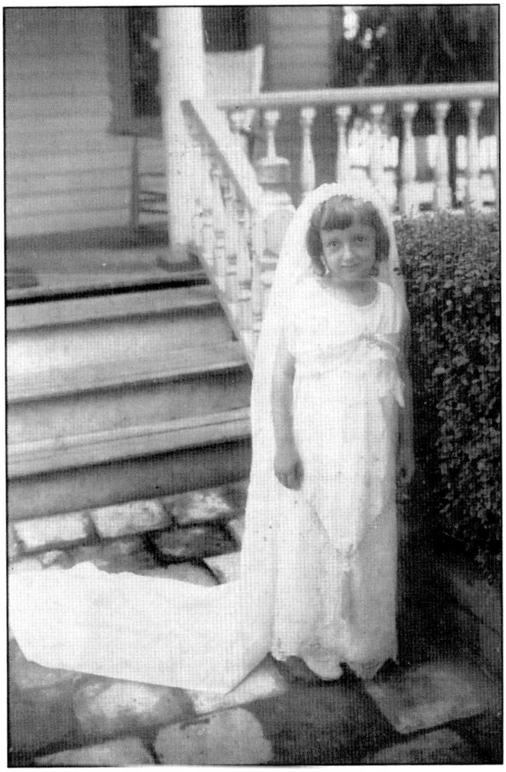

Possibly dressed for a Tom Thumb wedding, Jewel Parrott stands in front of the family home on Dennis Avenue in this *c.* 1916 photograph. The house once stood where the parking lot of Hancock-Elmore Funeral Home is today. Jewel was a daughter of Warley and Florence Parrott. (Barrie Cunningham Hardwick.)

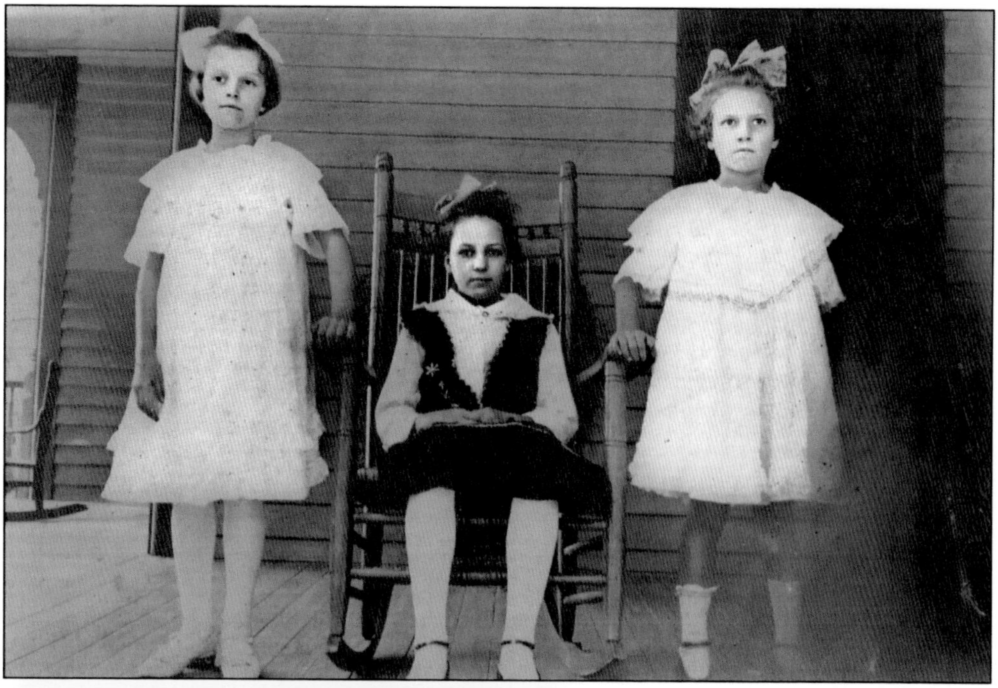

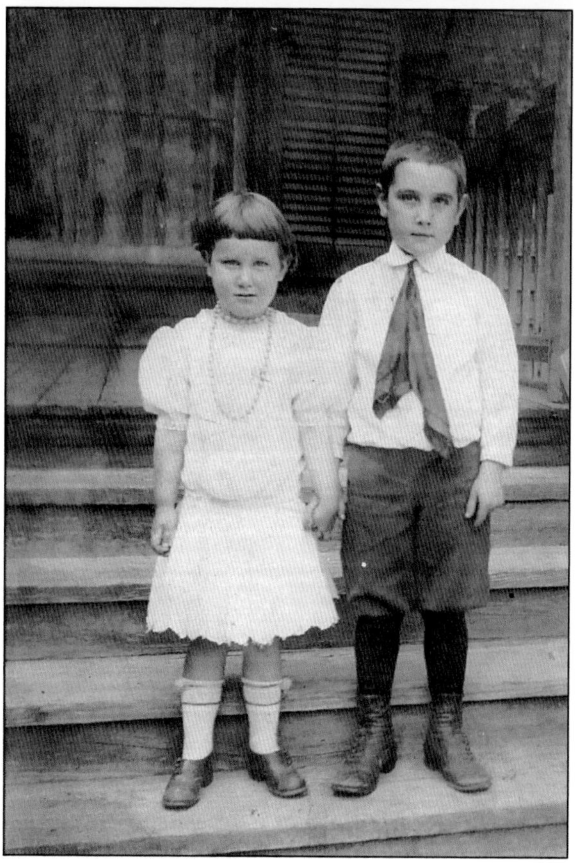

The daughters of Wallace and Novella Chaplin Davis are pictured on the front porch of their home about 1915. From the left are Tola, Thelma, and Kathleen Davis. The family lived in the Alcott section of Lee County where their father farmed. Tola married Julian McLendon, Thelma married Alva Kelley Sr., and Kathleen married Cliff Knight of Darlington. (June McLendon Jennings.)

Fred and Lina Stuckey's children Ashby Lee and Harriett Saye are pictured on the steps of their home around 1913. This photograph was probably taken in Mayesville, South Carolina. While they were still children, the family moved to Bishopville and resided on Heyward Street. Ashby married Louise Lavina and retired from Shaw Air Force Base. Harriet married Henry Watson.

From the left are John, Bessie, and Luther Truesdale about 1902. The children of James J. and Maggie Young Truesdale, they grew up several miles outside of Bishopville on the Browntown Road where James Truesdale farmed. Luther is the father of Liston Truesdale and is best remembered as the engineer for the Bishopville Fire Department. (Liston Truesdale.)

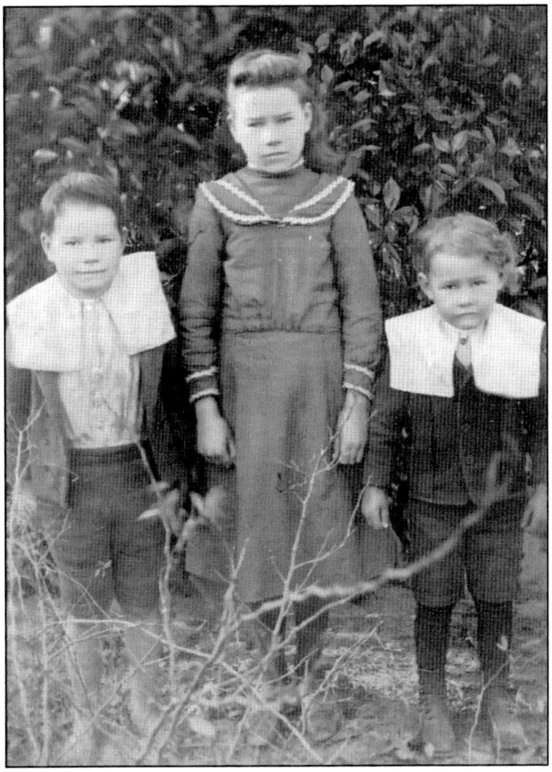

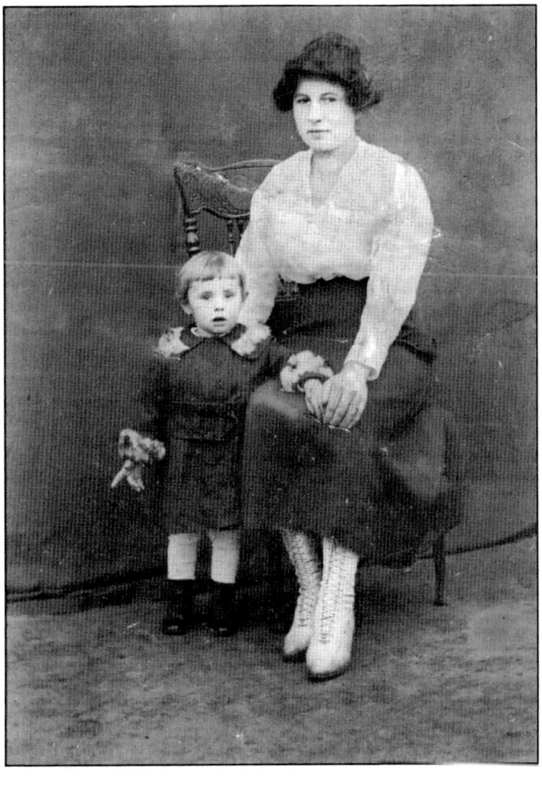

Elma King Brown is photographed with daughter Louise Brown (Davis) around 1917. Elma was the wife of Gene Brown who, for many years, served in the elected capacity of county cotton-weigher. After the cotton was ginned and the buyers made their offers, the farmers would take the bales to the platform behind the old depot to be weighed, as it was purchased by the pound. Brown also worked at the train depot, and his wife would assist in the delivery of freight to local merchants. (Betty Brown Truesdale.)

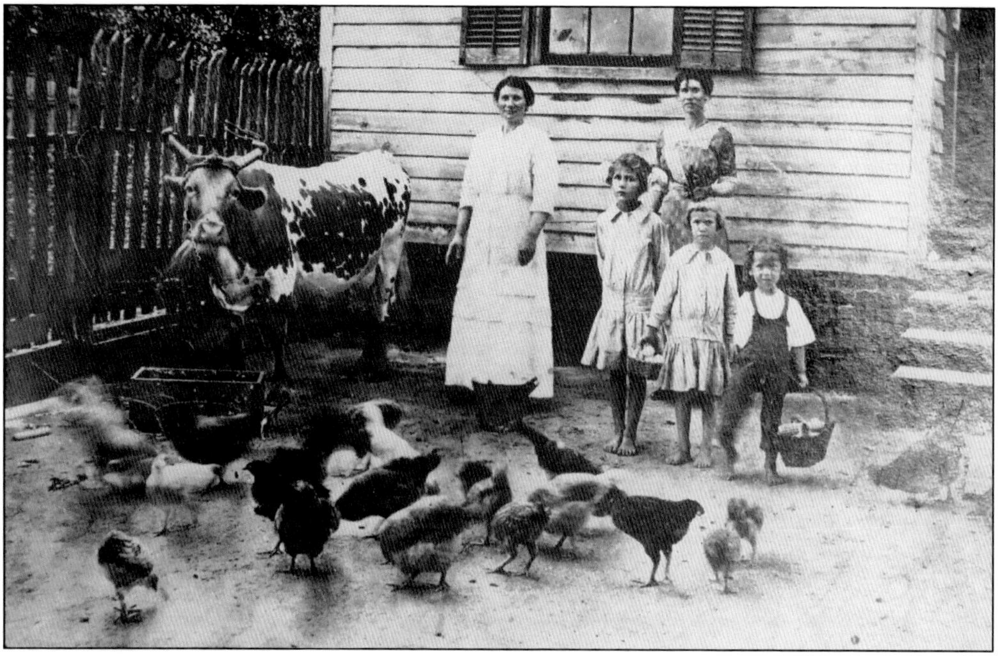

At the beginning of the 20th century, Jacob Gallun peddled his way to Bishopville where he set up a permanent shop. He and his wife, Mary, lived in town almost 30 years and had five children. Pictured above at the family home around 1913 are, from left to right, Daisy Belle (the cow), "Auntie Mama" (Eva Seidman Berman), Mary Seidman Gallun, and Jacob and Mary's children Dena, Mollye, and Louis. Brothers Marvin and Elmore were not yet born. Mary's sister, Eva, was married to Simon Berman, and they also lived in Bishopville. Around 1925, the Galluns relocated to Bladensburg, Maryland, where they operated another general store. (Charles Gallun.)

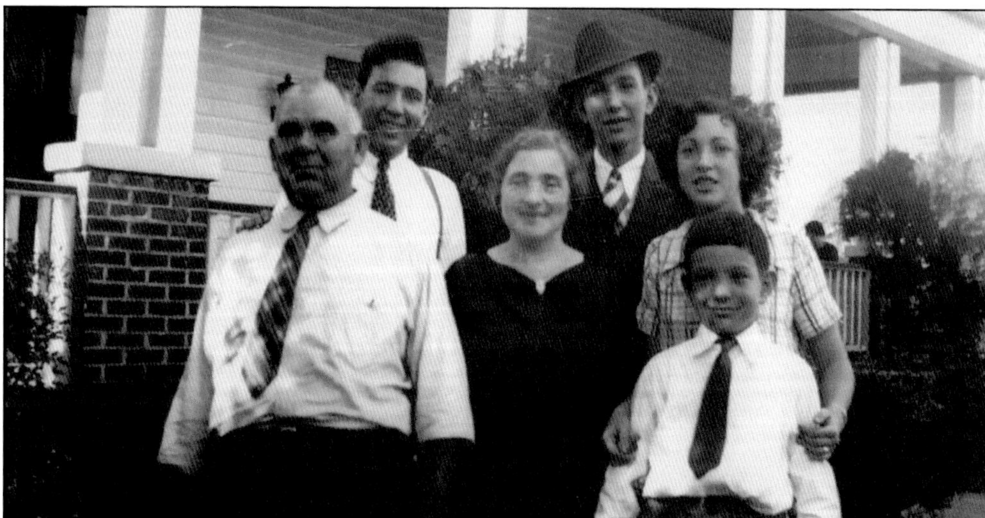

Frank and Nettie Cahn Levenson stand in front of their Heyward Street home with their children in this c. 1935 photograph. Behind the Levensons are their sons Sam and Leonard (with hat). Daughter Ella is holding onto her little brother, Jacob, who keeps trying to run off. In 1967, at the age of 76, Frank Levenson was Bishopville's oldest active merchant, having been in business since 1910. (Ella Levenson Schlosburg.)

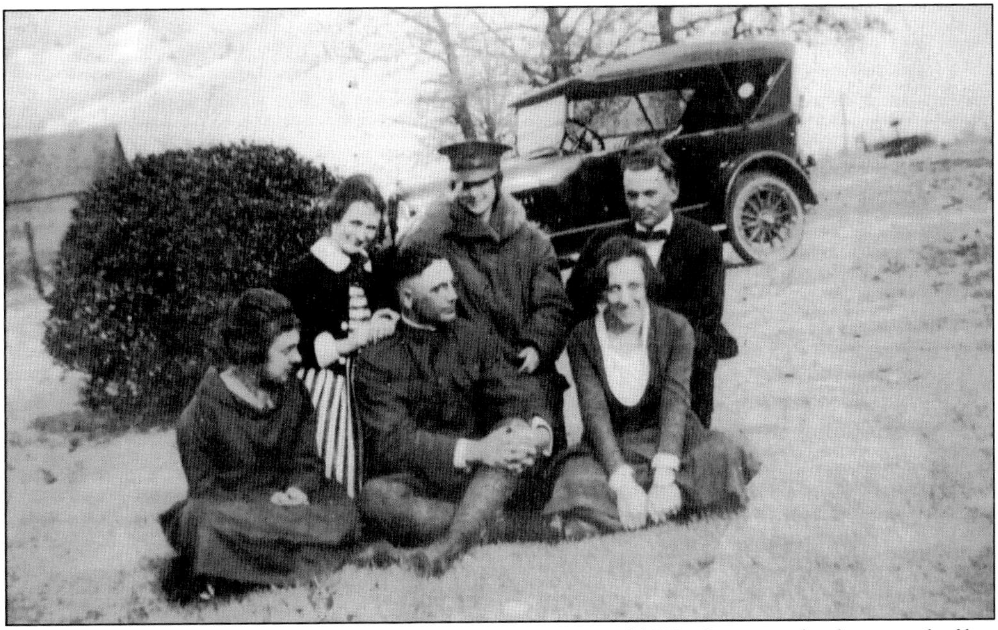

Alva Leslie Woodham, preparing to leave for service in World War I, sits in the front yard of his parents' Stokes Bridge home. The son of Willis Josey and Jane Dalrymple Woodham, he later married Vera Chappell, and they were the parents of Margery Woodham (Jeffords) and Alva Woodham Jr., known by all as "Tunky." Sister Gertrude Woodham is seated behind him with her hand on his shoulder, and another friend models his cap with a salute. (Margery Jeffords.)

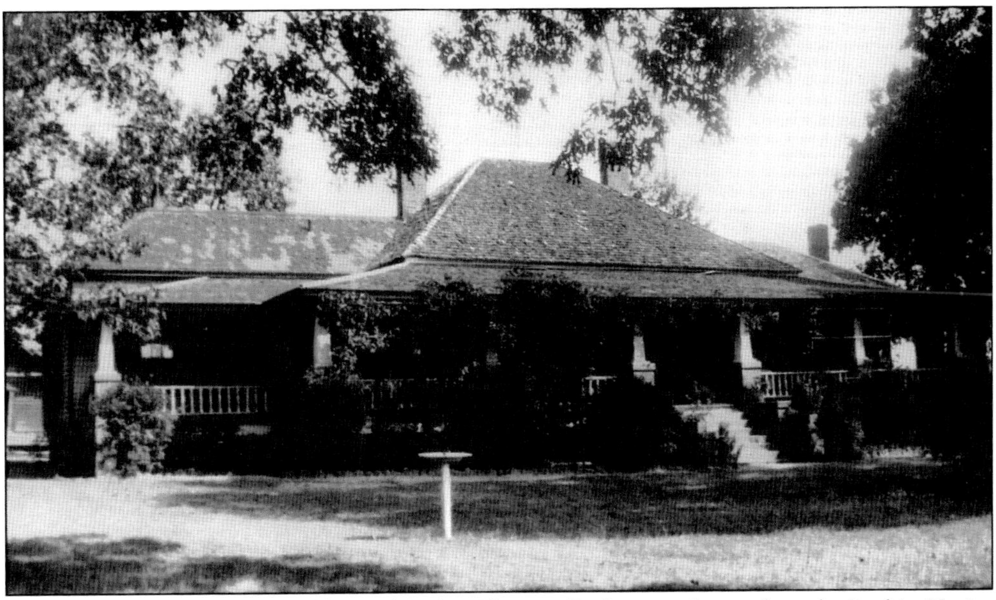

The residence of William Peebles and Esther Fleming Baskin was located on the Baskin-Heriot Road about 3 miles north of Woodrow, South Carolina. The Baskins raised their children, William Jr., Elizabeth (Massey), Adville (Walkup), and Norwood, here. William Sr. served as Lee County's first clerk of court and subsequently was a successful cotton farmer. Son William Jr. was an attorney, banker, and farmer who represented Lee County in the South Carolina Senate from 1938 to 1958. (Elizabeth Massey Booth.)

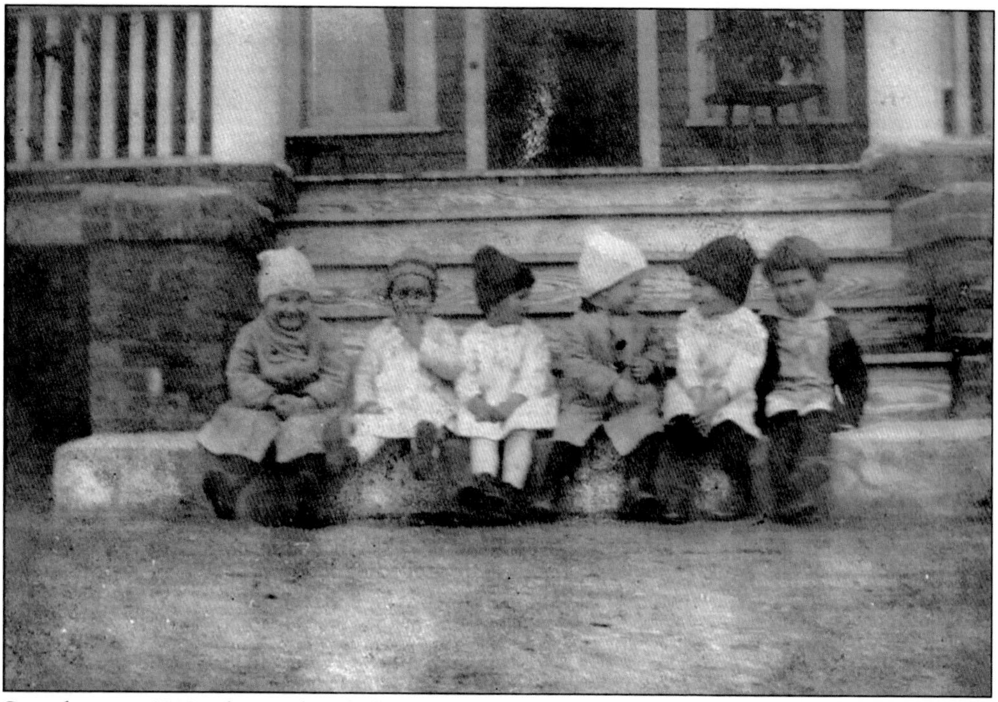

Seen here in 1918 taking a break from playing are, from left to right, Ruth Martin Stuckey (Stevenson), Frederick (Bubba) Reames, Dorothy Scott, Joe Stuckey Jr., Mary Hearon (Lane), and Tom McLeod Jr.

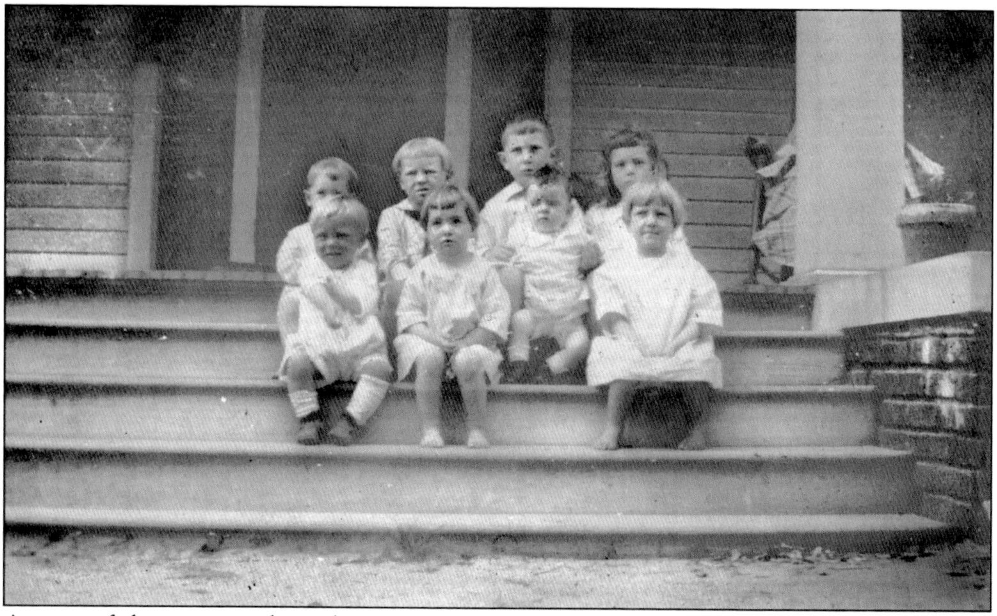

A group of playmates are shown here around 1921, seated on a front porch. From the left to right, they are (first row) Dowling Woodham, Zilphia Ruffin (Lewis), George H. (Scoot) Martin, and Frances Harris; (second row) Ben Stuckey (Quinn), Gus Woodham Jr., Joe Stuckey Jr., and Mabel Ruffin (Rudisill).

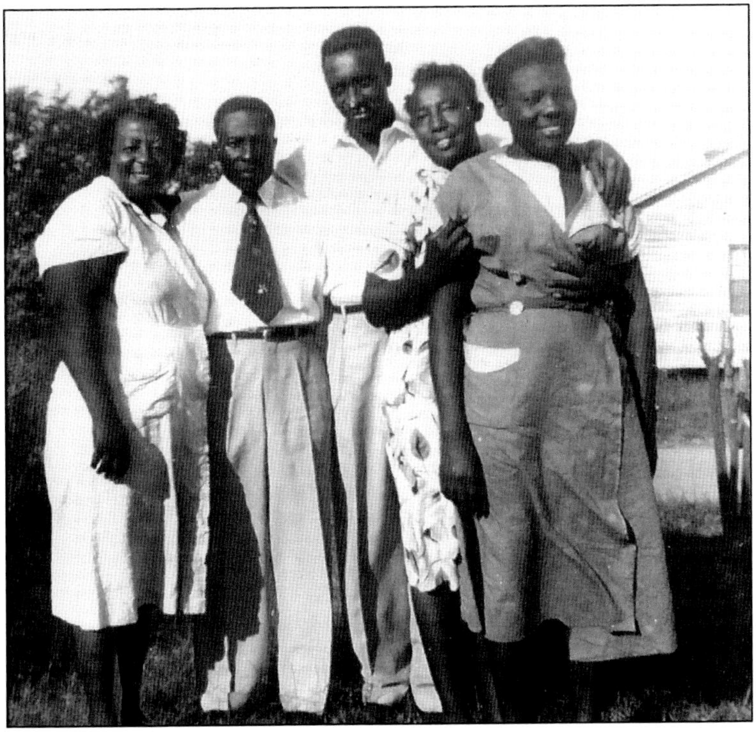

Robert Melton (second from left) is pictured at the funeral of his mother, Mary Marche Melton, in 1953. To Robert's right is his sister, Louise Kelly. To his left are brother James E. "Muddah" Marche and sisters Blanche McDonald and Janet Lockwood. Robert was married to the former Bertha Lockwood. He was McLeod Pharmacy's best-loved clerk and served nearly four terms on city council. (Karen Melton Stevens.)

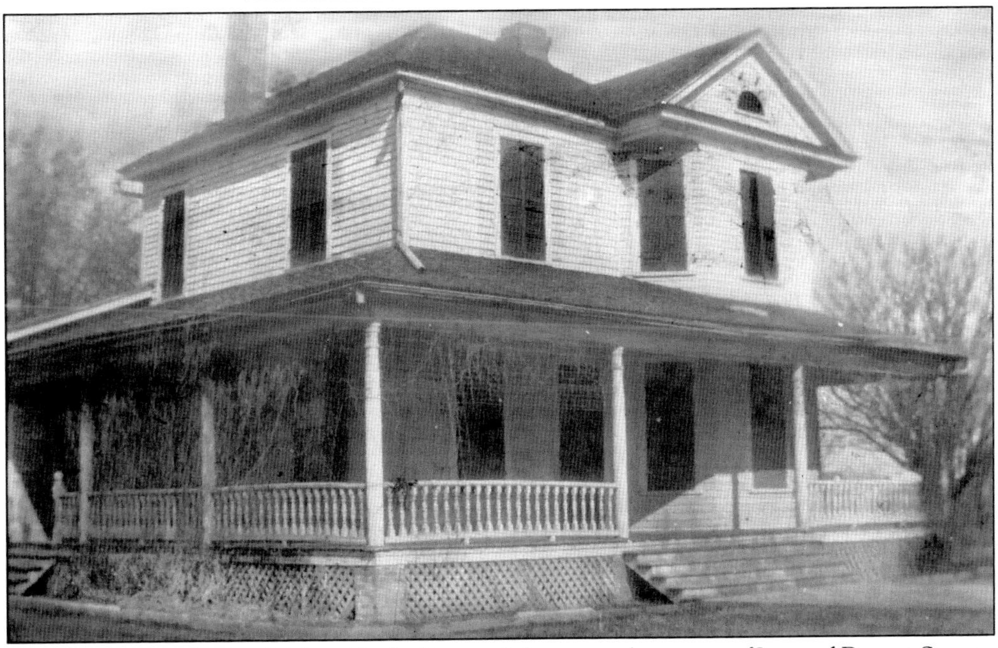

In 1904, Thomas Gordon McLeod built this stately home on the corner of Lee and Durant Streets. In 1906, McLeod was elected lieutenant governor of South Carolina and in 1922 was elected governor. The 1920 U.S. Census lists the McLeod family residing at this address, but in 1927, the house was purchased by the Stuckey and Woodham Insurance Agency and the following year was sold to Robert S. Latimer Sr., publisher of the *Lee County Messenger*. John and Patricia Latimer purchased the home in 1981 and reside in it today.

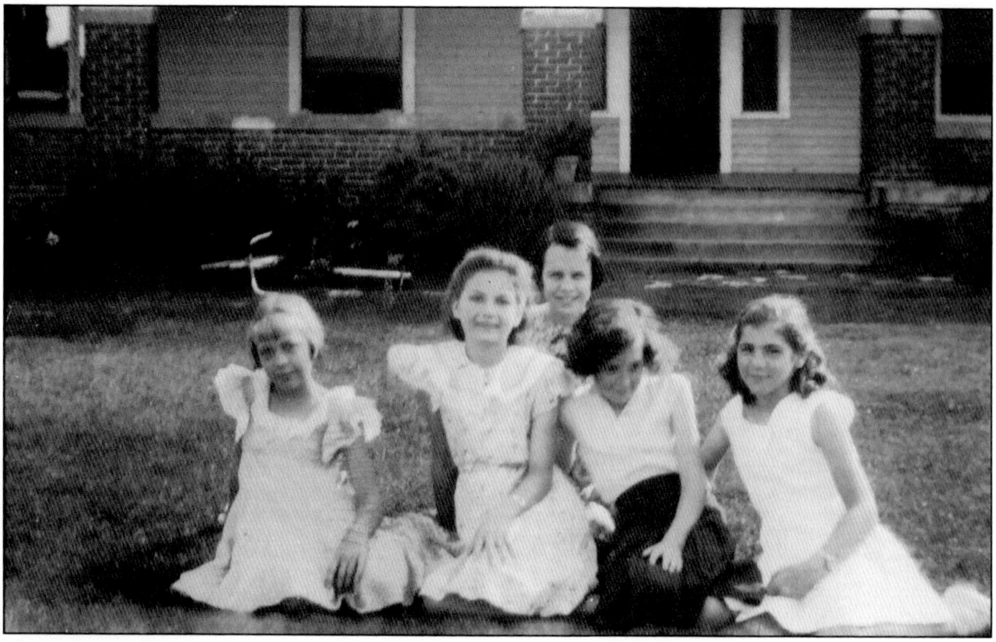

Playmates gather on the lawn of the Bradley Avenue home of Joe and Ruth Martin Stuckey in 1937. Pictured from left to right are (first row) Eleanor Reaves, Betty Milford, Katherine Martin (McCutchen), and Margery Woodham (Jeffords); (second row) Martha Wilson (Alexander). Betty was a first cousin to Katherine and to Cile Stuckey, who took the picture. (Lucile Stuckey.)

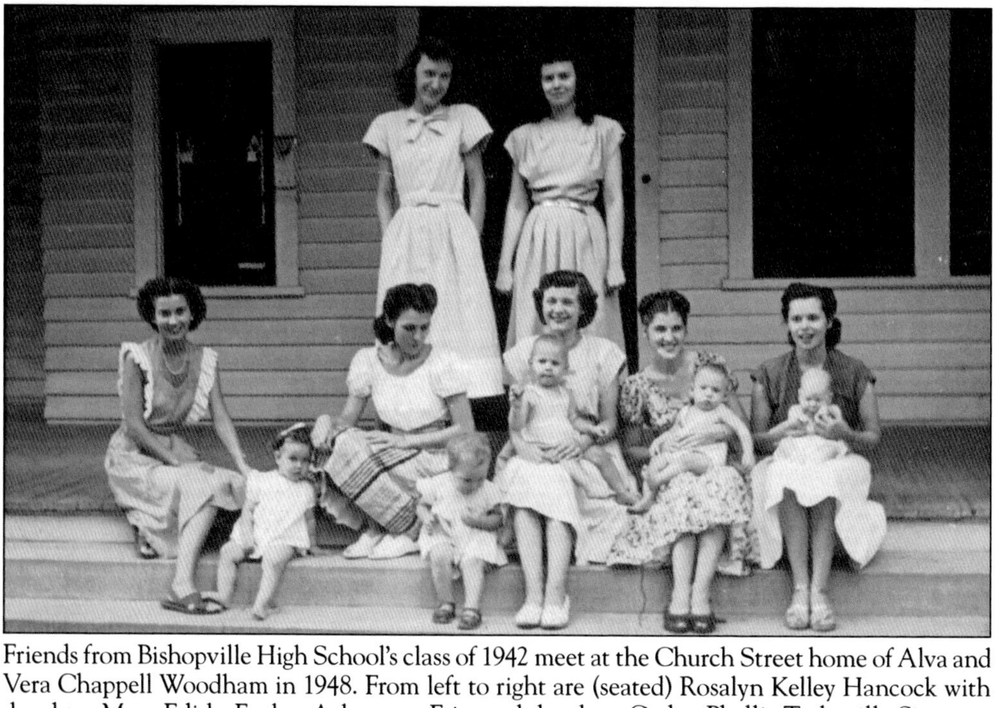

Friends from Bishopville High School's class of 1942 meet at the Church Street home of Alva and Vera Chappell Woodham in 1948. From left to right are (seated) Rosalyn Kelley Hancock with daughter Mary Edith, Evelyn Ackerman Fritz and daughter Cathy, Phyllis Turbeville Sizemore and son Ray Jr., Margery Woodham Jeffords and son Michael, and Anna Blanche Tarrant with daughter Patricia; (standing) Cile Stuckey and Martha Wilson (Alexander). (Lucile Stuckey.)

Two-year-old Arthur Ginsberg poses for a photograph in 1924. The youngest son of Sam and Fannie Ginsberg, Arthur was best known as co-owner (with his wife, Frances) of Ginsberg's, a women' dress shop started by his father in 1929. The Ginsbergs were the parents of three girls, Nancy, Beverly, and Sally. (Frances Ginsberg.)

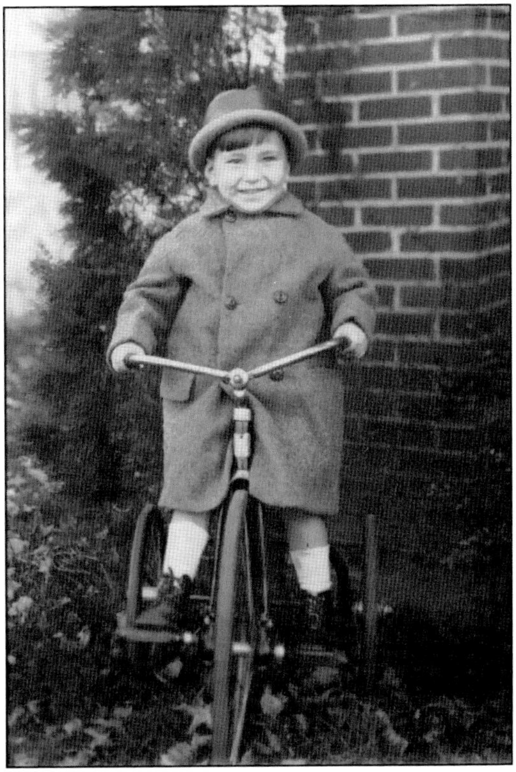

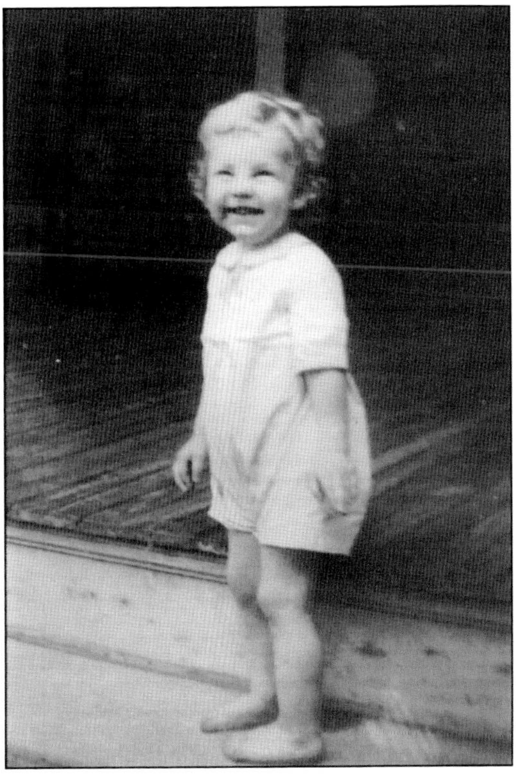

The darling little boy in this photograph is Frank DesChamps III, son of Frank Jr. and Maude Adams DesChamps. He was the brother of Margaret and Ralph DesChamps. The family suffered a tragedy in 1928 when they were involved in an automobile accident on a return trip from Maude's hometown of Abbeville, South Carolina. Sadly, Frank, who was 20 months old at the time, did not survive. (Ralph DesChamps.)

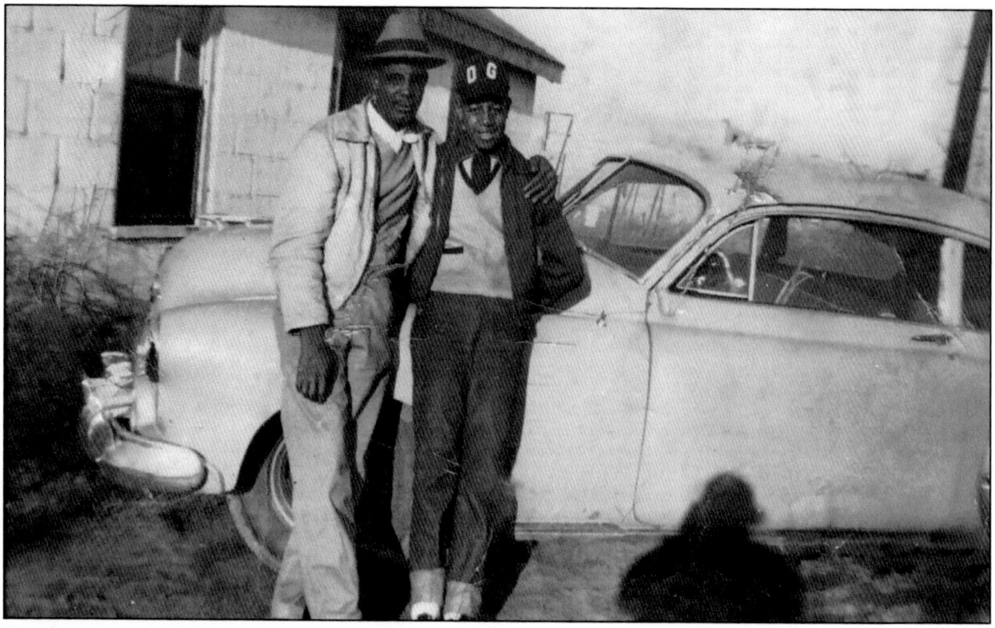

Brothers Joe and Dixon Gass were the sons of Joe Sr. and Carrie Boone Gass and are pictured in the front yard of their home off Highway 34. Joe Gass Sr. was a farmer, and when he died at a young age, Joe Jr. took over his responsibilities. Dixon finished college and for many years held the position of assistant registrar at Florence Darlington Technical College. The young men had two sisters, Carrie and Catherine Gass. (Carrie Gass.)

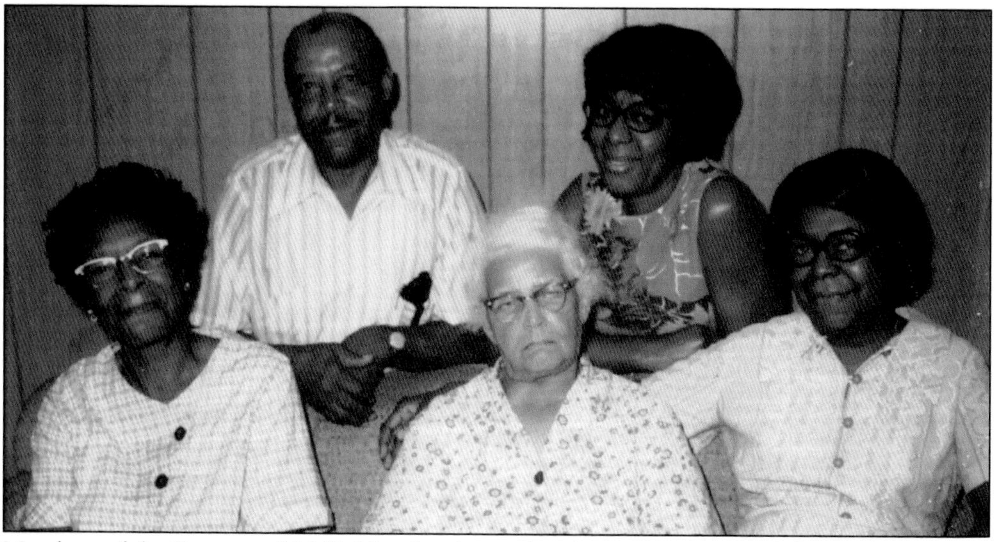

Members of the Boone and McFadden families gather for a picture. From left to right, they are (first row) Carrie Boone Gass, Cherry McFadden, and Marie Boone Hilton; (second row) Joshua McFadden and Carrie Gass. Cherry McFadden was the mother of Joshua and the wife of Sanko McFadden III. The first Sanko McFadden was brought to this country on a slave ship from Africa. His son, Sanko, hauled cargo on a wagon pulled by mules. After he completed a haul through a blizzard nearly frostbitten, his owner emancipated him and gave him a portion of land on which he could build a home. He made his land available for others to join him in worship. The church that was eventually built on the site became New Haven United Methodist Church. (Carrie Gass.)

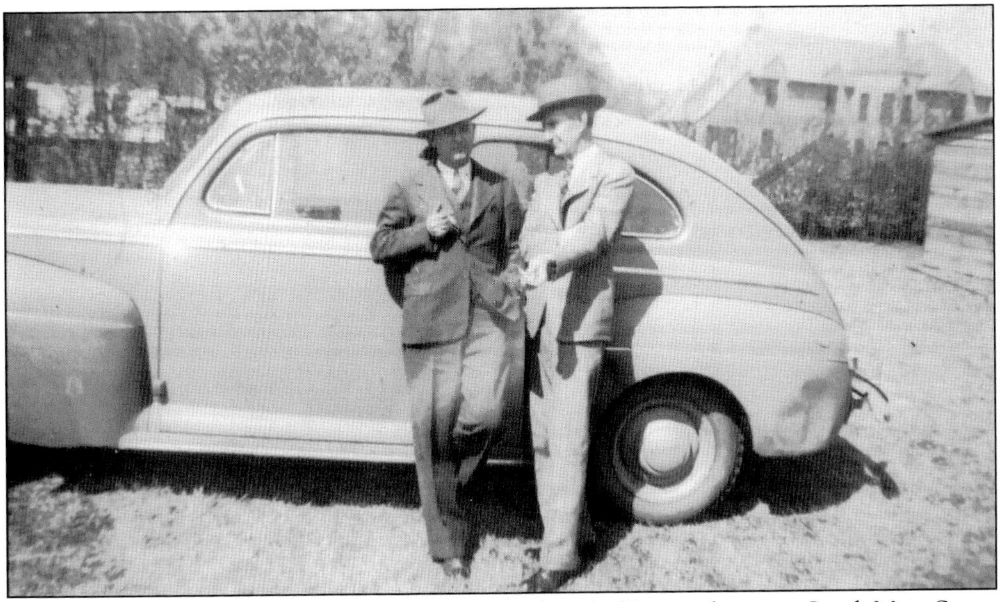

Buddy Dickinson and Ernest Martin chat in the backyard of Ernest's home on South Main Street in this picture from the early 1940s. The house once stood between Roland Elmore's filling station and the residence of N. J. and Alethea Laney. Ernest and his wife, Annie, were the parents of Katherine Martin (McCutchen) and George Hayes "Scoot" Martin. (Retta Dickinson Tindal.)

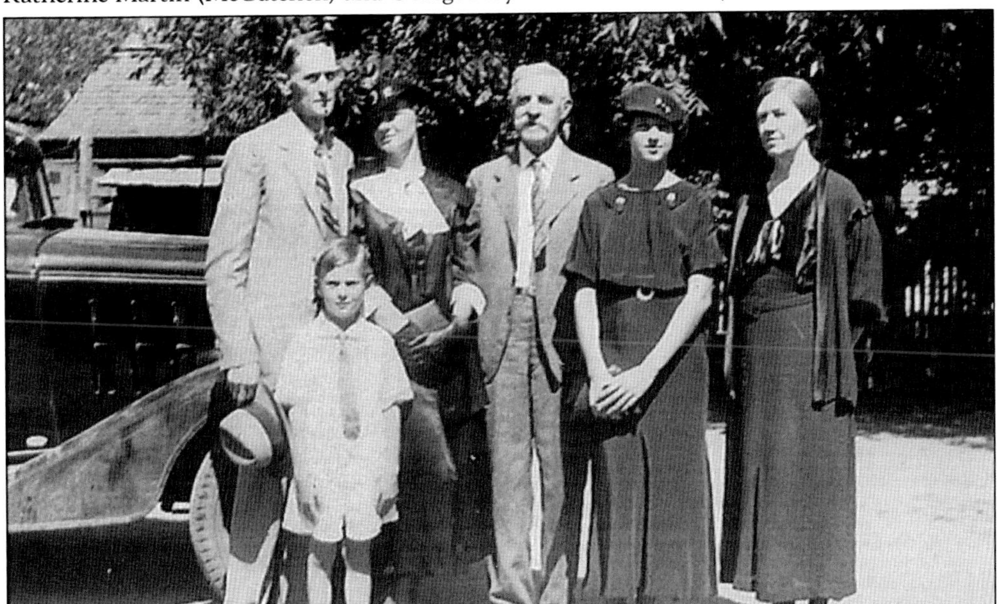

Members of the Stephenson and Pittman families gather for this 1932 photograph. From left to right are E. H. Pittman, Christine "Tina" Pittman, Grandpa (T. E. H.) Stephenson, Vivian "Bibber" Pittman, and Birdie Stephenson Pittman. The young boy is Henry Pittman. Tina, Bibber, and Henry were the children of E. H. and Birdie. Grandpa was Birdie's father. The Pittmans lived in the home on North Main Street that is now the Blossom Shop. In the days when Highway 15 saw heavy vacation traffic, Birdie posted a tourist sign at her home advertising rooms for travelers to rent. (Henry Pittman.)

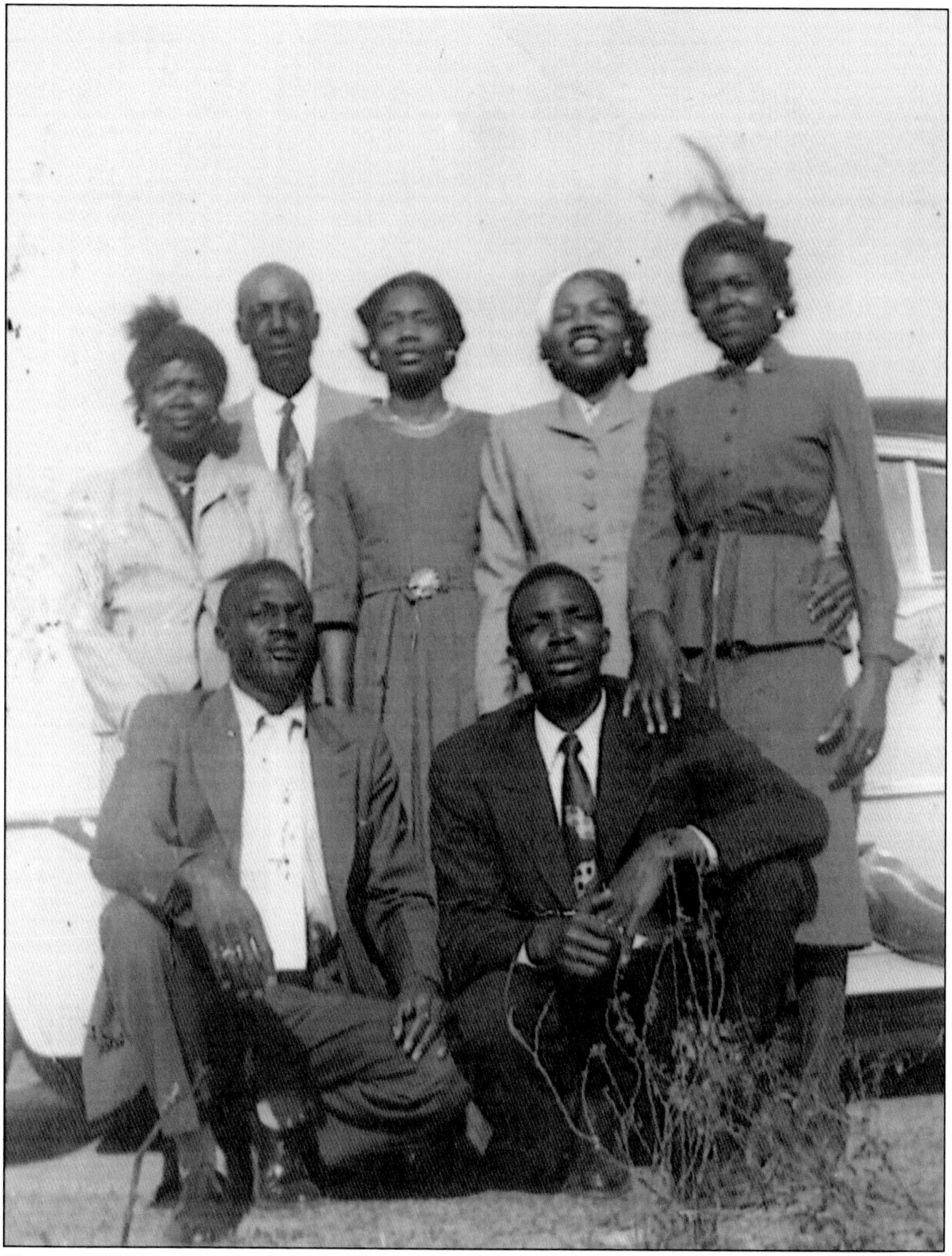

Henry and Ethel Isaac and their children are pictured near their home in Elliott about 1948. Seen from left to right are (first row) Henry Jr. and Daniel; (second row) Ethel Isaac, Henry Isaac, Rosa Lee, Bernice, and Anna Lua. Originally from Wisacky, Henry Isaac had purchased a farm in Elliott the same year this photograph was taken. (Bernice Isaac Bradley.)

Five

SCHOOL DAYS

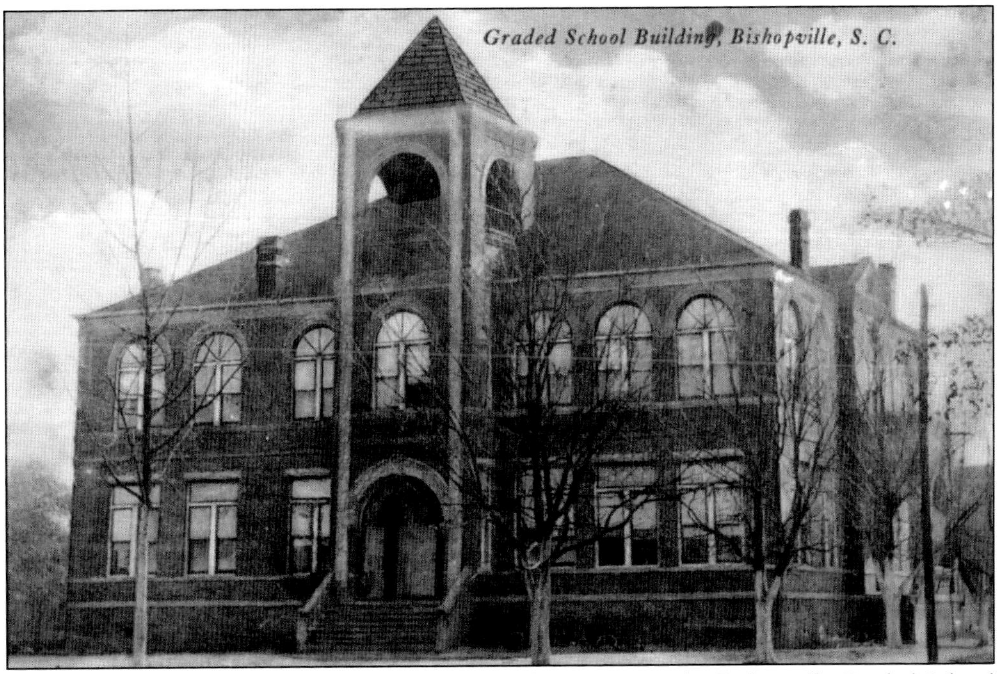

In the August 27, 1891, issue of the *Bishopville Eagle* newspaper, the Bishopville Graded School advertised its six departments: Primary, Academic, Collegiate, Commercial, Music, and Art. Built in the late 1800s, the school served students for miles around until the early 1920s when a high school was built on Ridge Street and the graded school became the primary school. The Bishopville Graded School was located on the property bounded by North Main and College Streets. It was situated behind where the old Bishopville High School is today.

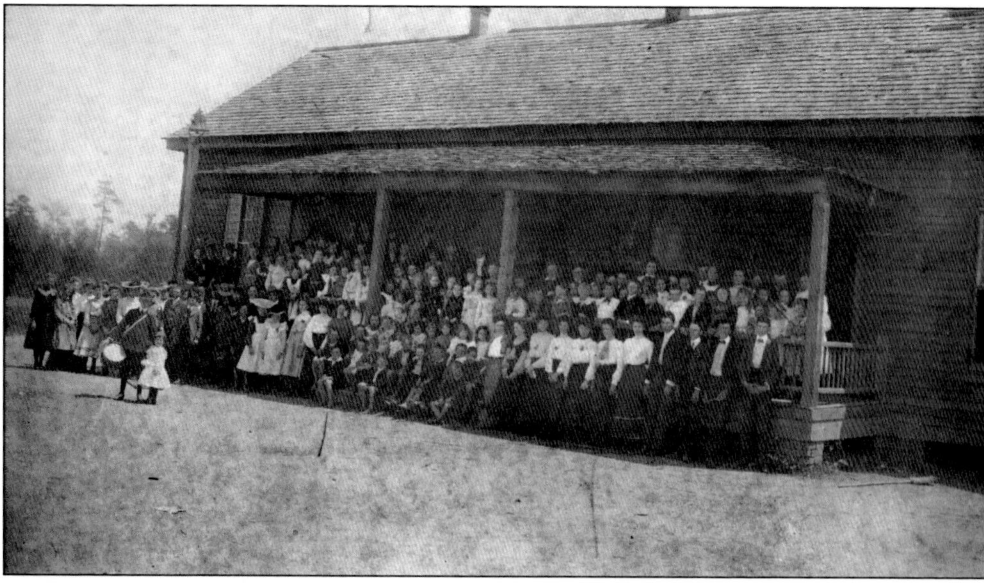

Students gather for a class picture outside the old wooden schoolhouse that served Bishopville in the 19th century. The yard has been freshly swept for the picture, as indicated by the broom off to the side. (Lee County Historical Society.)

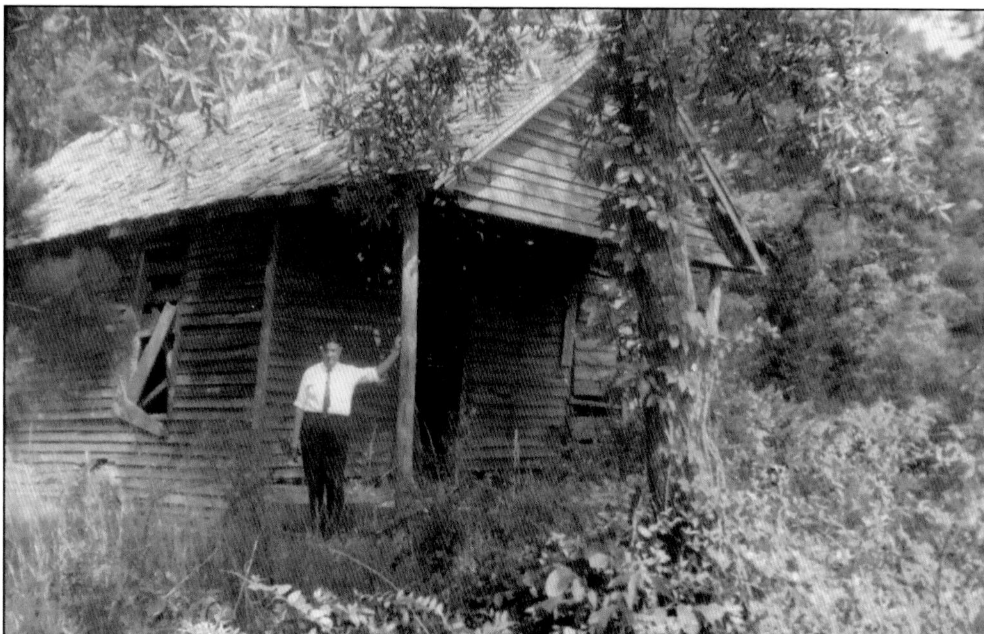

James Albert Stuckey (Jeff) stands at the remains of the Oak Grove School in Manville in this 1950s photograph. Constructed in 1897, this one-room schoolhouse served about 40 children between the ages of six and 21 during a school year. A long-bodied stove provided heat, and each patron of the school was asked to furnish one load of wood during the school year. Teachers at the turn of the 20th century included Catherine McLaurin, Jeannette McCutchen, Virginia Cooper, Minnie Scarborough, Jennie Huggins, and Evelyn Wilson. Teachers' salaries were $20 per month, and student tuition was $140 per year. (Ruthie Stevenson Bowman.)

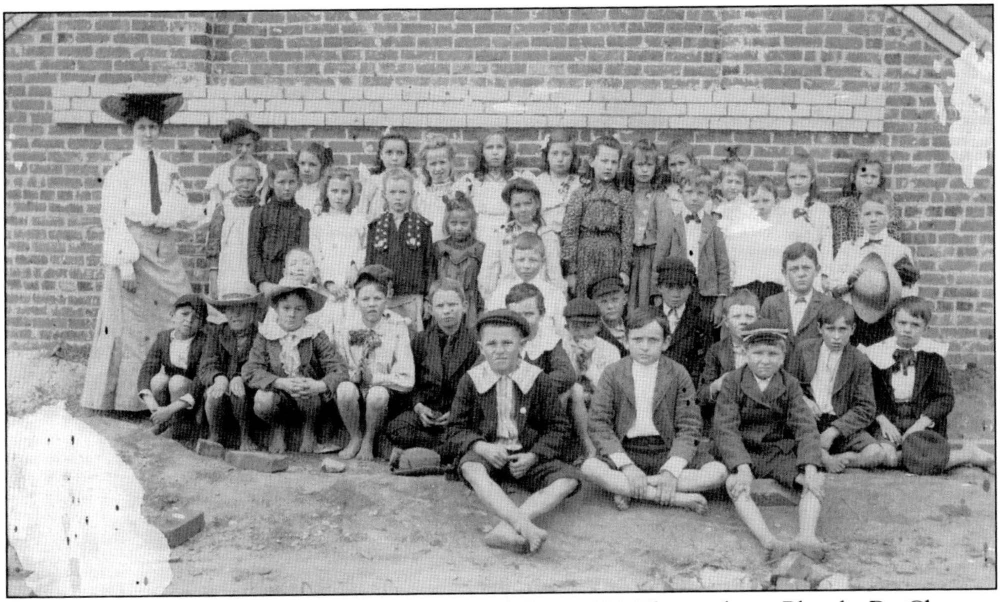

Students sit outside the Bishopville Graded School about 1899. The teacher is Blanche DesChamps. Some of the children identified are Jennie Butler, Marguerite Manning, Olive Carnes, Ora Lee Hearon, Gladys Hearon, Alethea Fleming, Rosamond Dixon, Ray Levy, Myrtle James, Louise Manning, Lurene McLure, Lurena Munn, Annette Parrott, Frank DesChamps, Jake Parrott, Algernon King, Carrol Simpson, Carl Scarborough, Harry Livingston, Hazel Parrott, Robert McCutchen, McLeod McClure, Ted Stuckey, George Blackwell, Leonard Shaw, Aubrey Wilson, ? Tallon, ? Clyburn, and ? Scarborough.

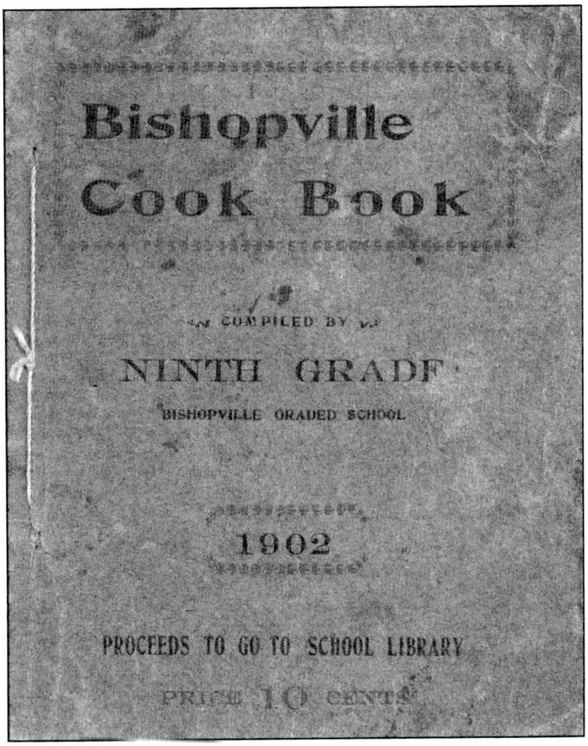

School fund-raisers are not a new invention, as evidenced by the cookbook published by the Bishopville Graded School's ninth grade in 1902. Full of advertisements from local merchants, proceeds were earmarked for the school library. Recipes were submitted by such familiar names as Mrs. W. A. James, Mrs. W. L. Parrott, Mrs. R. H. Pittman, Mrs. H. S. Cunningham, Mrs. Manly Smith, and Mrs. R. Y. McLeod, and included chess pie, spiced grapes, "cocoanut" pudding, and strawberry acid.

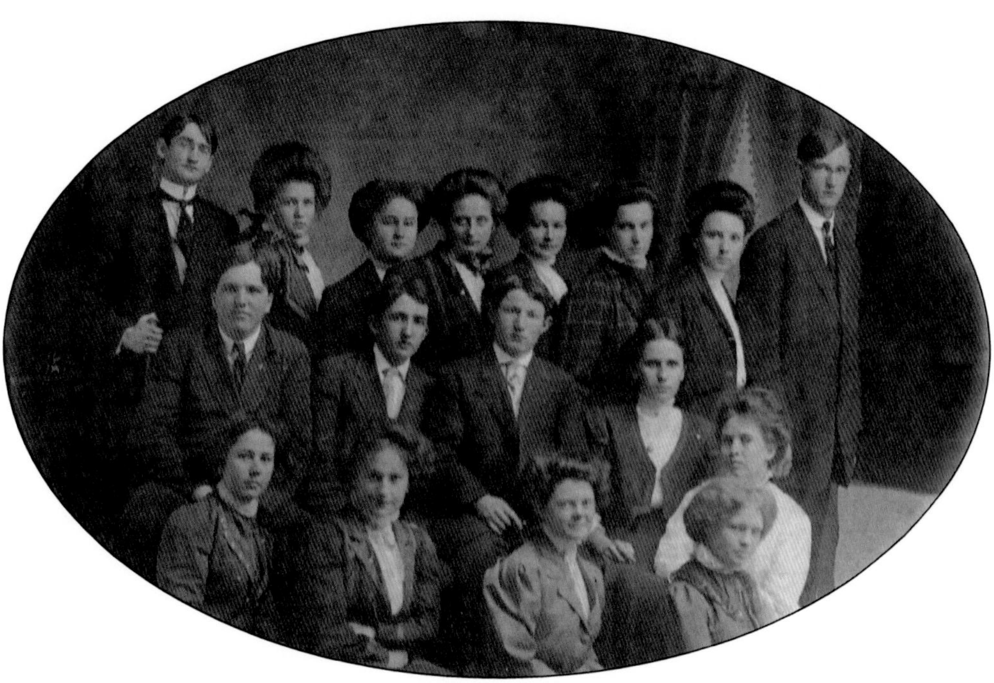

The first record of an educational institution in present-day Lee County can be found in the journal of local planter John Baxter Fraser. In late January 1803, he penned, "Schoolhouse and all completed. Jno. Deloney Harvey, schoolmaster . . . began school today." This entry was followed less than a month later by, "Harvey fired. Drunkard." Just over 100 years later, the Bishopville High School class of 1909 sat for this picture. The first young man in the second row appears to be Marion Wilson; the young lady on the far right is identified as Bertha McCutchen. (*Lee County Observer.*)

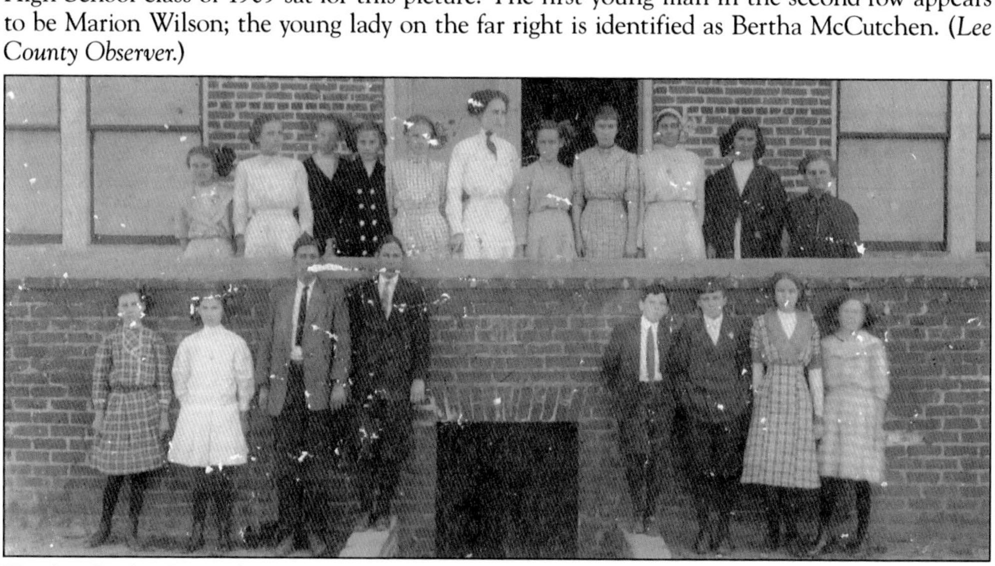

Teacher Ruth Martin (center, in white) is shown around 1913 with her class. Graduates of the class of 1913, though not necessarily in this photograph, were Blanche Gertrude Ackerman, Eulalie Shaw, Nettie Marie Boykin, Emma Lurena Munn, Mary Lucile McLeod, Gladys Harriet Hearon, Mildred Lee Gunter, Mabry McCoy, Susan Emma Heriot, Jake L. Parrott, and George Richard Cousar. Other teachers that year were Eleanor N. Chappell and Madge Gregory; G. B. Dukes was superintendent.

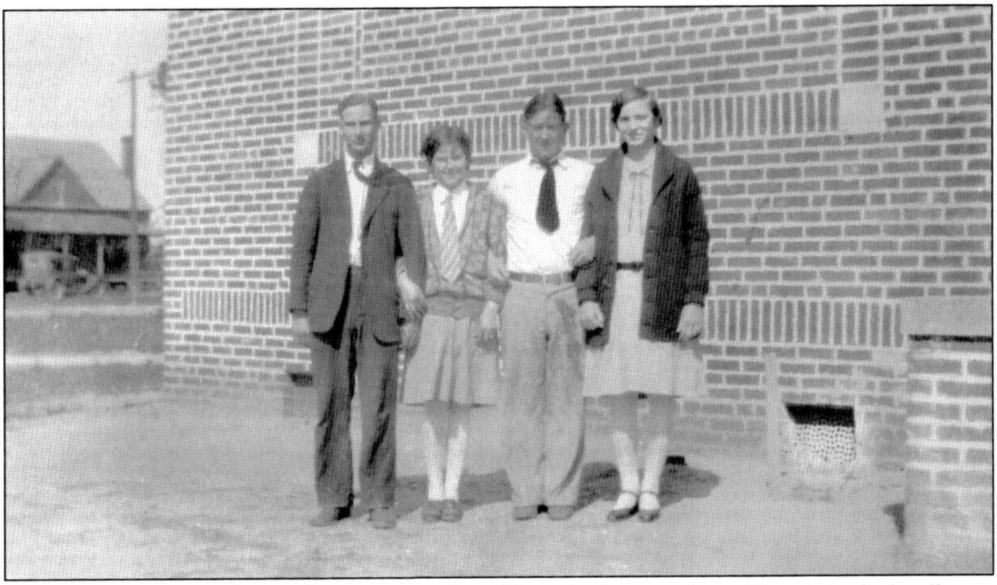

The Lynchburg Graded School was organized in 1902 with three teachers. The original schoolhouse was a white frame building situated south of Highway 76. Several years later, a modern brick building was erected for the school. When a new Lynchburg High School was constructed in 1925, the old building was converted to the grammar school, which it served as until 1950. The high school ceased to operate after 1966, but the 1925 building continued on as the grammar school. The girls in the above photograph are Frances Stokes and Annie Mae Hickson. The boy on the far left is Henry Hodge. (Betsy Redick.)

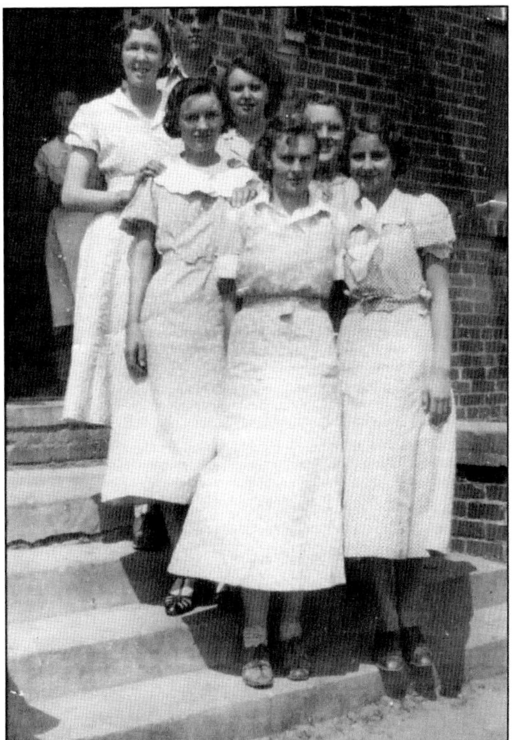

Elliott High School served the community from 1913 until 1945. The two-story brick building was located on Highway 401. When the school closed, students attended Bishopville High. The Elliott High School class of 1934, seen here from left to right, included (first row) Mary Welsh and Christine Smith; (second row) Abbie Law and Doris Carter; (third row) Billie Mooneyhan and Alice Hill; (fourth row) T. W. Watson. (Christine Smith Shirley.)

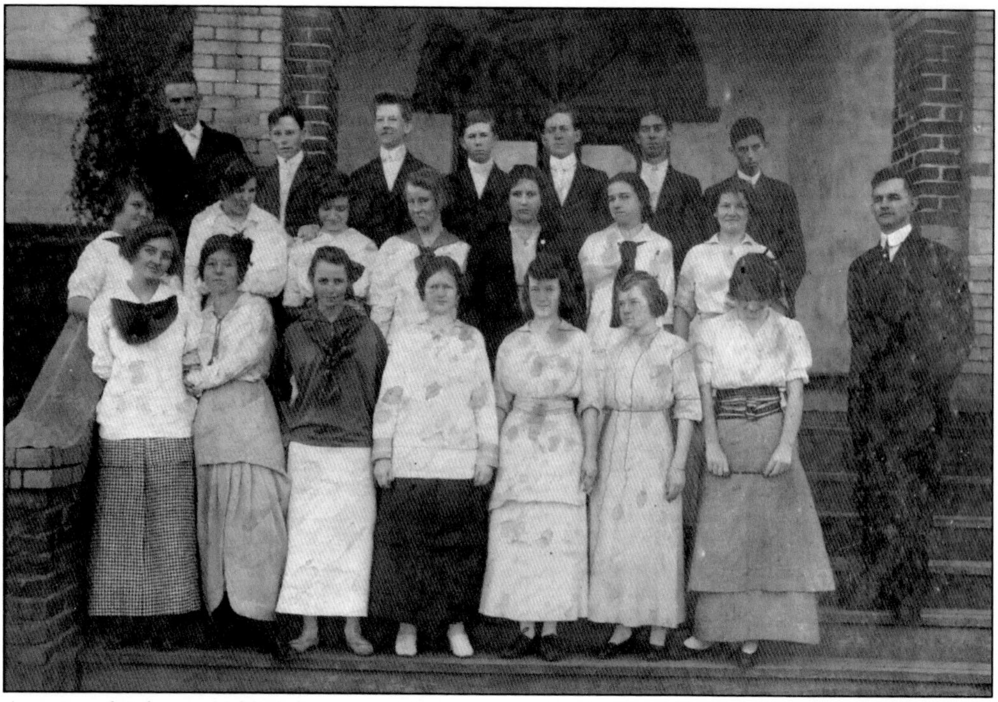

A group of girls gets tickled about something just as the photographer snaps the picture in this c. 1914 photograph. The moment was captured on the front steps of the Bishopville Graded School. (Lee County Historical Society.)

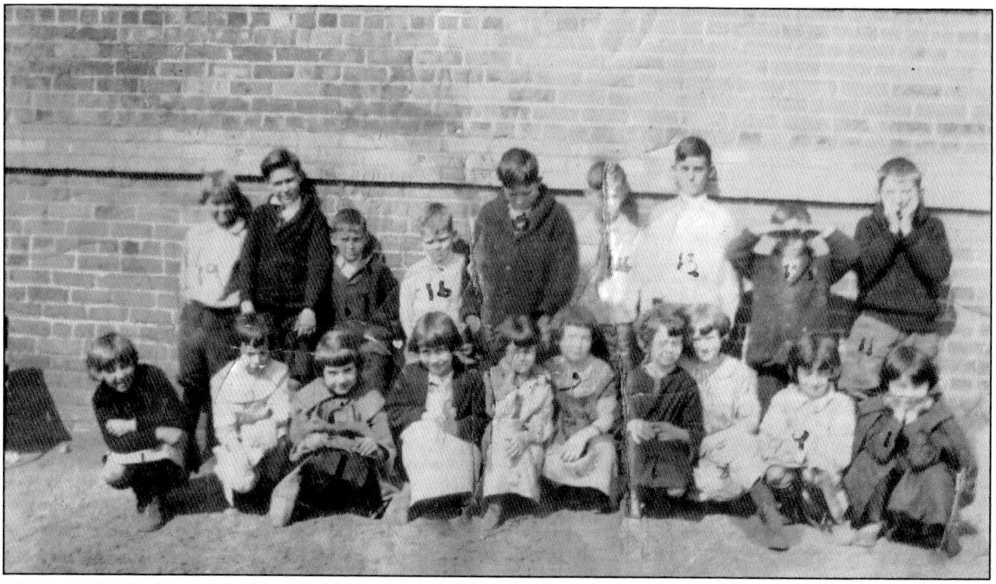

Here is the Bishopville Graded School third grade class of 1923. The second and third girls in the first row are Betty McCutchen (Austin) and Ruth Martin Stuckey (Stevenson). Other girls include (in no particular order) Clara F., Minnie Green Moore, Marion Ruffin (Stephenson), Eleanor ?, and Mary J. C. The boys include (in no particular order) ? McCutchen, Marion S., ? S., Jorome Weatherly, Richard D., Harold Dickinson, James McCutchen, and ? R. (Ruthie Stevenson Bowman.)

Rebecca "Aunt Beck" Dennis (left) and her sister, Theo, sit for a photograph at the beginning of the 20th century. In 1916, Aunt Beck donated a parcel of land so that a school might be built for African American children. The original buildings, two wooden-framed structures, burned, and in 1936, the old brick Dennis High School, which stands on Cedar Lane, was constructed. When a second Dennis High was constructed in 1954, the old building was converted to use for the primary school. (Robert Jennings.)

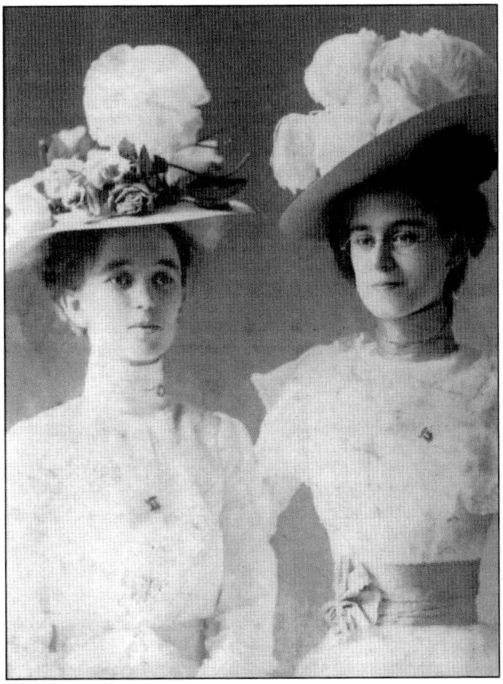

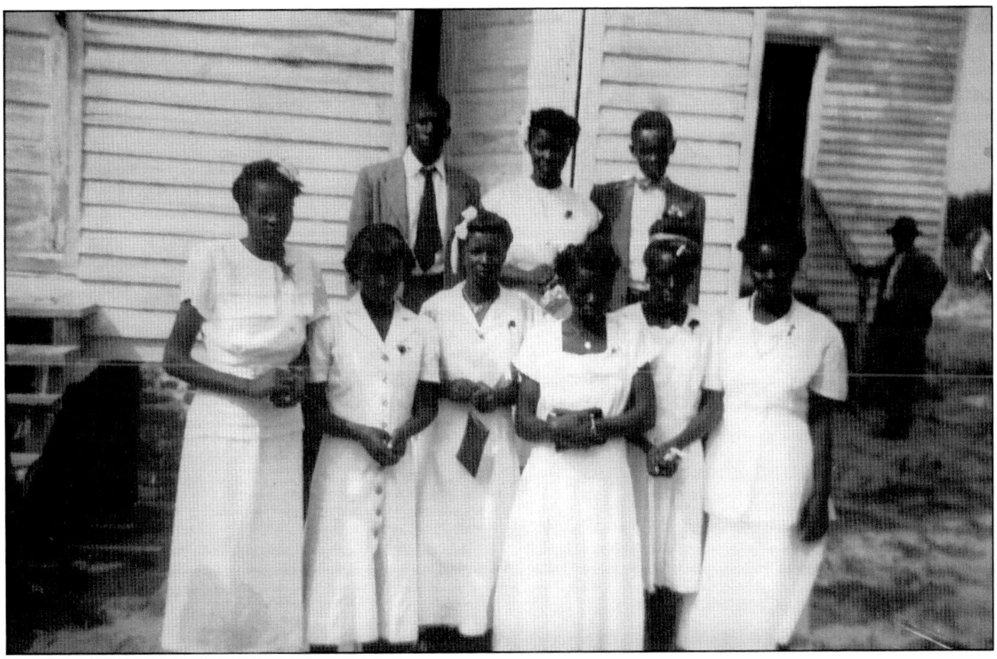

After Bernice Isaac finished Allen University, she taught at the Ionia School, pictured above about 1950. The wood-framed building had been a school for white children, and when it closed, it was repurposed for the African American community. It consisted of three classrooms and lacked indoor plumbing; heat was supplied by wood stoves, with the fuel provided by parents. Bernice taught the first and second grades, Carrie Burgess taught third and fourth grades, and Carrie's husband, the Reverend L. B. Burgess, was the principal and taught fifth and sixth grades. (Bernice Isaac Bradley.)

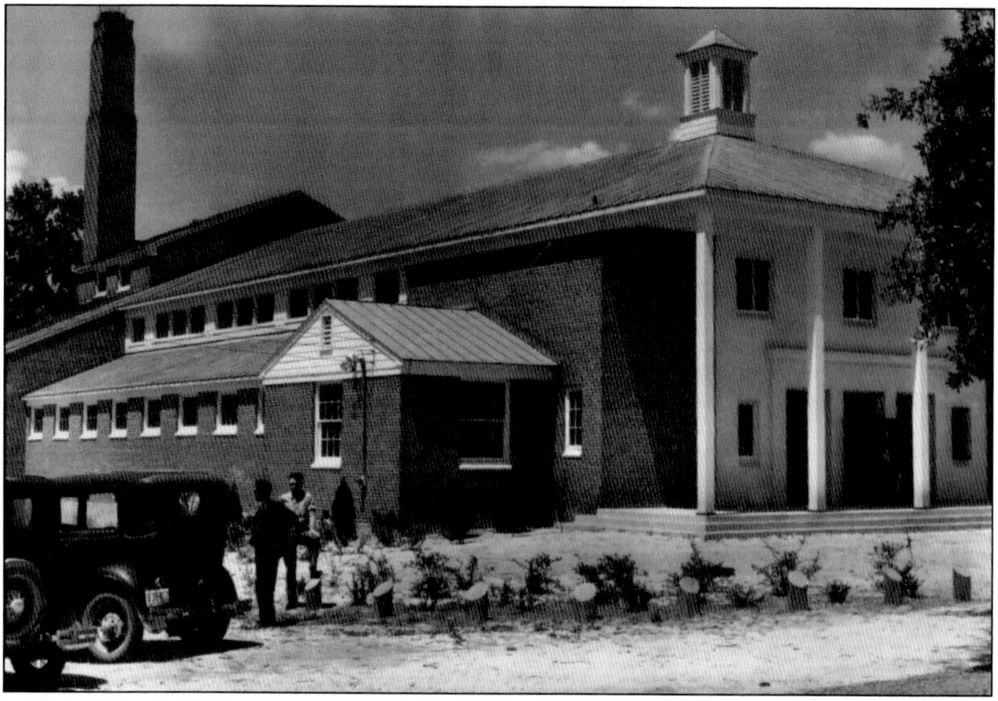

In the 1930s, the U.S. government purchased land in the Mechanicsville community for the Ashwood Project. In 1935, families from all over the state resettled in Ashwood, where their homes and farming necessities were mortgaged from the government. Above is the Ashwood Gym, which was designed for sports but also served as a place for assemblies, graduation, and even movie shows. Ashwood-Central school remained in operation until the 1979–1980 school year. The gym still stands and has been extensively renovated. (Betty Brown Truesdale.)

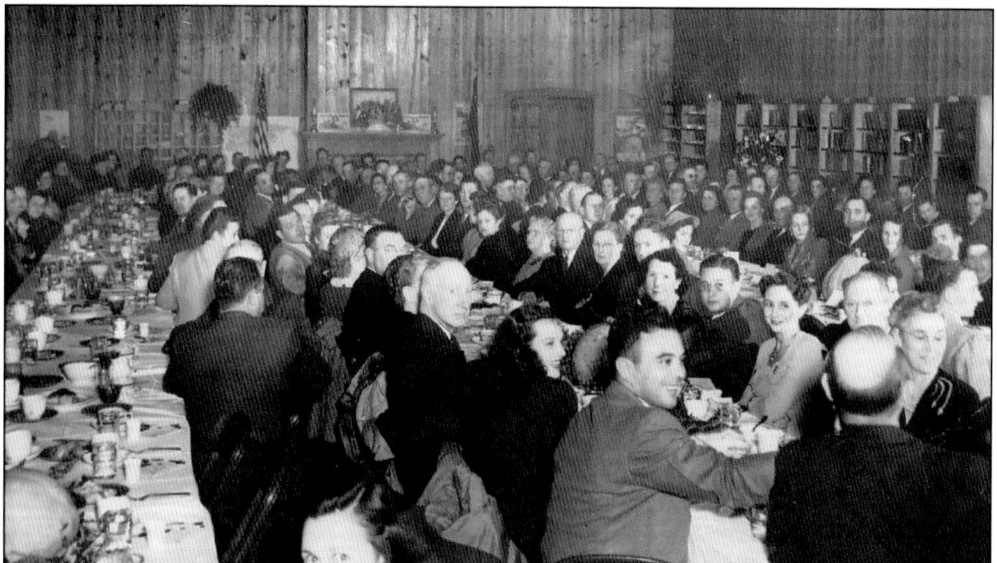

This fund-raiser for the Ashwood school library was held in the library itself around 1940. Visible in the foreground are Irven and Estelle Traub, Robert and Christine Muldrow, Jeff and Alice Stuckey, Joe and Ruth Stuckey, and V. S. and Anna Goodyear. (Judith Austin Watkins.)

Bernice Isaac graduates from Dennis High School in 1944. At the time of this photograph, the Isaac family lived in Wisacky, and Dennis was the only high school for African American students in Lee County. Those who did not have transportation had to walk the several miles into town. It was not until 1948 that Clarence McFadden began operating a school bus for African American children, at his own expense, so that rural students would have reliable transportation to school. (Bernice Isaac Bradley.)

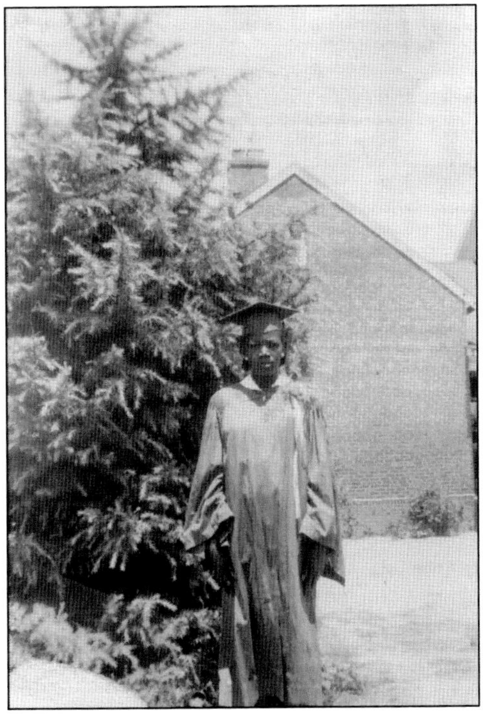

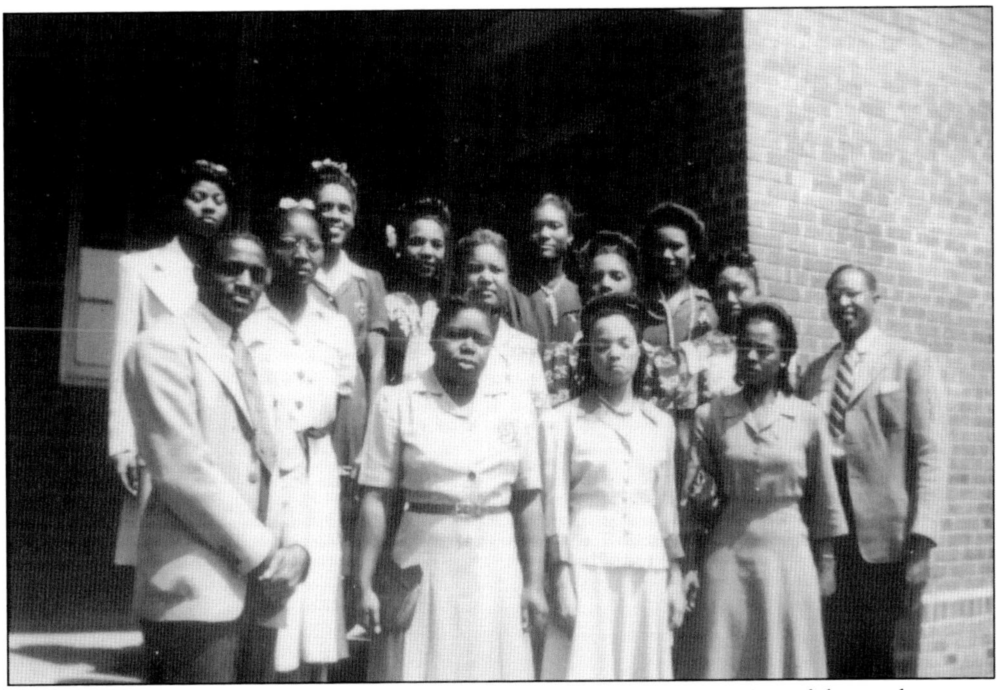

Pictured above are Dennis High School faculty and staff about 1944. Most of the teachers were not Bishopville natives but came from nearby towns such as Sumter, Cheraw, and Columbia. The men pictured are principal I. C. Brown (on left) and Mr. McKnight. Female teachers included Mrs. Williams, Mrs. Chirp, Mrs. Richardson, Mrs. Burton, Mrs. Gregg, Mrs. Sawyer, Mrs. Taylor, Mrs. Black, and Mrs. Murry. (Bernice Isaac Bradley.)

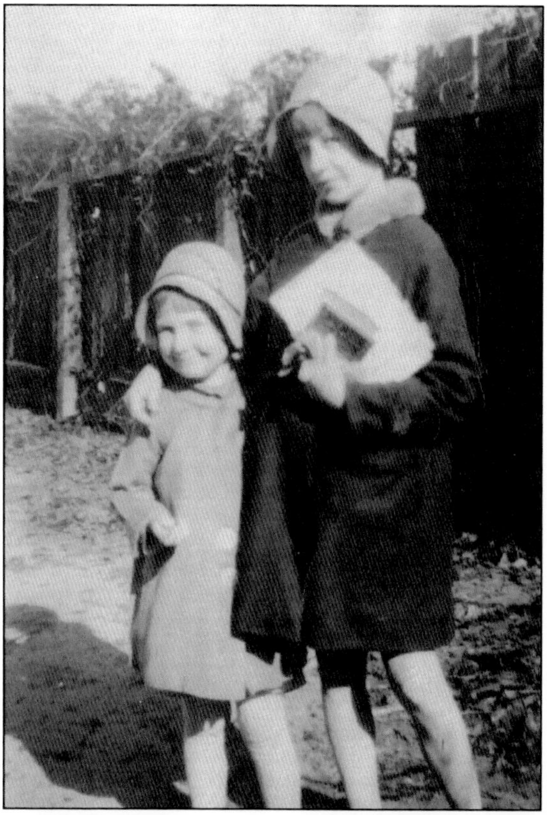

Five-year-old Cile Stuckey says goodbye to her sister, Ben, who is heading to the grammar school in this 1930 picture. At the time, white elementary students attended class in a small wooden building located next to the high school on Ridge Street. The girls' home was on Heyward Street, and school was a short walk away.

Mrs. McCoy's 1951–1952 fourth grade class stands on the steps of the grammar school for its picture. From left to right are (first row) Jane Fergurson, Sylvia Skinner, and Christine Smith. Others in the picture include (in no order) Frankie Kelley, Mary Ann Baskin, Barrie Cunningham, Billie Raye Dampier, Barbara Reynolds, Alma Joyce Smith, Joyce Walters, Brenda Cumalander, Suzanne McCutchen, Carey Kilgore, Johnny Reames, George O'Kelley, Val Green, Dickie Bridgeman, John Hope Shuford, Jimmy Moore, Butchie Williams, and Jimmy Dowling. (Barrie Cunningham Hardwick.)

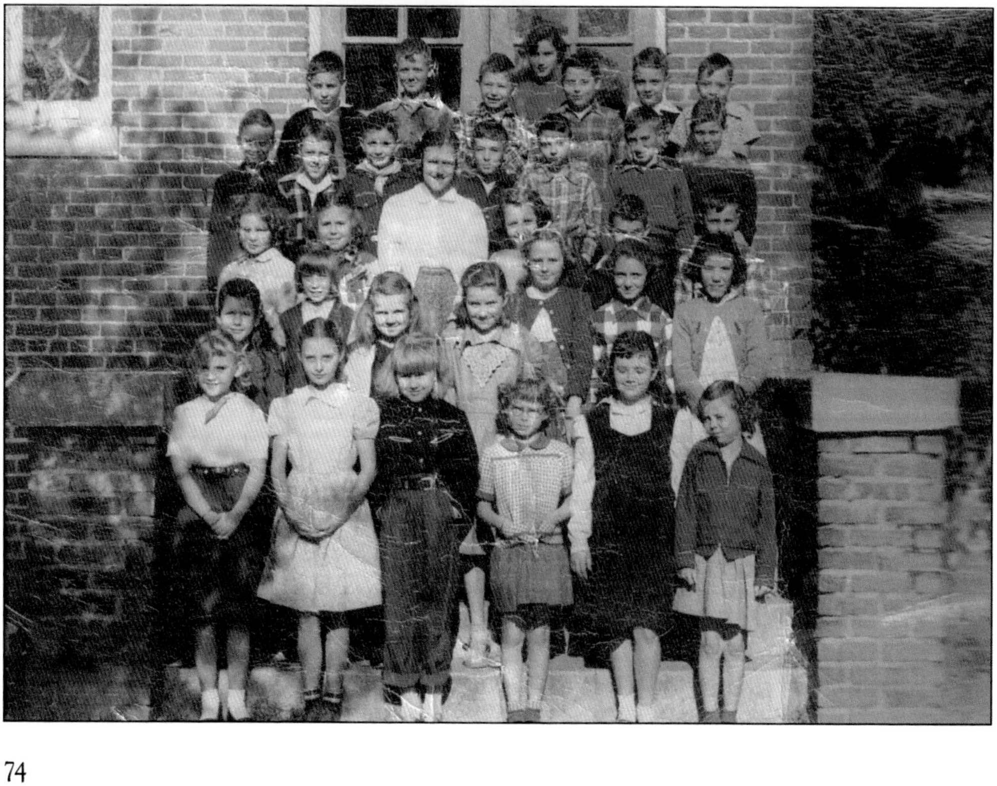

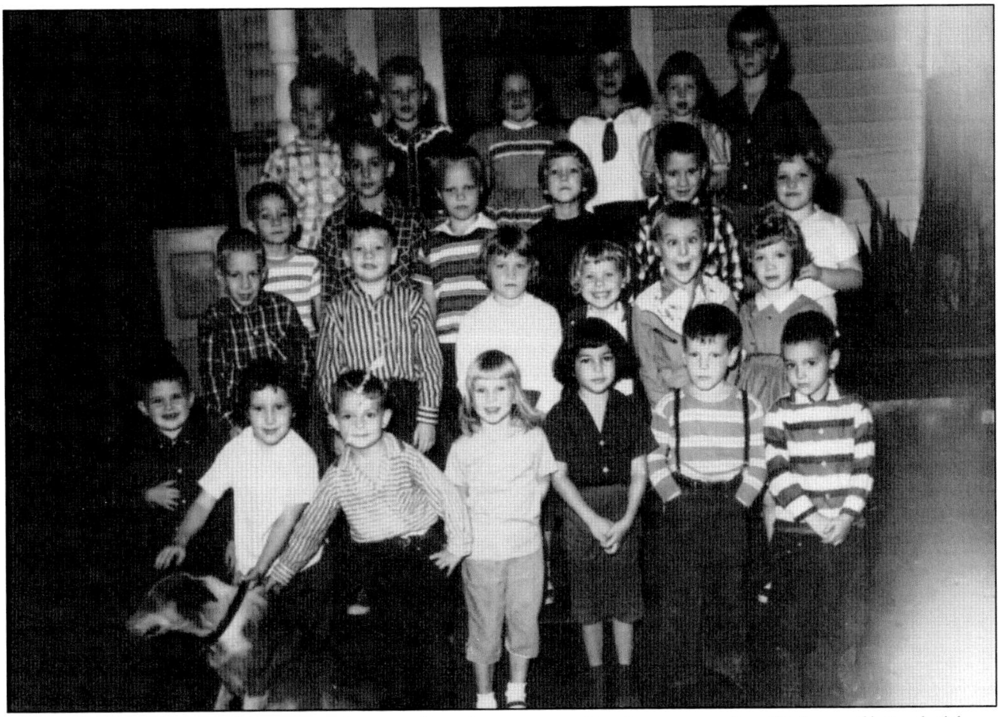

For many years, Jewel Cunningham offered a private kindergarten for Bishopville's children in her home on Ridge Street. Seen from left to right in this c. 1955 class photograph are (first row) Pierce O'Kelley, Ann Martin, John Law, Lynn Latimer, Beverly Ginsberg, Mike Jordan, and Leslie Heaton; (second row) Bill Stuckey, Blake Dennis, Karen Farver, Sally Olmert, Jackie Robinson, and Martha Woodham; (third row) Graham Stokes, Terry Levenson, Bubba Barnes, Donna Walden, Luther McCutchen, and Christine Walukewicz; (fourth row) Chip Smith, Marion Woodham, Jane Drayton, Sally Scurry, Teenie McCutchen, and Jimmy McCutchen. (Barrie Cunningham Hardwick.)

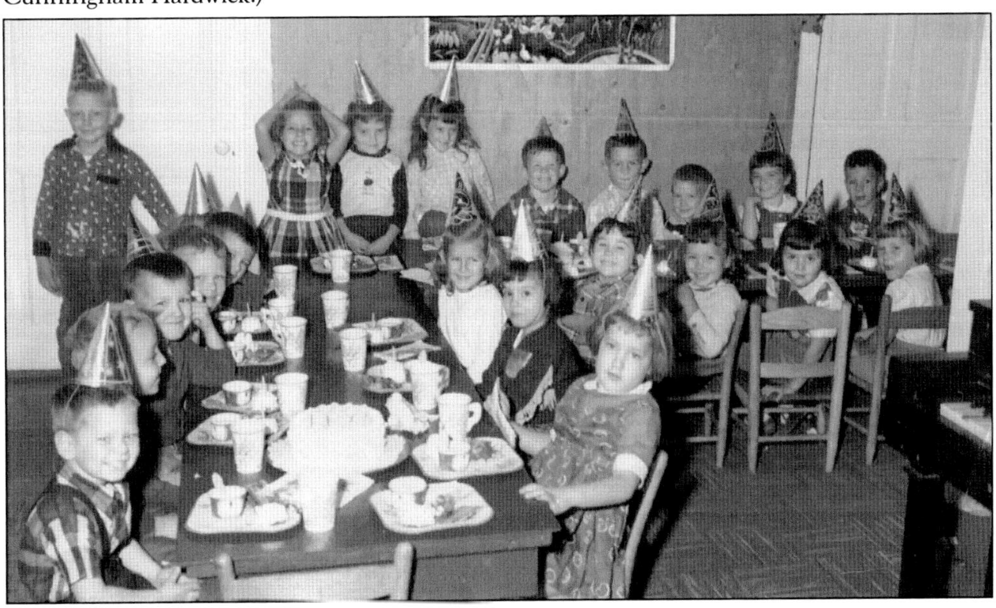

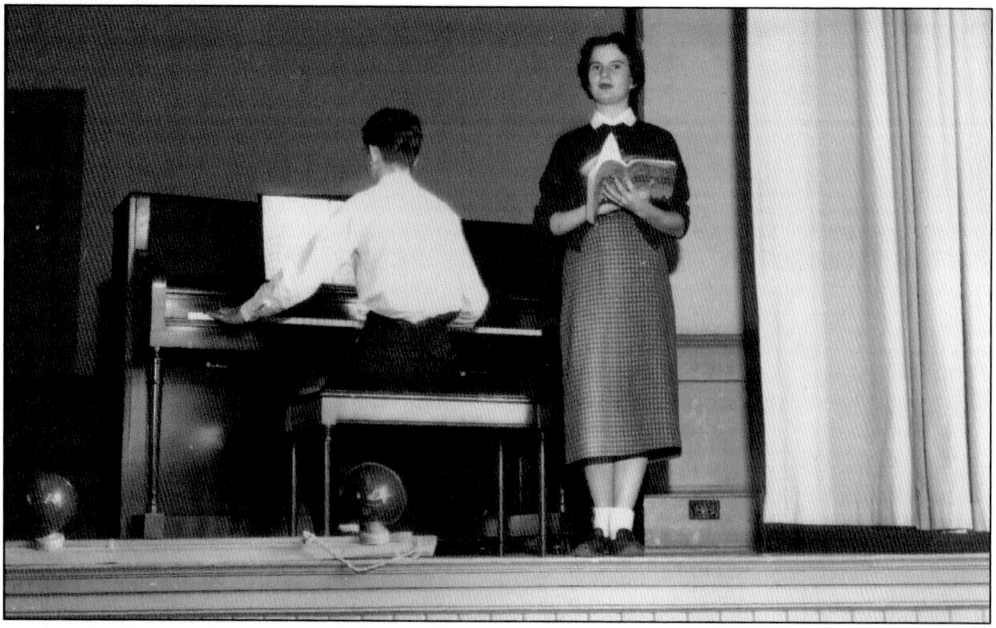

High school student Boochie DuRant (Swearingen) practices her musical repertoire in the auditorium of the grammar school on Ridge Street. When this picture was taken in 1954, the school had just acquired new draperies for the stage and a new piano. Prior to 1937, the school had served as Bishopville High. (Lee County Public Library.)

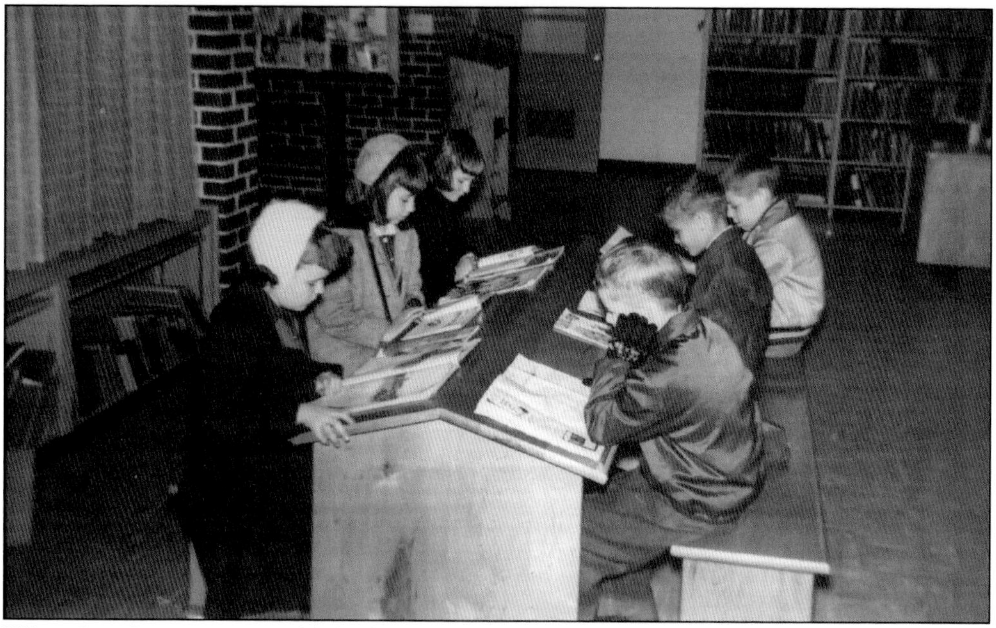

When Lee County was established in 1902, the Bishopville Library Association was already a year old and boasted 39 members and 772 books. Here a group of young readers enjoys the children's corner of the new Woodward Public Library in 1954. The facility was made possible through a bequest of the late Hosea Wilson Woodward, who left Woodward Park and $30,000 for the construction of a library. In 1954, two thousand five hundred books were added to the collection. (Lee County Public Library.)

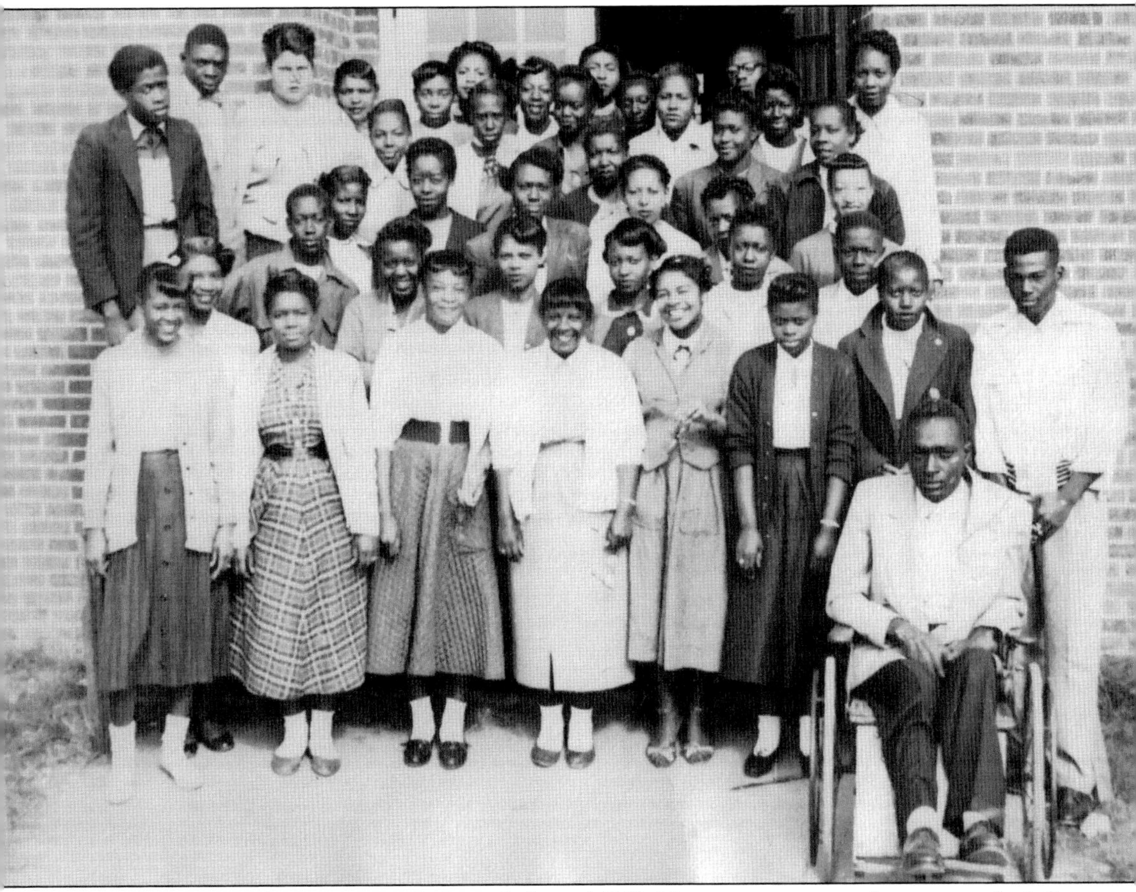

Pictured above is the Dennis High School class of 1953. The young man on the top row, far left (wearing the dark coat) is none other than local blues legend Drink Small. Other classmates seen here are (in no particular order) Shirley Morgan, Eva Mae James, Bertha Reece, Carrie Gass, Minnie Joe, Katie Dixon, Catherine Williams, Fannie Dorgan, Pearline Toney, Doreatha Toney, Elizabeth Charles, Mary Nelson, Annie Cooper, Dollie Joe, Mary Mack, Rosa Davis, Ella Mae Mickens, Mary McDuffie, Thelma Hickman, Ruth Jackson, Jannie Murphy, Luncinda Brunson, Amie Wilson, Bessie Simon, Luvenia Simon, Louise Price, Ruth Smith, Everlina Benjamin, Josephine Benjamin, Dorothy Lowery, Rufelia Lowery, Willie Mae Scarborough, Dollie Thomas, Ada Bell Frierson, Freddie Greene, Cellestine Wilson, Alice Carter, Pearl Wells, Mack Phillips, Lucius Sylvester, Fred White, Johnnie Fortune, Clarence Wilson, Ray Bradley, Eddie Lee Isaac, Levi Pearson, James Scott, Moses Toney, and Walter Durant. Note the disproportionate ratio of boys to girls. It was still quite common during this period of time for young African American men to quit school at an early age and go to work on the family farm. (Carrie Gass.)

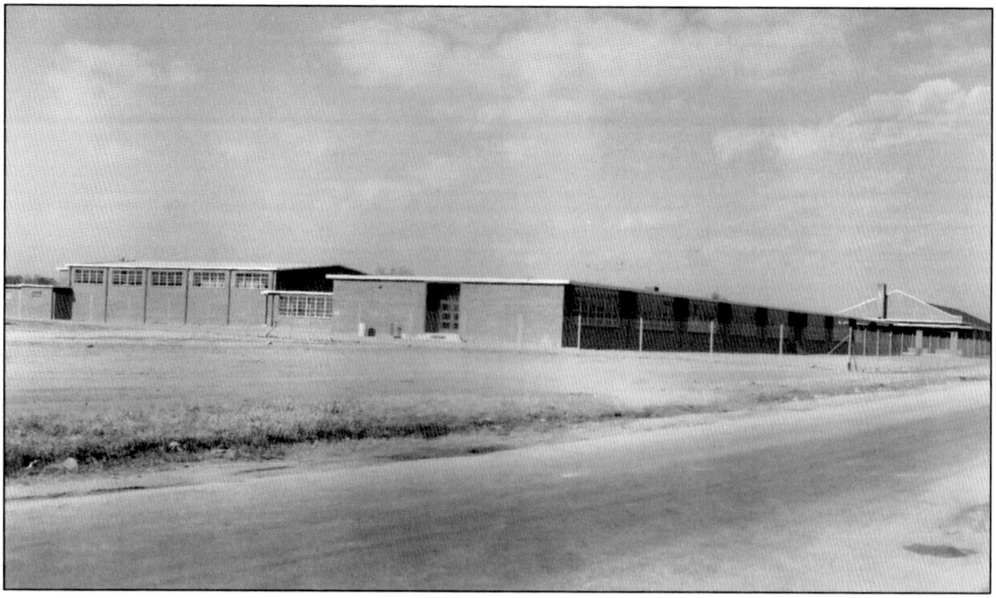

In 1953–1954, a new building was erected for Dennis High School, and the old building was renovated for use as Dennis Primary School. Pictured above is one of the new classrooms. While there was still disparity between the black and white educational systems, the new school was a far cry from the little brick building that had served students since 1936. No longer did the students have to build a fire in the big heater in the auditorium during the winter months or run to the outhouse between classes. (Lee County Public Library.)

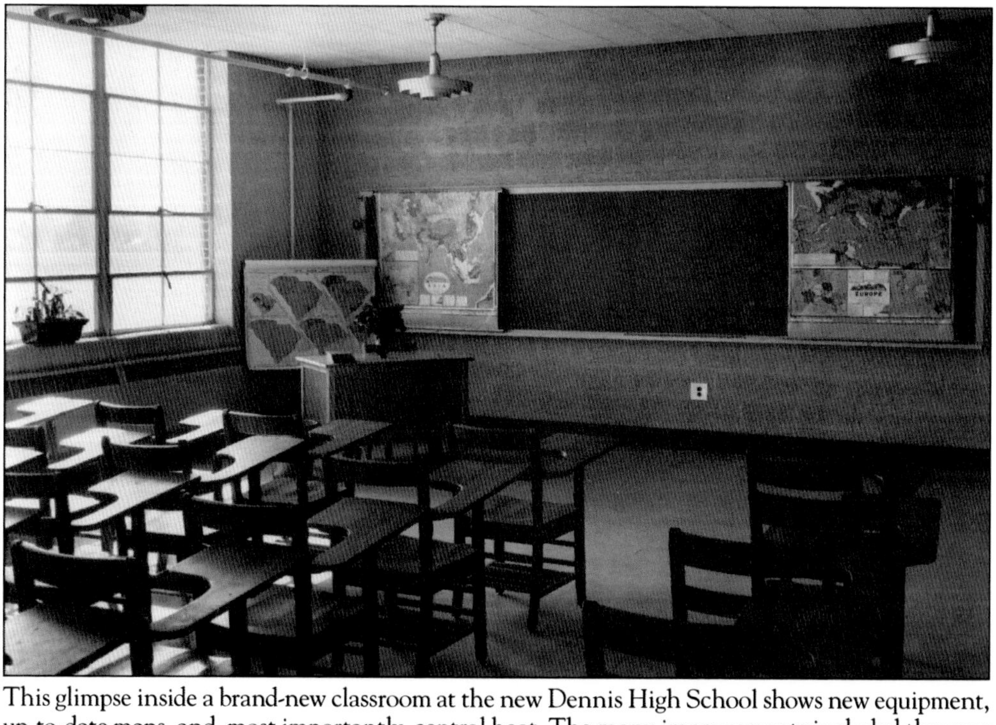

This glimpse inside a brand-new classroom at the new Dennis High School shows new equipment, up-to-date maps, and, most importantly, central heat. The many improvements included the very first gymnasium for the area's African American students. (Lee County Public Library.)

Bishopville High School principal J. H. Stafford takes a break on the bumper of a car in the high school parking lot in this 1941 photograph. Stafford also taught history and in later years served as school superintendent.

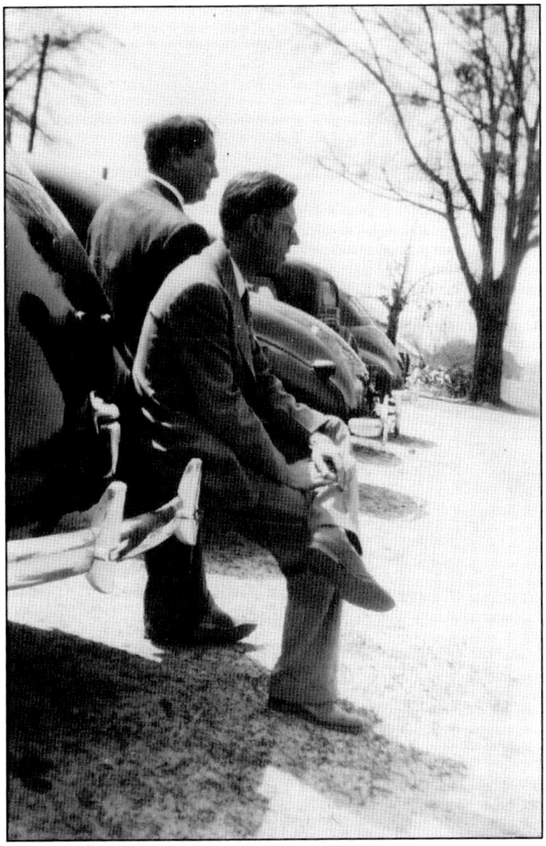

An anonymous author wrote of Louise Graham in the 1923 Bishop yearbook, "Louise is verily 'neat as a pin' both in personal appearance and in schoolwork." Her students from the early 1940s, when this photograph was made, remember those same characteristics. Sometime after this picture was taken, Graham married Lee County sheriff James Wilson.

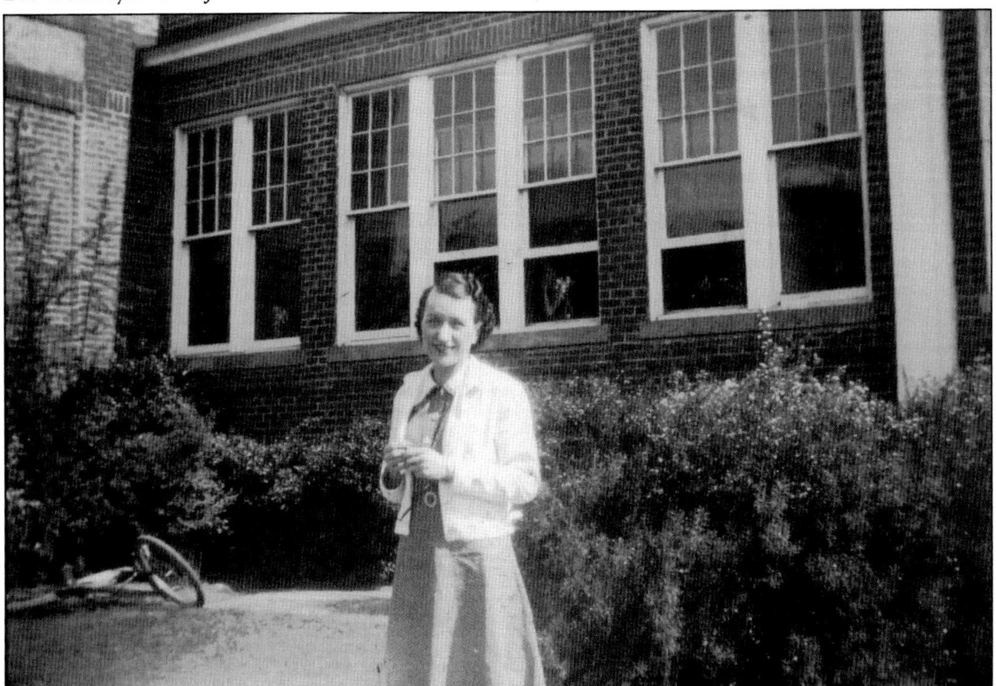

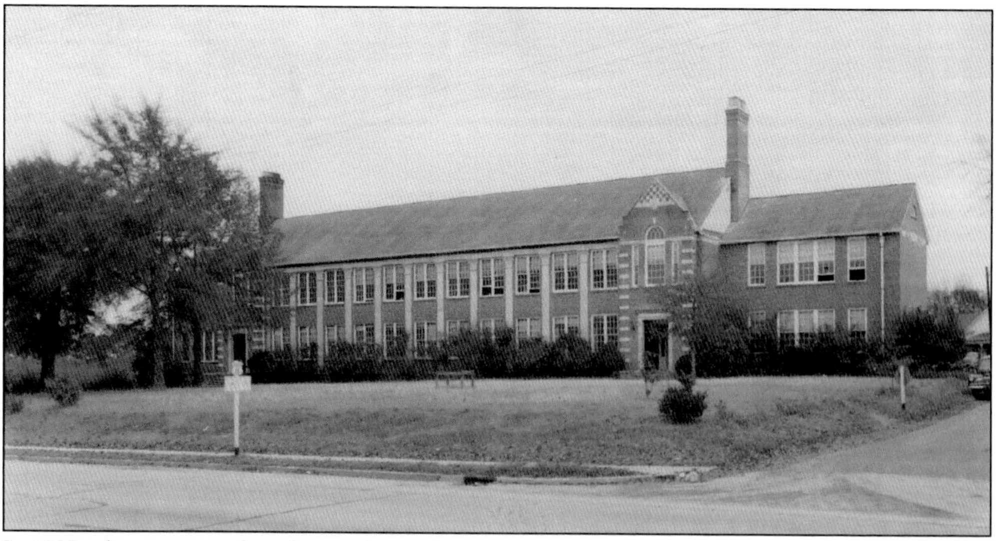

In 1937, what is now referred to as the "old" Bishopville High School welcomed its first students. In fact, the school was completed midway through the year; the class of 1937 commenced its senior year at one school and graduated from the new Bishopville High the following spring. Some of the funding for the new school, which was built to relieve overcrowding of the Ridge Street School, came from the Public Works Administration. This photograph dates from about 1940. Additions to the building were made in 1956, and a new gymnasium was added in 1965.

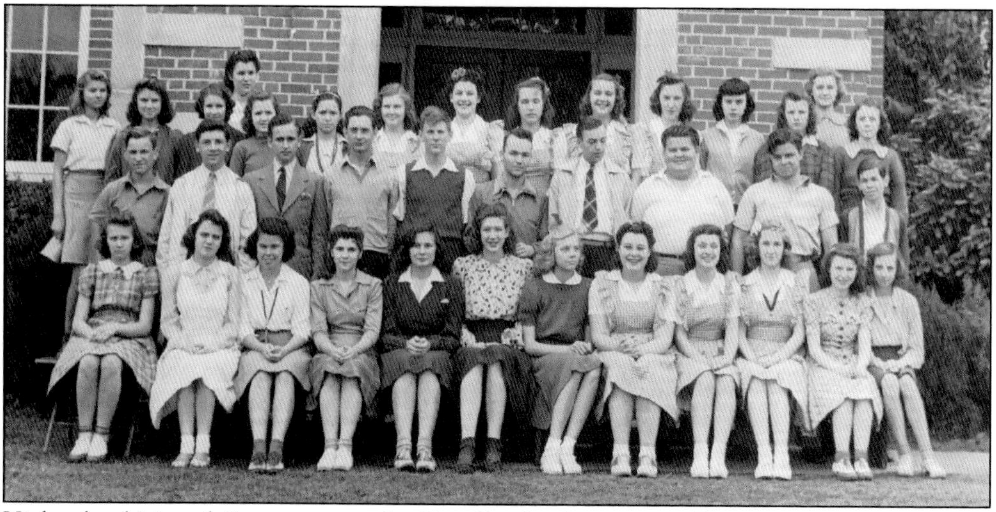

High school Mental Contests were the Quiz Bowls of yesteryear. The 1941–1942 BHS mental contestants are shown here. From left to right are (first row) Betty Ann Lee, Willie Kate Craven, Louise Cousar, Margery Woodham, Olive McIntosh, Sarah McCutchen, Eleanor Reaves, Rita Slesinger, Beverly Woodward, Esther Lee Tindal, Sarah Winifred Cook, and Julia Josey; (second row) Julius Skinner, Allan Sindler, Don Grant, Lavern Dalrymple, Henry Pittman, John Marion Rhame, Billy Reaves, Jared Smith, Ben Ford, and Guy Smith; (third row) Udene Davis, Sarah Hall, Mary Cheatham, Evelyn Ackerman, Janet Turner, Ann Moore, Elwanda Truesdale, Helene Cahn, Christine Sellers, Mary Elizabeth Blanchard, Lucile Stuckey, Martha Wilson, Elizabeth Barfield, Inez Hyatt, and Carolyn Webb. Team member Elaine Galloway was absent from the picture. Students who excelled on the local examination competed at the state finals in Columbia. (Georgia Lucile Stuckey.)

Six

RECREATION AND ORGANIZATIONS

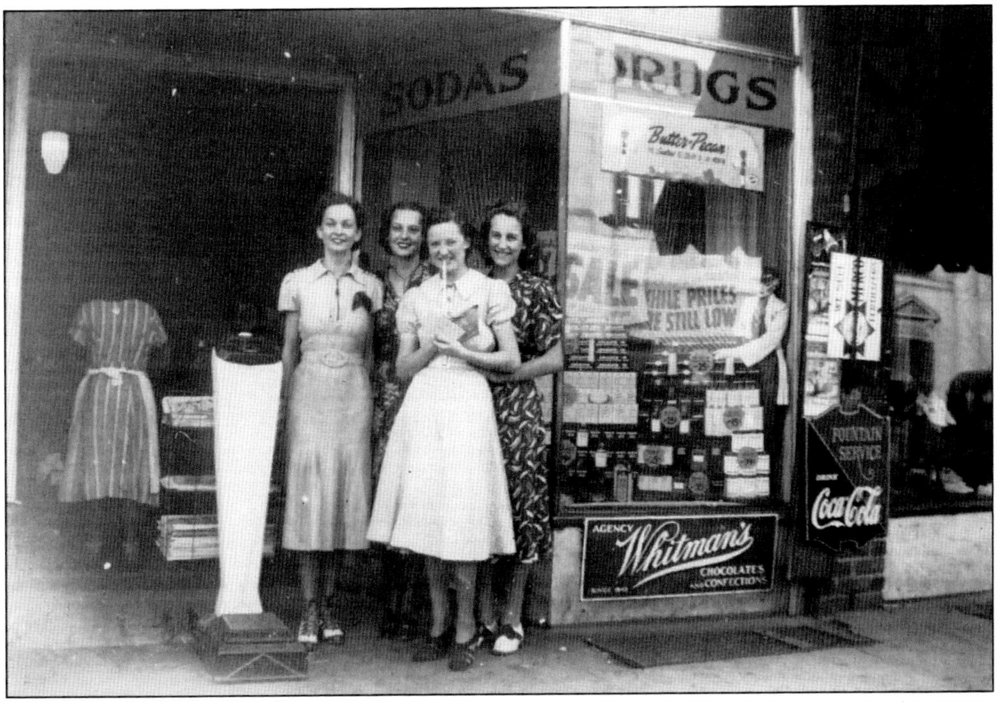

These pretty girls are on their way to enjoy fountain drinks at DuBose's drugstore in this 1930s photograph. Rosa Margaret Perrin (Kilgore) is standing directly beside the scale, and Dot Carnes (Ellen) is next to her in the white dress. The other friends are unidentified. The drugstore was originally owned by Dr. S. B. DuBose. In 1929, Dr. DuBose hired G. Herman McElveen as a pharmacist, and in 1935, Herman bought a half-interest in the firm. In addition to his responsibilities at the drugstore, Herman was mayor of Bishopville for many years.

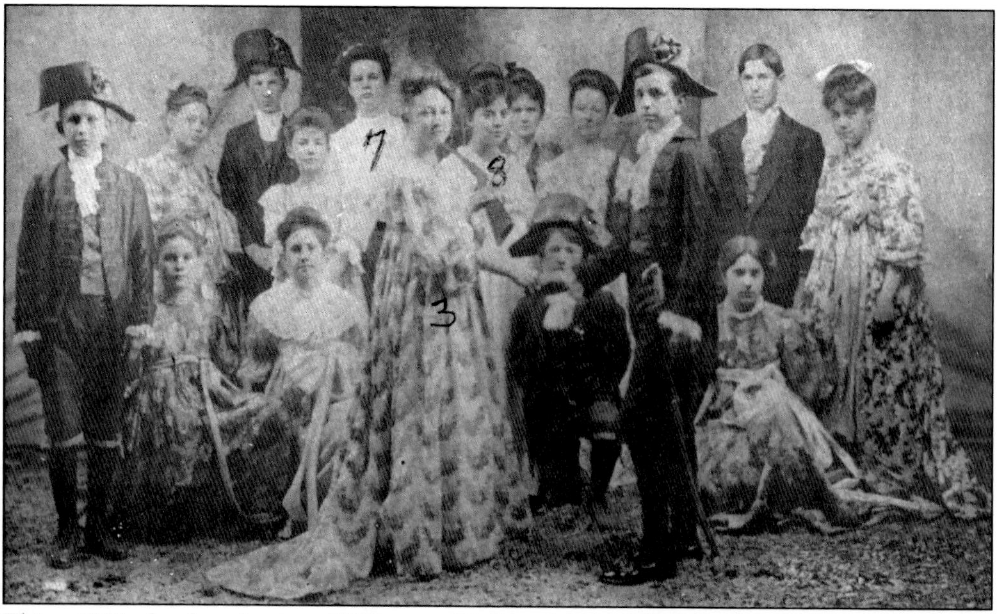

This *c.* 1905 school production of Gilbert and Sullivan's *H.M.S. Pinafore* featured Lila Moore, Leila James, Mae Moffatt (3), John Rhame, Lide Kilgore, Susie Reynolds, Sadie Smith (7), Geraldine Moore (8), Nita Taylor, Tiny DesChamps, Russell Shaw, Eva Weatherly, and Melisha M. Levy (13). (SCCM.)

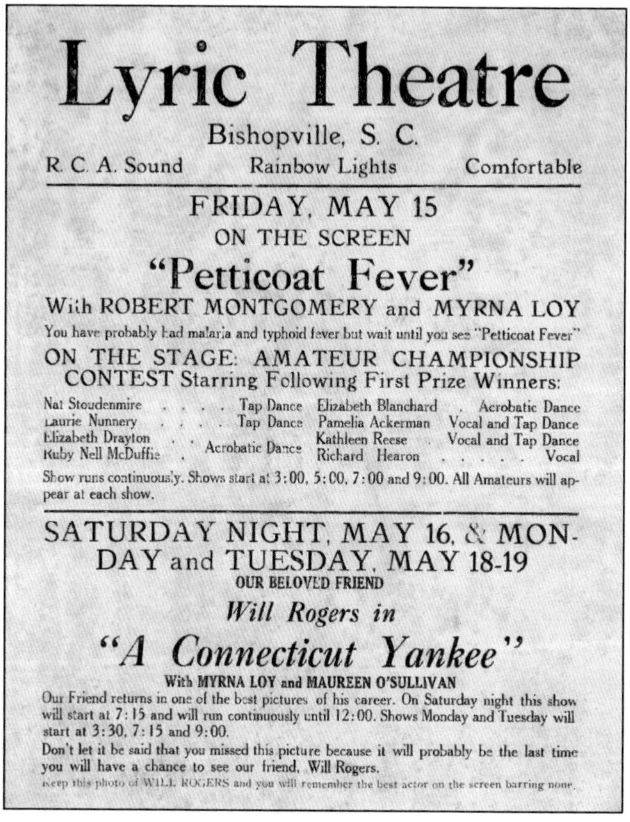

Lyric Theatre

Bishopville, S. C.

R. C. A. Sound — Rainbow Lights — Comfortable

FRIDAY, MAY 15

ON THE SCREEN

"Petticoat Fever"

With ROBERT MONTGOMERY and MYRNA LOY

You have probably had malaria and typhoid fever but wait until you see "Petticoat Fever"

ON THE STAGE: AMATEUR CHAMPIONSHIP CONTEST Starring Following First Prize Winners:

Nat Stoudenmire	Tap Dance	Elizabeth Blanchard	Acrobatic Dance
Laurie Nunnery	Tap Dance	Pamelia Ackerman	Vocal and Tap Dance
Elizabeth Drayton	Acrobatic Dance	Kathleen Reese	Vocal and Tap Dance
Ruby Nell McDuffie		Richard Hearon	Vocal

Show runs continuously. Shows start at 3:00, 5:00, 7:00 and 9:00. All Amateurs will appear at each show.

SATURDAY NIGHT, MAY 16, & MONDAY and TUESDAY, MAY 18-19

OUR BELOVED FRIEND

Will Rogers in

"A Connecticut Yankee"

With MYRNA LOY and MAUREEN O'SULLIVAN

Our Friend returns in one of the best pictures of his career. On Saturday night this show will start at 7:15 and will run continuously until 12:00. Shows Monday and Tuesday will start at 3:30, 7:15 and 9:00.

Don't let it be said that you missed this picture because it will probably be the last time you will have a chance to see our friend, Will Rogers.

Keep this photo of WILL ROGERS and you will remember the best actor on the screen barring none.

A 1936 playbill from the Lyric Theatre on Main Street announces that the Friday feature film will be preceded by an amateur talent show performed by some very familiar contestants. In the days before television, movie theaters showed not only the popular films of the day but newsreels, cartoons, and the occasional stage show. A line at the bottom of the bill notes, "It will probably be the last time you will have a chance to see our friend, Will Rogers." Rogers had died the previous year. (SCCM.)

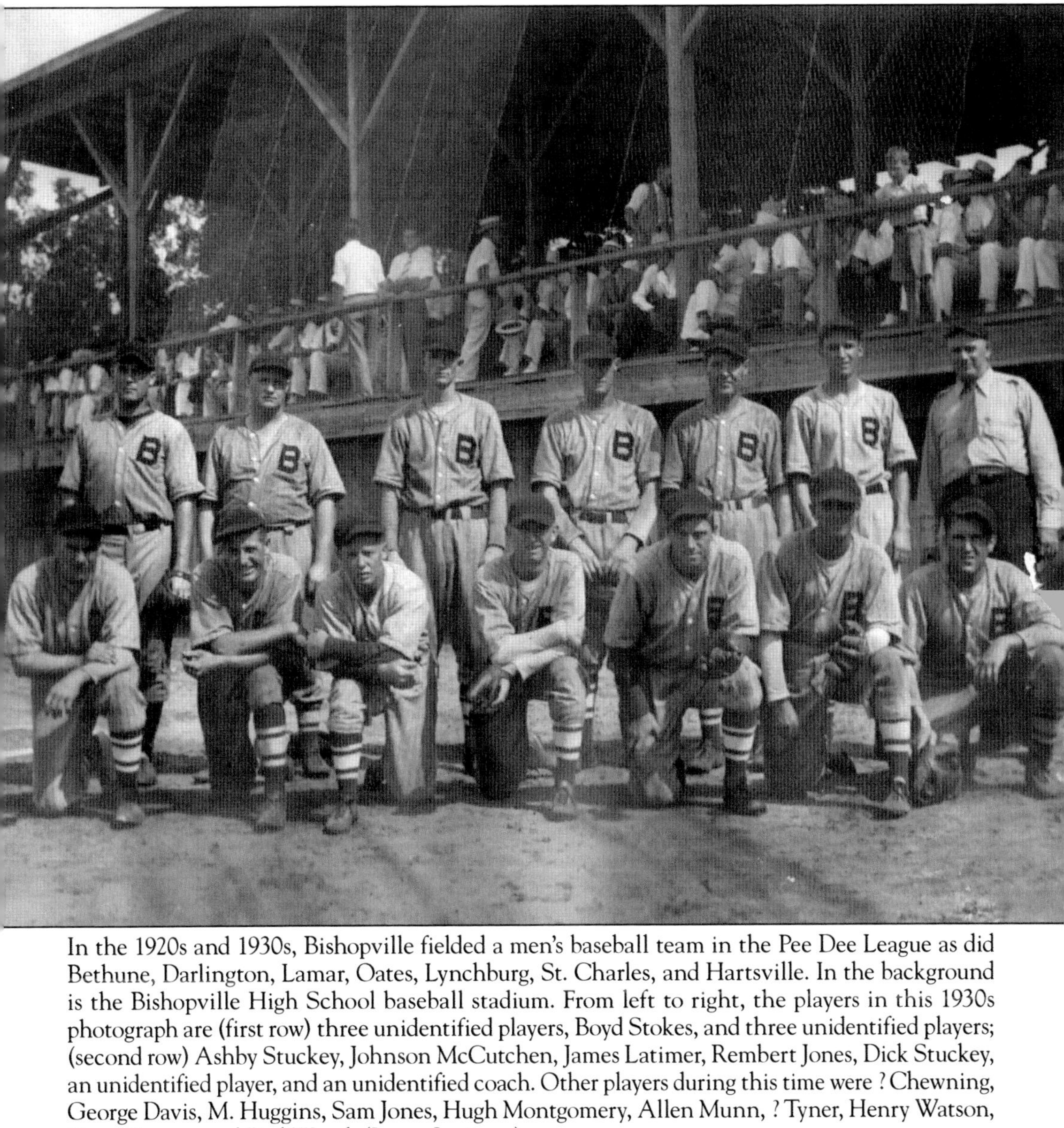

In the 1920s and 1930s, Bishopville fielded a men's baseball team in the Pee Dee League as did Bethune, Darlington, Lamar, Oates, Lynchburg, St. Charles, and Hartsville. In the background is the Bishopville High School baseball stadium. From left to right, the players in this 1930s photograph are (first row) three unidentified players, Boyd Stokes, and three unidentified players; (second row) Ashby Stuckey, Johnson McCutchen, James Latimer, Rembert Jones, Dick Stuckey, an unidentified player, and an unidentified coach. Other players during this time were ? Chewning, George Davis, M. Huggins, Sam Jones, Hugh Montgomery, Allen Munn, ? Tyner, Henry Watson, Tom Watson, and Red Wood. (Laura Latimer.)

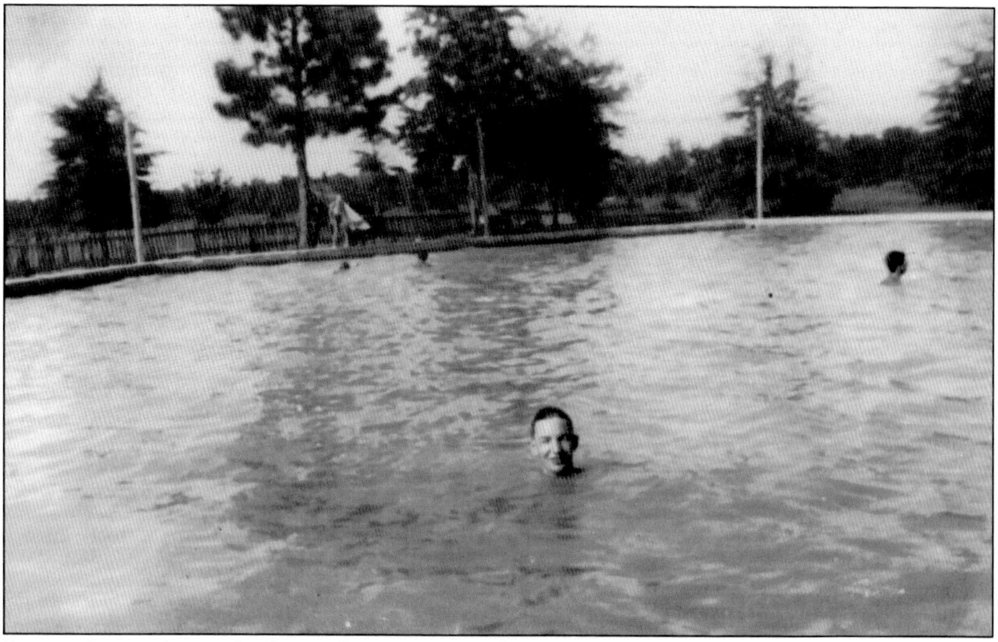

Sonny Carnes beats the heat of a South Carolina summer at Denny's Pool in 1940. Several generations of Bishopville youth spent many a summer's day swimming in the artesian-fed pond and enjoying a frozen candy bar or two from the concession stand. Known by earlier generations as Lake Delano, the facility was later owned and operated by the Denny family. With a jukebox and a small dance floor, the pool is remembered by teenagers of the 1950s and 1960s as the place to be on a summer weekend night. (Retta Dickinson Tindal.)

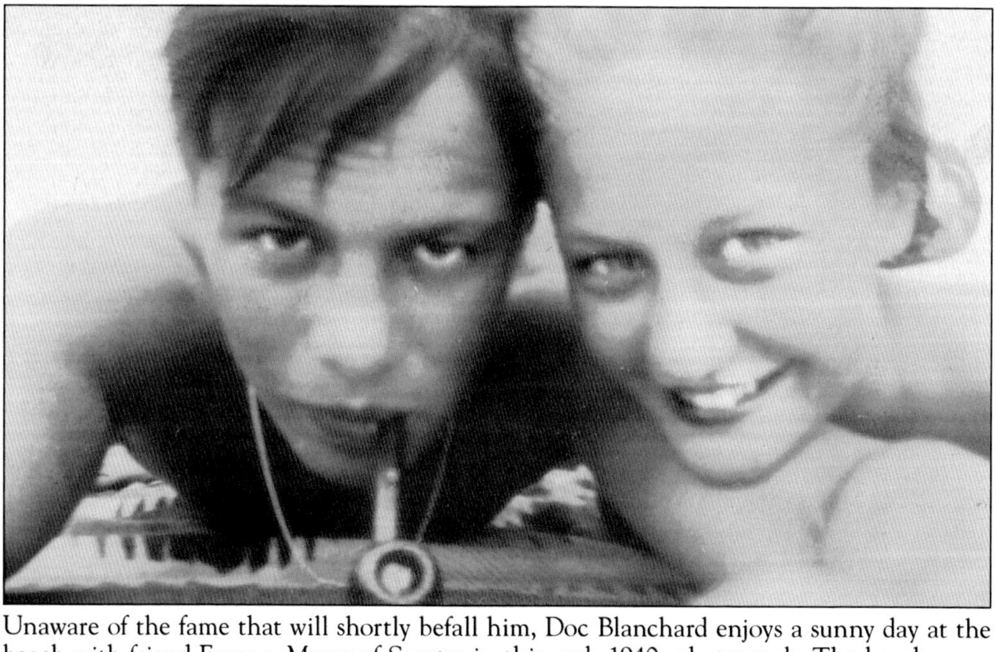

Unaware of the fame that will shortly befall him, Doc Blanchard enjoys a sunny day at the beach with friend Frances Moses of Sumter in this early-1940s photograph. The beach party also included Frances's first cousin, Woonie Skinner (Dickinson), and Sonny Carnes. (Retta Dickinson Tindal.)

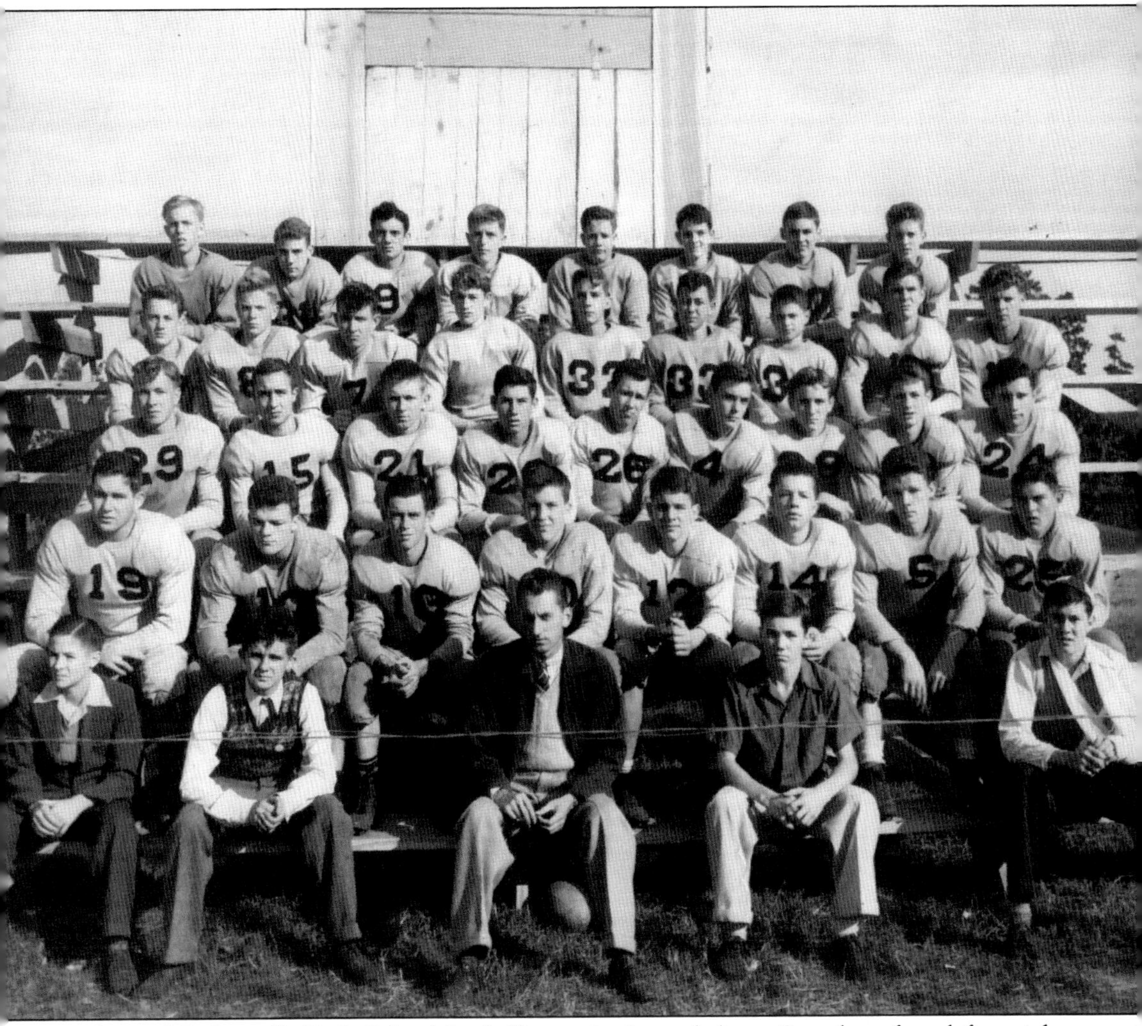

The 1945 Bishopville High School football team is pictured above. Seen here from left to right are (first row) Tommy Jordan, Luther Moore, coach J. O. Willis, ? Pate, and Joe Stoudenmire; (second row) W. S. Huggins, Leonard Pate, Thurston Stuckey, James K. "Bubba" Alexander, Jacob Jennings, Alva Kelley Jr., Gerald Pate, and Max DuBose; (third row) ? Stokes, Raymond Strickland, Billy Stewart, Bobby Merck, Liston Truesdale, Laddie Brealey, Willis Woodham, J. W. Jones, and Howard Brown; (fourth row) unidentified student, Buster Brown, unidentified student, Larry Stevenson, Tommy Jones, Lavern Stokes, Dan Laney Jr., Harold Hatfield, and unidentified student; (fifth row) Frank Huggins, Clifford Reaves, Johnnie Brown, Tom Alexander, two unidentified students, John Blackwell, and unidentified student. (Liston Truesdale.)

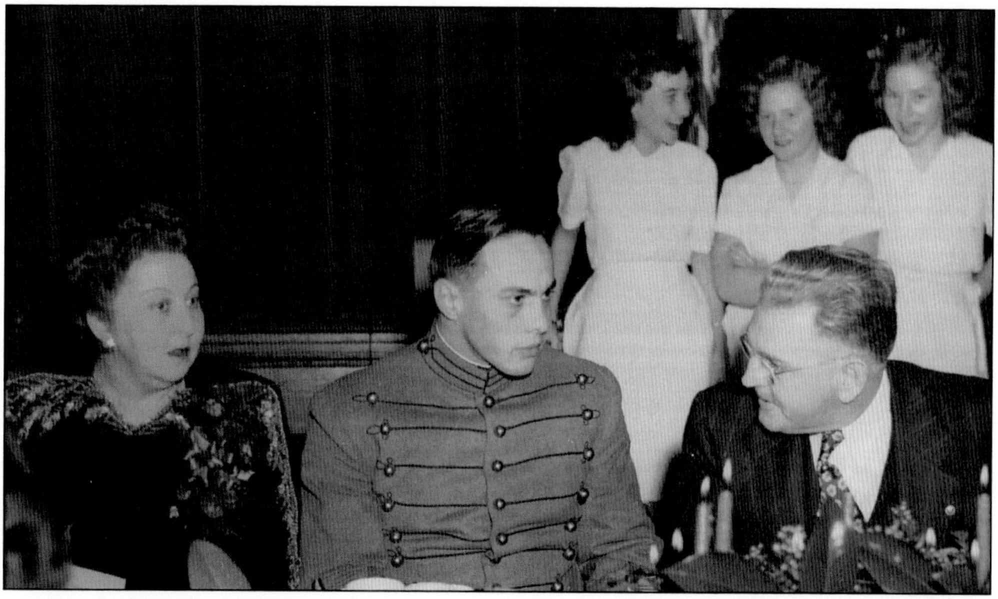

In 1945, Bishopville native and West Point cadet Felix A. (Doc) Blanchard was awarded the Heisman Trophy. The first junior classman to win the award, Doc scored 38 touchdowns and gained 1,908 yards in three years on the Army team. A banquet in his honor, sponsored by the Bishopville Rotary, Lions, Pilot, and Kiwanis service clubs, was held on December 27, 1945, in the high school auditorium. Many sportswriters, sports editors, and college football coaches, as well as friends and family, were in attendance. Above, he is seated at the table with his mother, Betty Tatum Blanchard, while Henry Jennings speaks. Below, Doc is shown signing autographs for a line of students. (SCCM.)

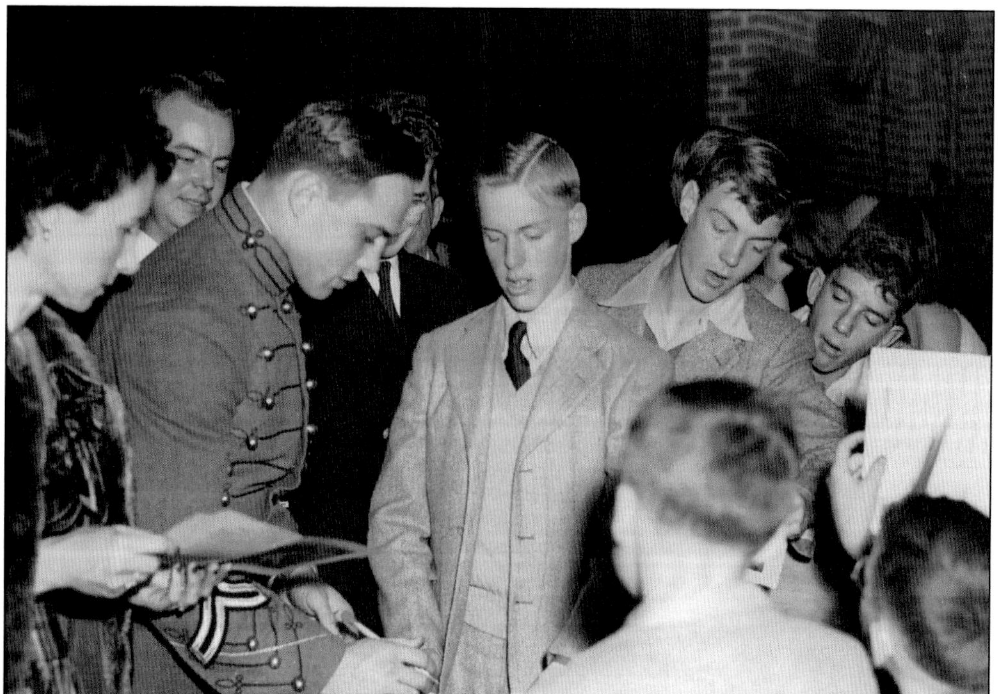

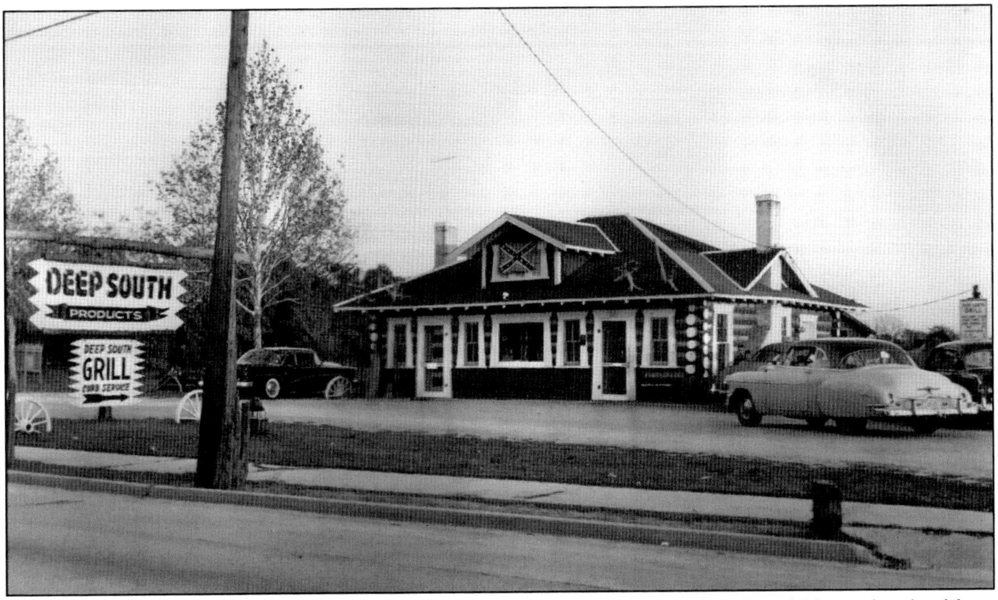

The Deep South Products Company opened in 1954 and was located in the old log cabin building on South Main Street. H. P. Moore Sr. was owner of the business and was assisted by his son, H. P. (Mocus) Moore Jr., and Rosa Lee O'Kelley. Products for sale in the shop, such as lamps, tables, planters, and figurines, were all manufactured locally, often with native products such as cypress and bamboo. The ceramics sold at the shop were made in Bethune. The Deep South Grill featured curb service and catered to students. (Lee County Public Library.)

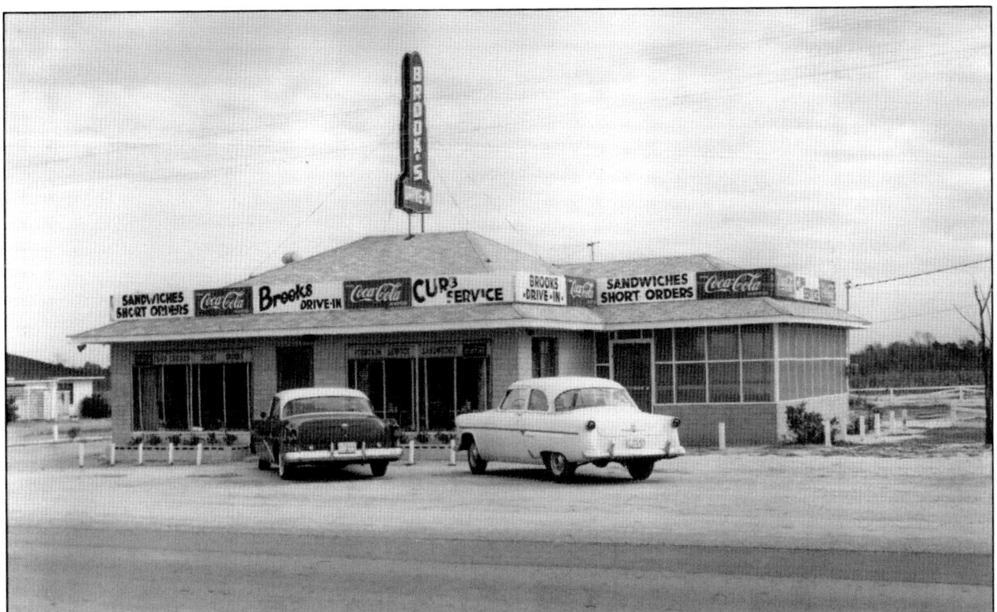

Originally opened in 1954, Brooks Drive-In, located on the Hartsville Highway, was a popular spot for high school students. The restaurant was owned and operated by Brooks Walters and his wife, Jackie. At a later date, the screened porch in the photograph was removed to enable additional curb service. The restaurant burned down, and in 1960, J. W. Davis bought the property and built Wayne's Drive-In, which was run by his son, Wayne. (Lee County Public Library.)

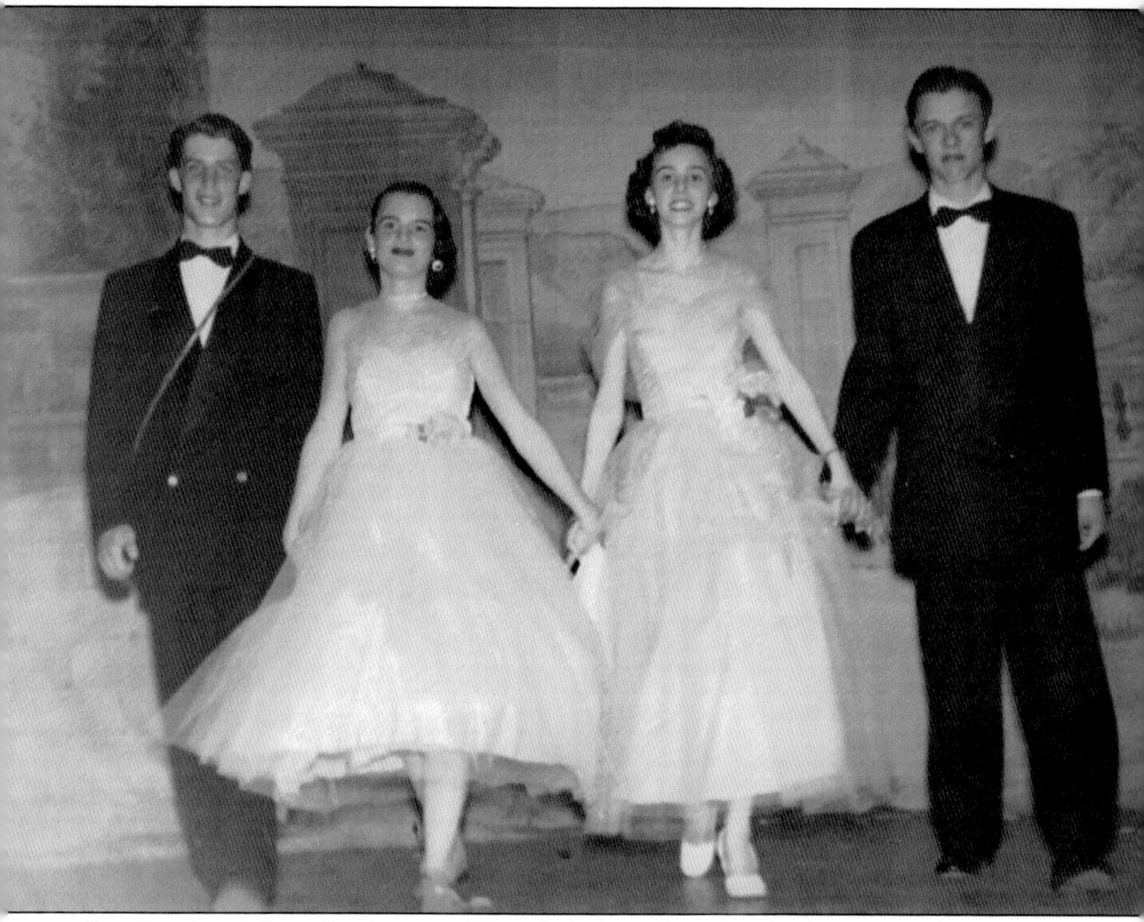

Seen here from left to right, the stars of the 1954 Bishopville High School operetta *Pickles* are David Quattlebaum, Boochie DuRant (Swearingen), Louise Hapeshis (McCutchen), and Ralph Shumaker. An annual tradition, the operetta featured members of the school's various musical groups. Band and chorus director Woodrow Tisdale was assisted by Mrs. Y. A. Montgomery, who taught music. By 1959, Shumaker was Glee Club director at the high school. (Louise Hapeshis McCutchen.)

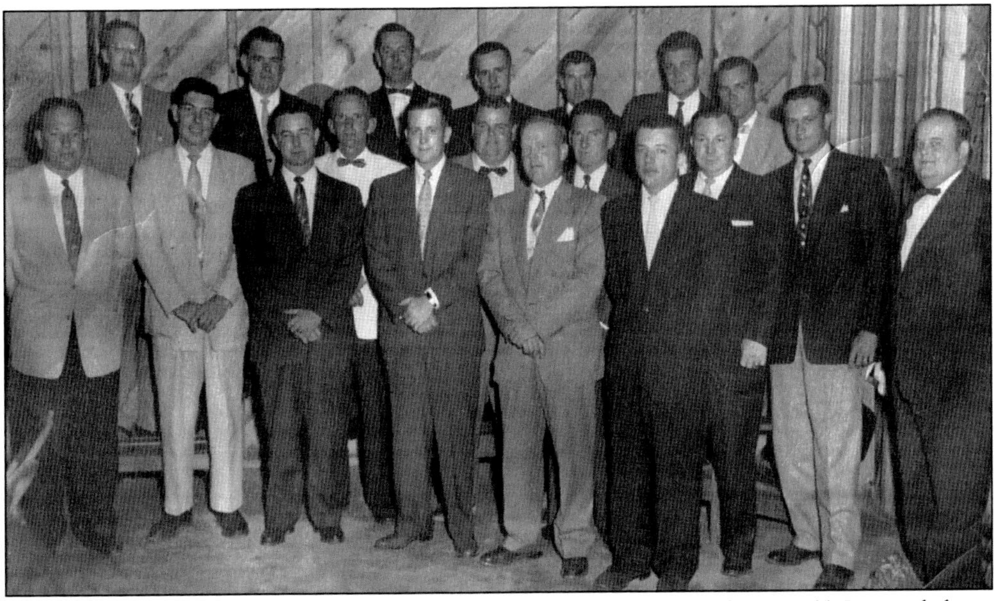

The Bishopville Junior Chamber of Commerce was chartered on March 30, 1955. Pictured above are charter members, from left to right, (first row) Wallace DesChamps, Harvey Shaw, Dick Alexander, and Alva Kelley Jr.; (second row) Arthur Ginsberg, Edward Watkins, H. B. Woodham Jr., Brent King, Edwin Wilson Jr., C. B. Player Jr., M. D. Hancock Jr., and Jared Smith; (third row) Charles Alexander, William Leach Jr., Hughey Tindal Jr., Don Grant, Robert Merck, W. B. McCutchen Jr., and Jim Sellers. Absent from picture were Chesley Hearon, H. P. (Mocus) Moore Jr., Joe E. Morris, Coye Stokes, Dan F. Laney Jr., Burnell Roberson, Liston Truesdale, Raymond Drayton, and Jack Gardner. (SCCM.)

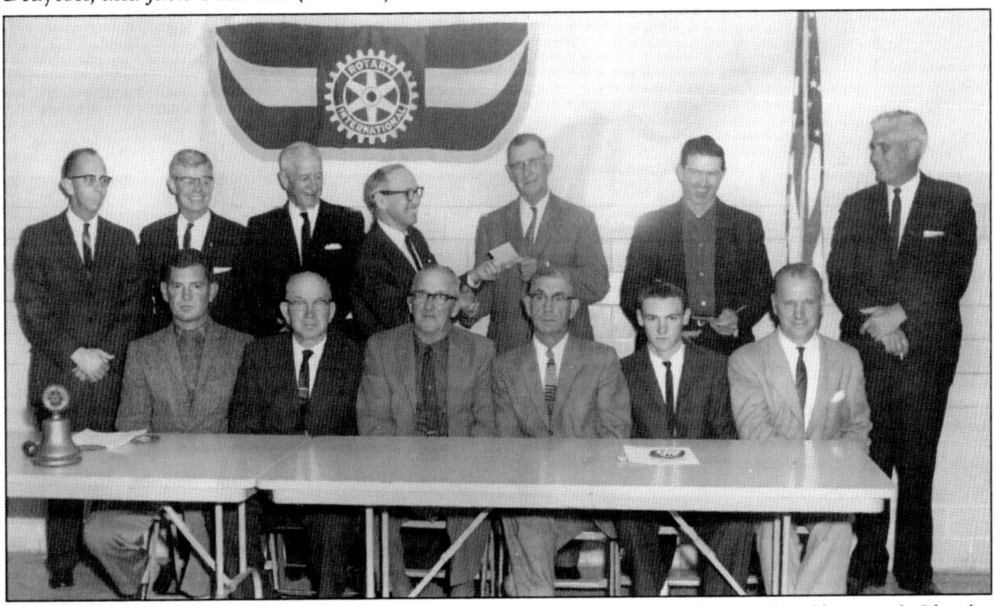

This c. 1955 photograph of Bishopville Rotarians includes, from left to right, (first row) Charlie Mimms Jr., Bill Player, John Blackwell, C. W. Mimms Sr., Fate Logan, and Frank Bouknight; (second row) Virgil Lindler, Joe Olmert, Bob Cooper, Sen. W. P. Baskin Jr., Charlie Josey, Fred DuBose, and Dilly Hammond. (SCCM.)

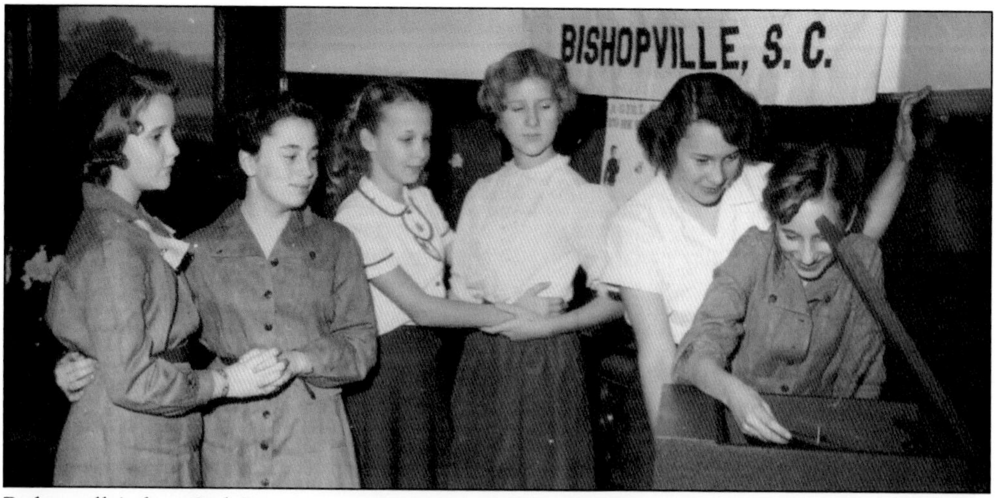

Bishopville's first Girl Scout troop was organized in 1943. Seen from left to right in this 1954 photograph are Jane Ferguson (Watson), Scoozie McLeod (Jones), Mary Ann McCaskill, Christine Smith, Betty Cheatham, and Harriette Stokes (Yarbrough). The girls are enjoying some new equipment provided through the efforts of the Finer Carolina Committee. At the time of this picture, the troop used the jury room in the courthouse for the site of its meetings. Troop leaders that year were Claribell Baskin and Mary Ellen Scurry. (Lee County Public Library.)

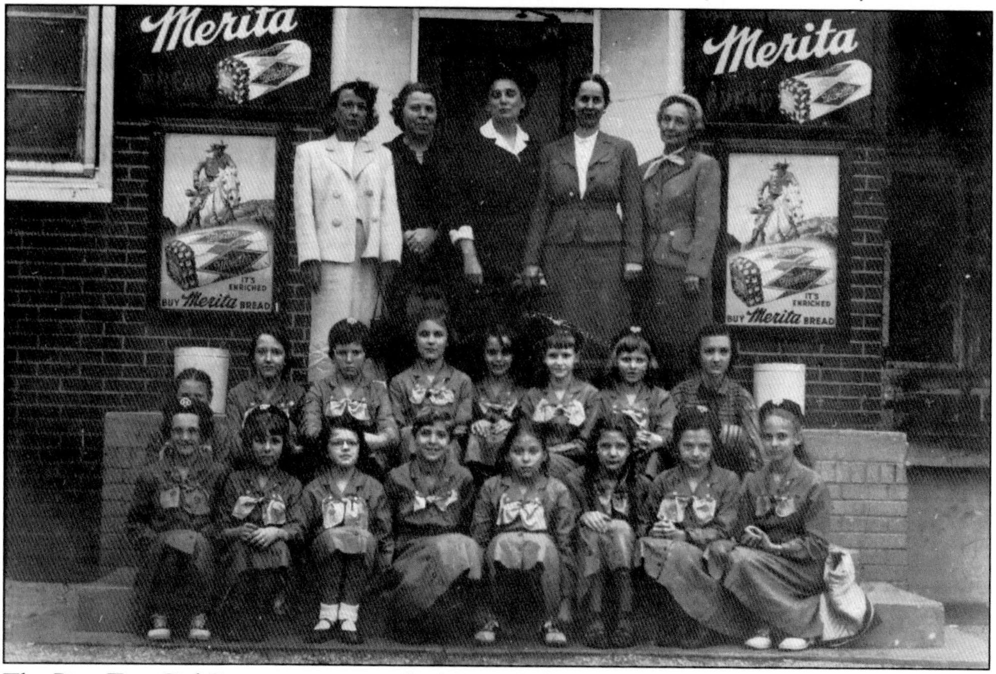

The Pine Tree Girl Scout troop visits the Merita Bakery in Florence on March 14, 1955. Troop No. 500 was led by Mary Quattlebaum and met in her home. Pictured from left to right are (first row) Ann Newsom, Carol Ann Gainey, Wilma Hancock, Linda Walters, Martha Nash, Susan Anderson, Patsy Skinner, and Virginia Quattlebaum; (second row) Ruthie Stevenson, Pam Cunningham, Harriet McCutchen, Judy Bryant, Irene Reames, Peggy Watson, Jean Shirley, and Harriett Foxworth; (third row) Willie Rose Gainey, Beulah Nash, Kathleen Bryant, Mary Quattlebaum, and Leila Flowers, aunt of Kathleen Bryant. (Ruthie Stevenson Bowman.)

Joan Pate, Bishopville High School class of 1953, represents Lee County at the 1955 Miss South Carolina Pageant in Columbia. The daughter of Hazel Pate Sr. and Wilhelmina Stuckey Pate, she is escorted here by Sen. William P. Baskin Jr. (SCCM.)

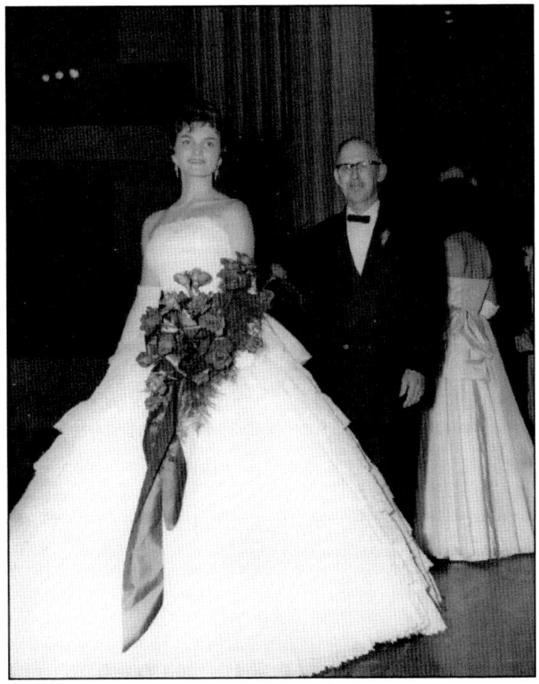

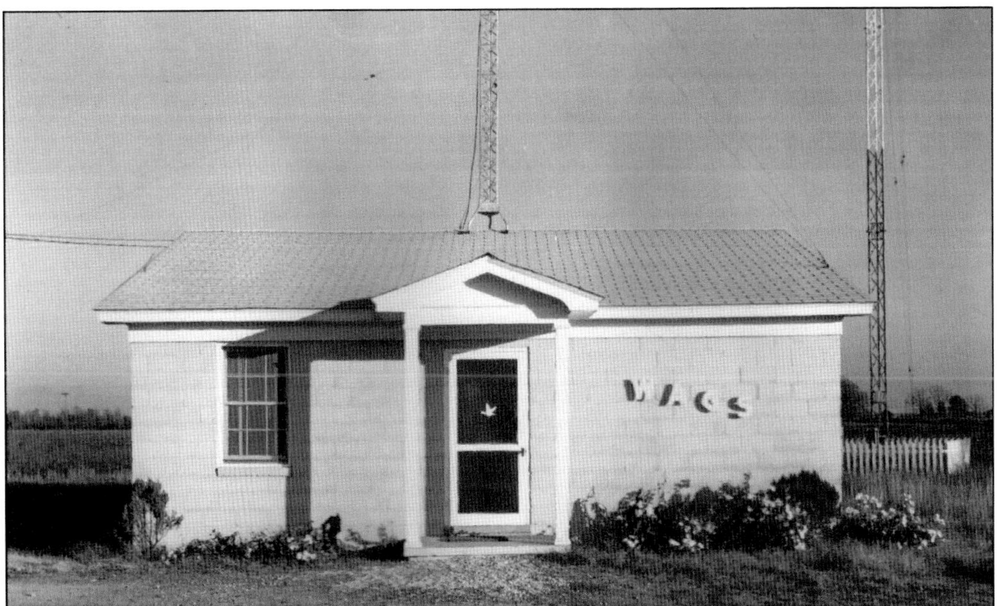

WAGS founder Howard Ginsberg had always been interested in the radio industry. While still a partner in Ginsberg's Ready to Wear, he learned the radio business from friends at stations in Hartsville and Sumter. For a brief time, he broadcast from a small room at the rear of his department store, but in 1954 he constructed the building pictured above. When asked, Ginsberg would say the call letters stood for "Where All Girls Shop"—referring to the family's dress shop. Early deejays were J. T. Nesbit, Joe Morris, Carl Watts, and Denny Smith. The station featured rock and roll, country and western, and live shows. In 1955, Ginsberg went to work for a radio station in Spartanburg and sold WAGS. It still broadcasts today. (Lee County Public Library.)

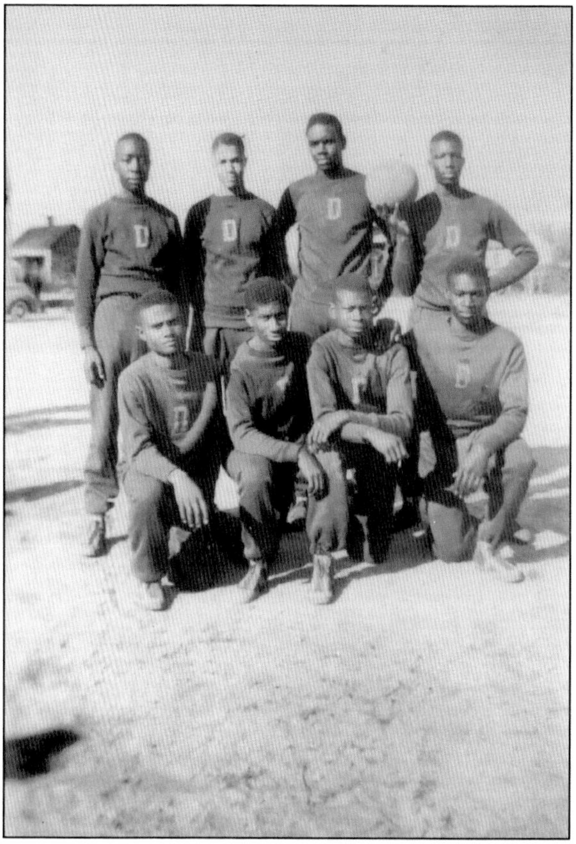

From left to right, this 1944 photograph of the Dennis High School basketball team features (first row) Otto Bradley, George Kelly, Sammie Lee George, and Phillip Bradley; (second row) Russell ?, James Cook, Herbert Williams, and J. T. McDonald. Prior to 1954 when a new building was constructed, Dennis students had no real athletic facilities. The team practiced and played on dirt courts across the road from the school building. Opportunities for competition were limited as there were no other high schools for African American students at the time in Lee County. When the new building was constructed, it featured the gymnasium pictured below. (Left, Bernice Isaac Bradley; below, Lee County Public Library.)

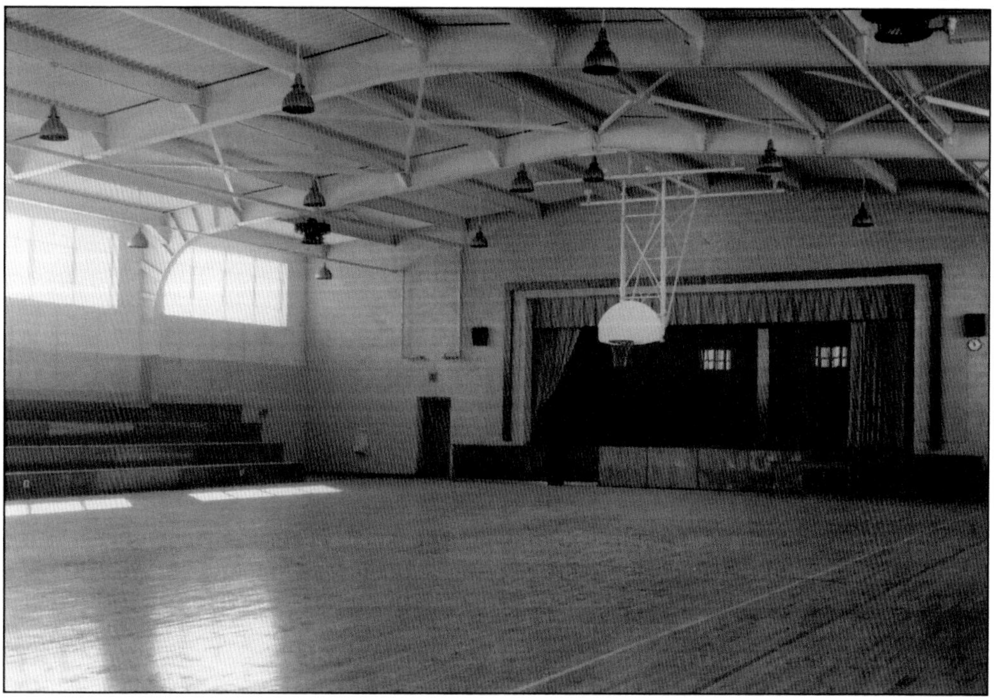

Seven

A Joyful Noise

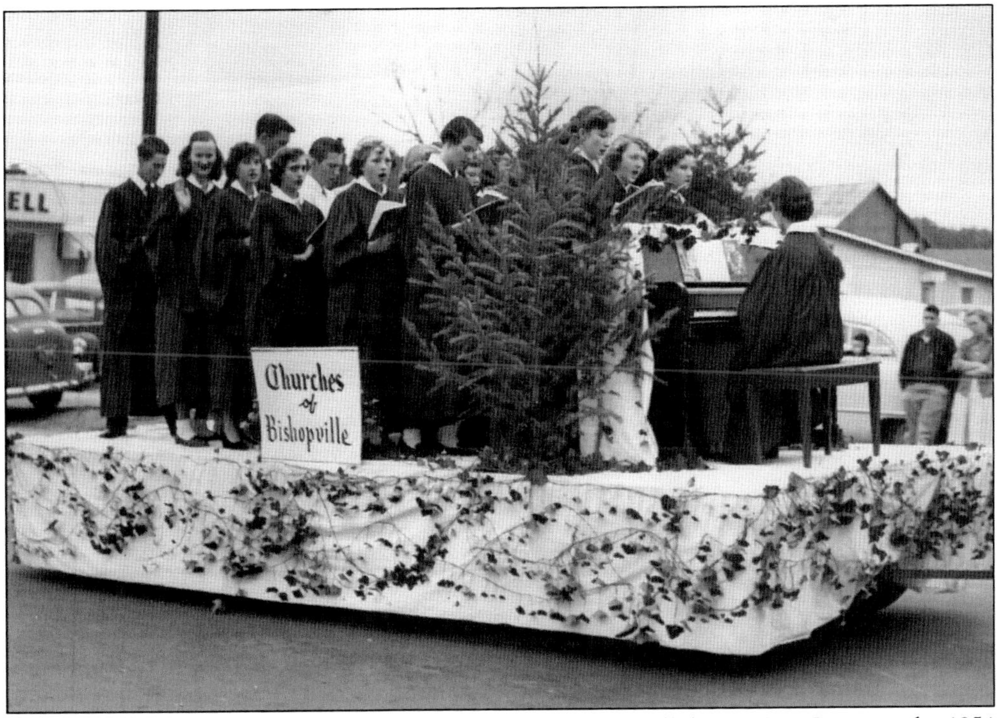

A float sponsored by the churches of Bishopville prepares to roll down Main Street in the 1954 Christmas Parade. Bishopville was home to most mainstream Protestant denominations and had a small Catholic chapel. The town's Jewish population once worshipped in the Masonic Hall above Sindler's menswear store. Methodist and Presbyterian congregations had existed since the early 1800s, followed by the Baptists later in the century. (Lee County Public Library.)

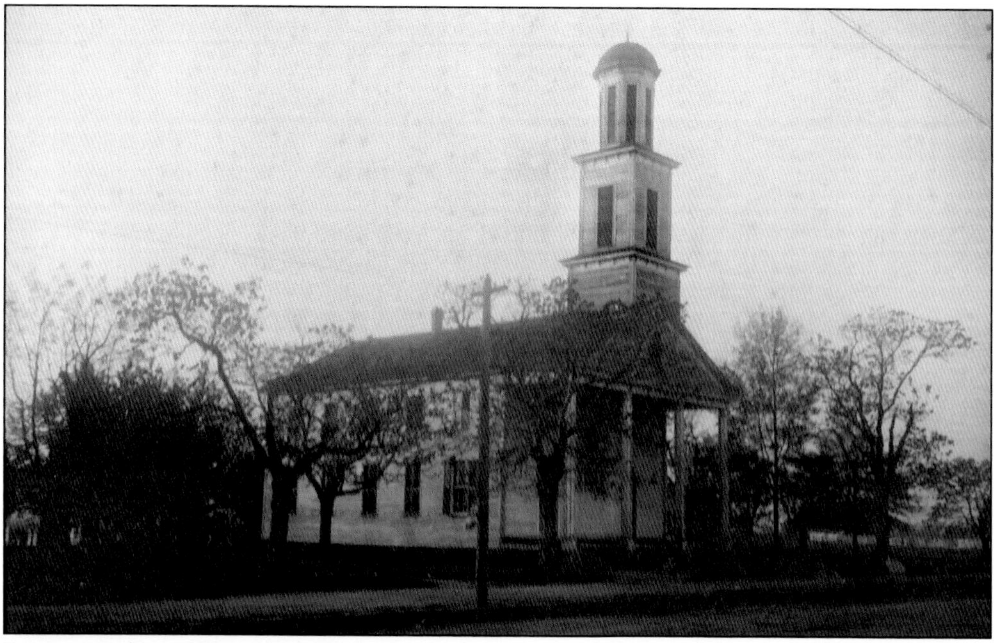

Former members of Mount Zion Presbyterian who wanted a church at Bishopville began construction of the above building in 1839 and had it completed by January 1840. This wooden clapboard church would serve its congregation until it was torn down in 1909. The brick church that stands today was completed in 1910. (Ralph DesChamps.)

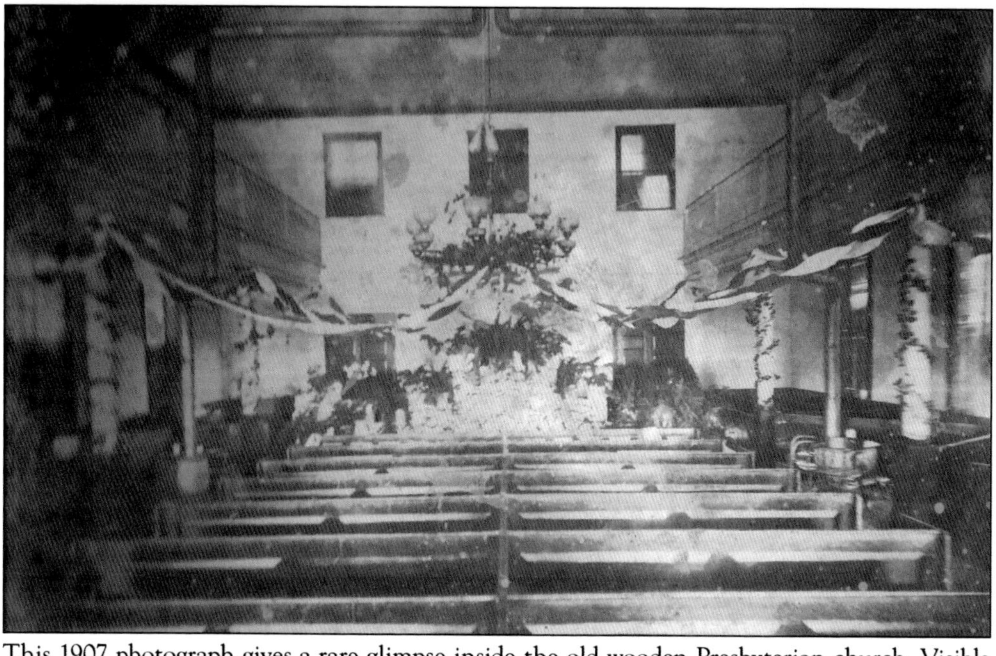

This 1907 photograph gives a rare glimpse inside the old wooden Presbyterian church. Visible are the slave galleries and wood stoves, as well as the magnificent chandelier. The sanctuary had been decorated for the November 20 wedding of J. Baron Kelley and Rebecca F. DesChamps, known to her family as "Little Rea." Baron was a downtown merchant, and Little Rea was a sister to Frank DesChamps. (Ralph DesChamps.)

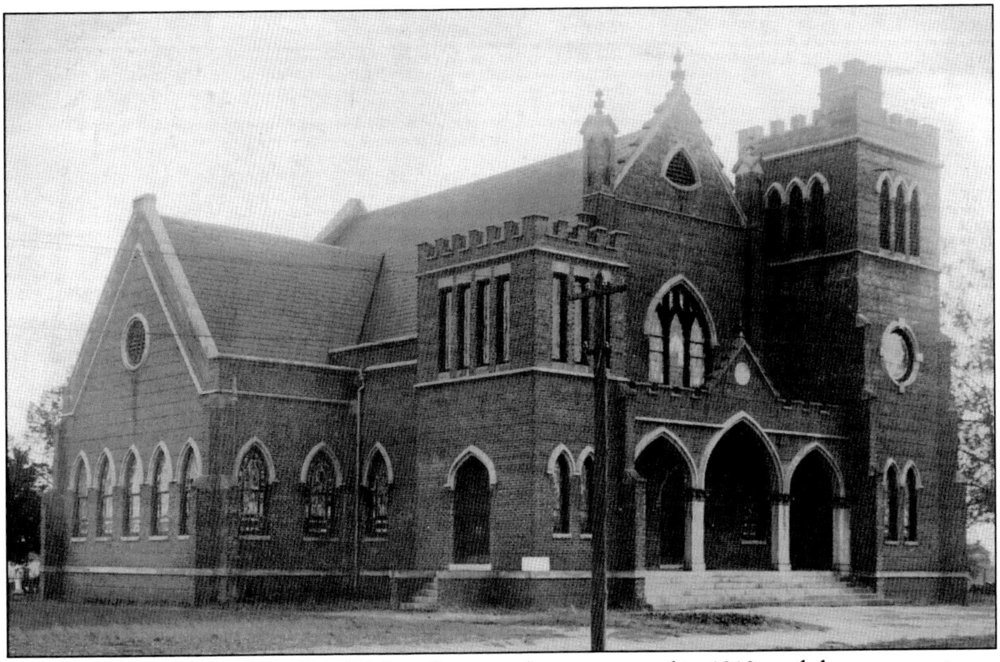

The Presbyterian church on South Main Street today was erected in 1910, and the new sanctuary was dedicated on April 23, 1911. An educational building was added in 1949 and was expanded in 1964. (Barrie Cunningham Hardwick.)

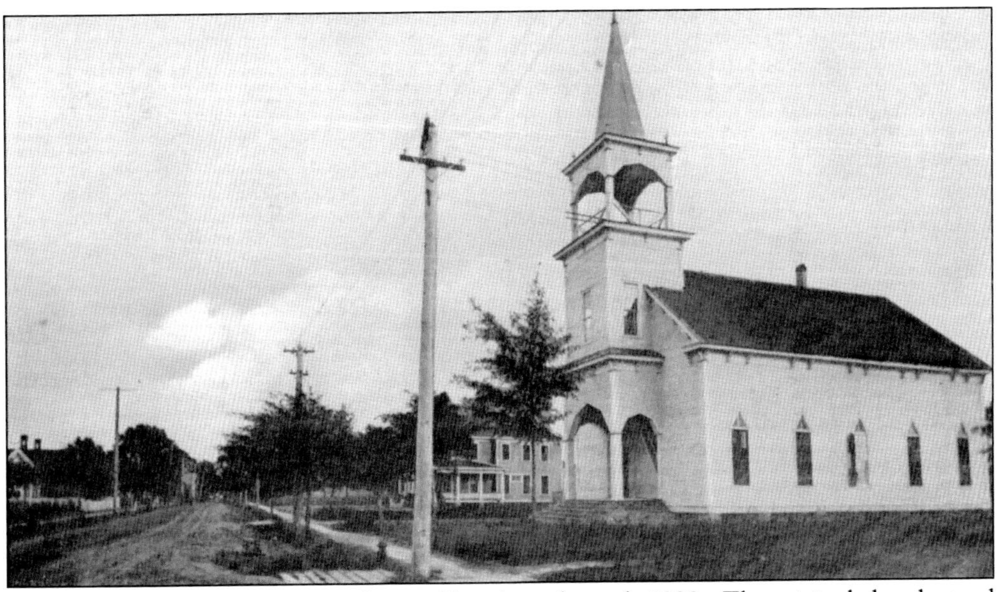

First Baptist Church began as Piedmont Church in the early 1800s. The original church stood across Highway 15 from the Piedmont Cemetery. In 1887, the church was destroyed by fire and reorganized later that year as Bishopville Baptist Church. A new building constructed on Church Street burned in 1895 when it was ignited by sparks from the nearby Phoenix Hotel, which had caught fire. The above view dates from 1908. Across the street in the far left of the photograph is the Elmore home, now Hancock-Elmore Funeral Home. (*Lee County Observer.*)

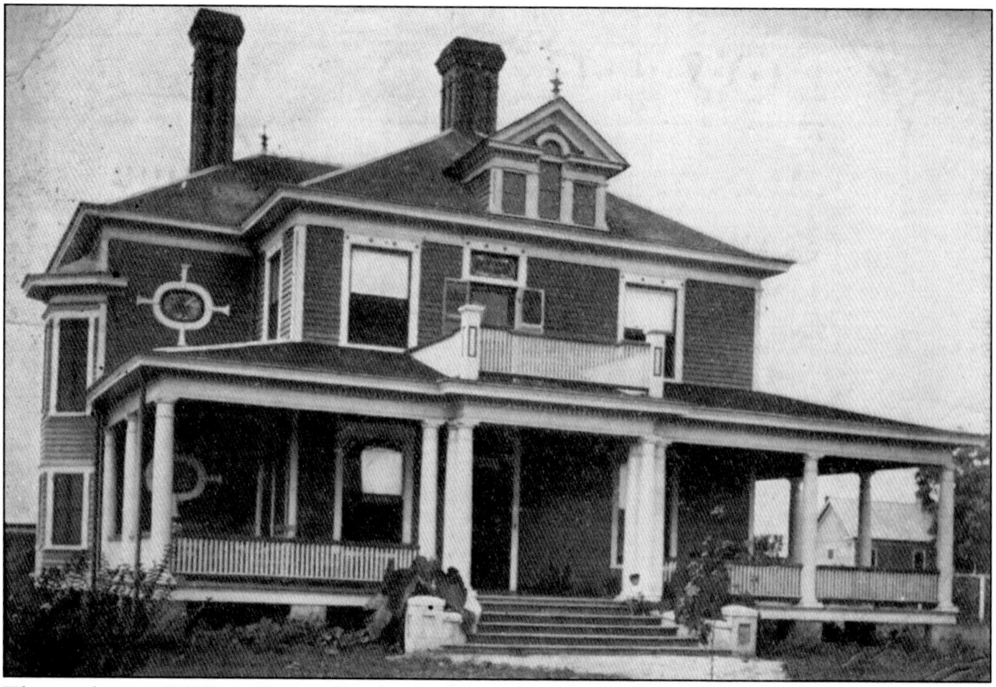

The residence of William Rogers Scarborough stood on West Church Street where the First Baptist Church parking lot is today. The church purchased the home in 1946 and used it for Sunday school rooms and as a recreation area. Scarborough helped organize the Bank of Bishopville in 1901 and served one term as the town's mayor. He and his wife, Rosa. had three children: William, Claud, and Hattie. (SCCM.)

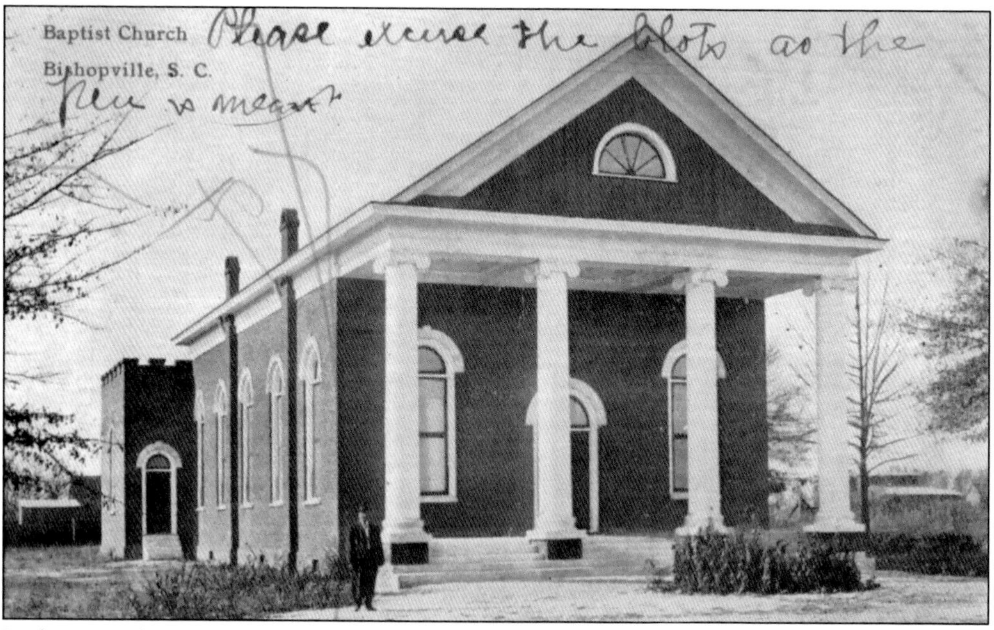

In this 1913 photograph, the Reverend M. M. Benson stands outside the Baptist church, which has recently been bricked over. In later years, the church added stained-glass windows, a steeple, an educational building with Sunday school rooms, and a dining facility. (Barrie Cunningham Hardwick.)

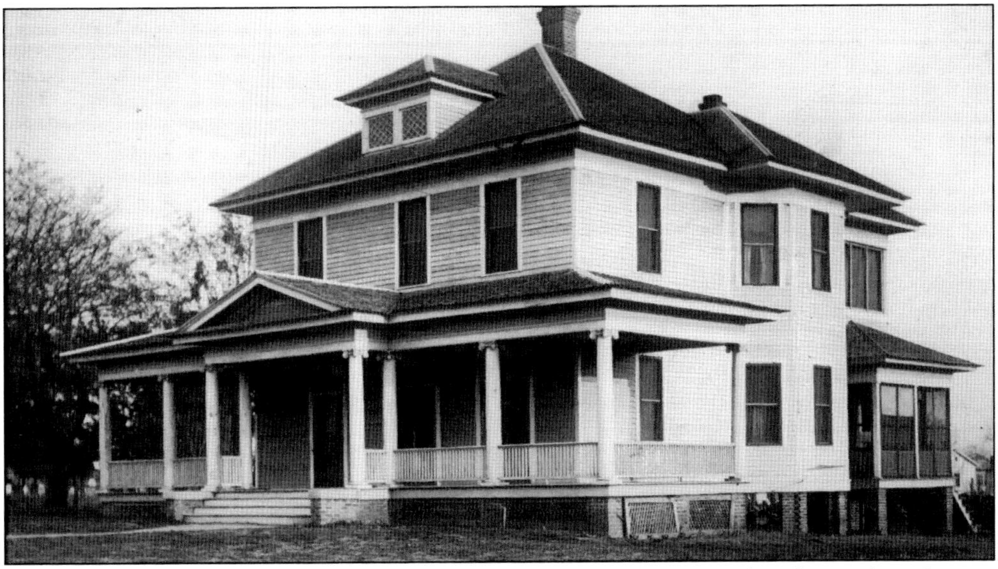

This stately home, formerly the manse of the Bishopville Presbyterian Church, stood on the east side of South Main Street, adjacent to the church. Over the years it served as home for numerous ministers and their families. Around 1970, the house was used to store county records while the courthouse was being remodeled. Not long afterwards, it was demolished to make room for additional parking and cemetery expansion. (SCCM.)

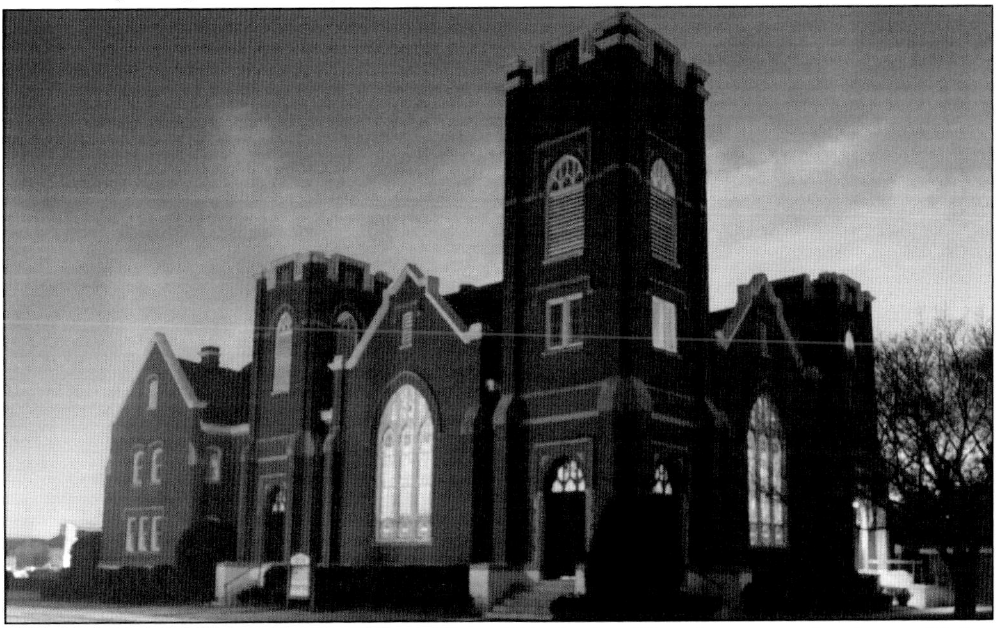

This nighttime photograph of Bethlehem United Methodist Church captures the gleam of lights from Main Street. Old Bethlehem Church was established in 1817 and located about 2 miles from Bishopville, where Bethlehem Cemetery stands today. In 1851, a larger church was erected near the original church, and the old building served as a schoolhouse. By 1884, the population of Bishopville had become centralized in the downtown area. For this reason, a new church was erected on Church Street. Over the next 30 years, the need for a more modern facility grew; the building pictured above was dedicated on August 2, 1914. (Photograph by Liston Truesdale.)

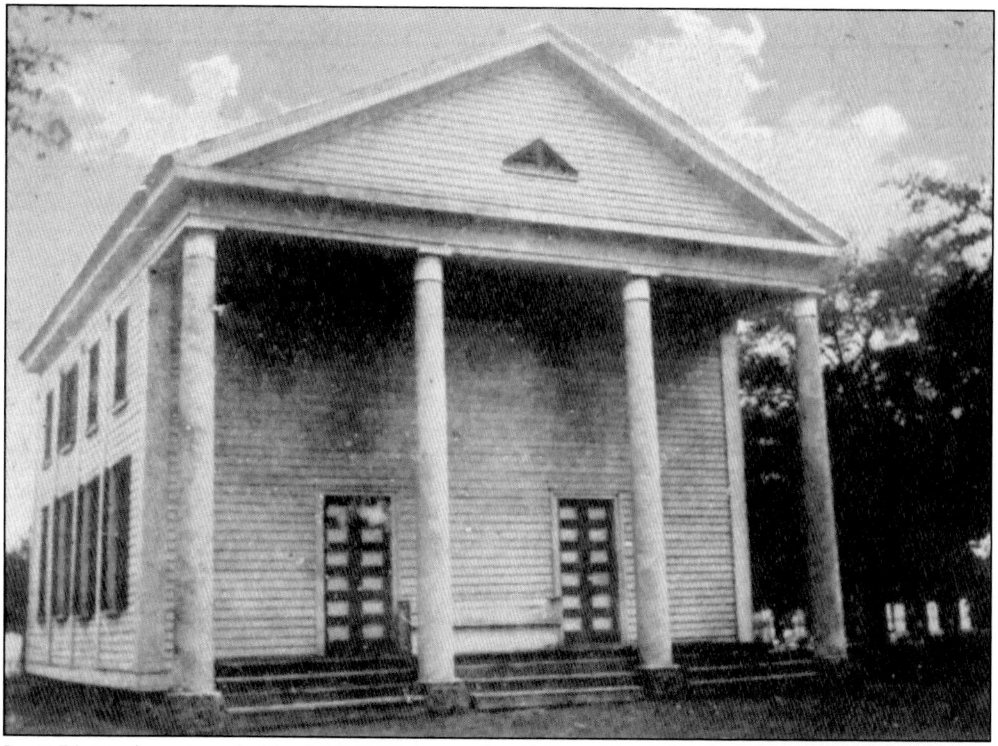

In 1855, Presbyterians led by Joseph Commander, Robert Commander, and James G. McIntosh organized and made plans to construct a church at Lynchburg. Land for the building was donated by Anna J. Law, wife of James R. Law and daughter of Robert English. The church was erected in that same year with help from the Methodists. The Reverend W. W. Wilson, who concurrently served the Bishopville Presbyterian Church, was the congregation's first minister. The cemetery to the rear of the church continues to serve as a burial ground for all denominations in the community. (Barrie Cunningham Hardwick.)

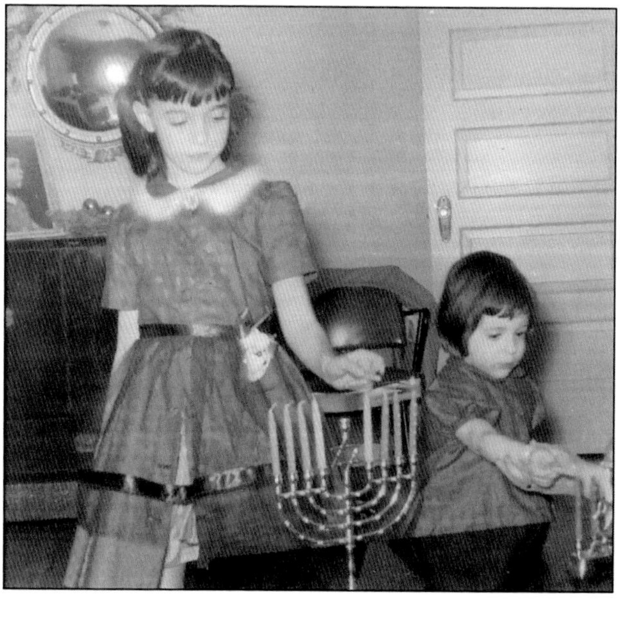

Jennie Krasnoff and her younger sister, Dixie, light a candle on their menorahs to celebrate the first night of Hanukkah, around 1955. Though Bishopville was once home to a bustling Jewish population, by the 1950s it had dwindled, and Jewish residents traveled to Sumter or Columbia for religious education and services. (Jennie Krasnoff Caine.)

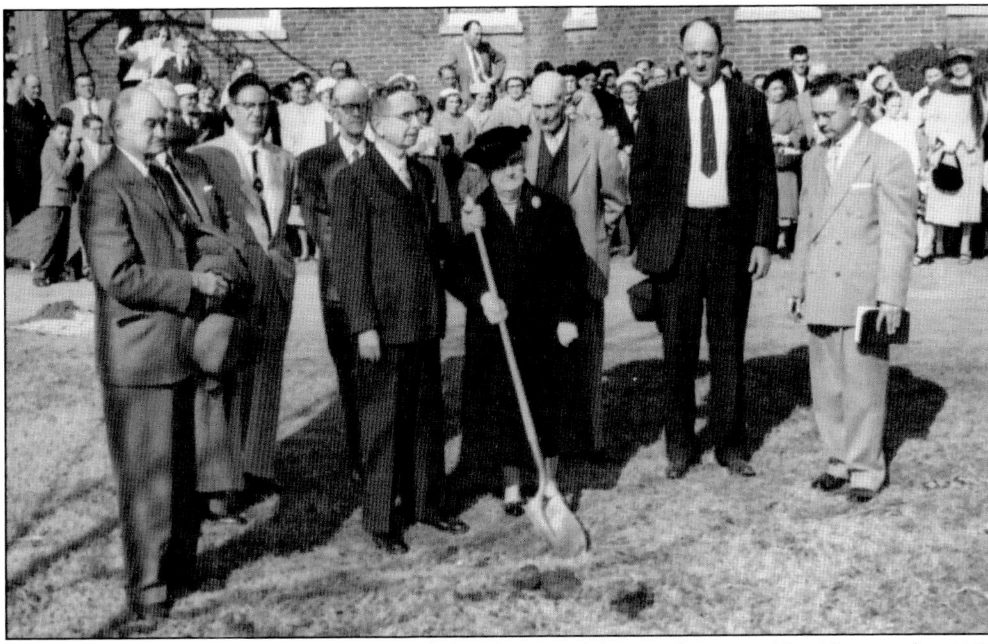

Members of the Lynchburg Baptist Church break ground for an educational building in this 1958 photograph. Holding the shovel are Tom Miller and Elma Hickson Tomlinson. Second from left is Floyd Cribbs, and third from left is H. A. "Bubba" Hickson. Jim Dougherty stands behind Miller. A Baptist congregation was organized at Lynchburg for the first time in 1876, and the original church was erected in 1879 on land purchased from J. A. Buddin. (Betsy Redick.)

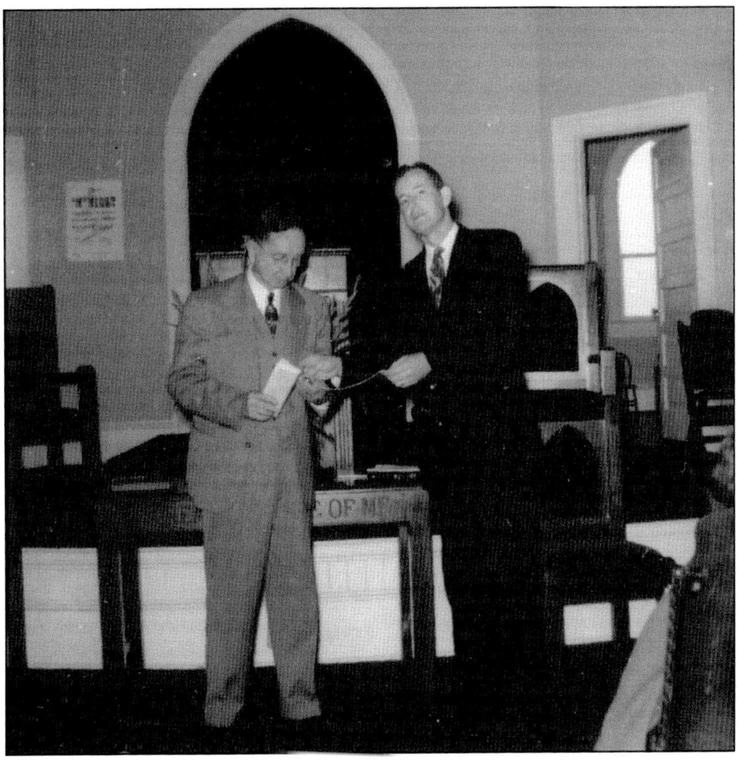

Pictured in front of the altar inside the church sanctuary are Tom Miller (left) and the Reverend Wallace Taylor. The current sanctuary dates from 1916. During the early to mid-1800s, Baptists, Methodists, and Presbyterians worshipped together in Lynchburg. (Betsy Redick.)

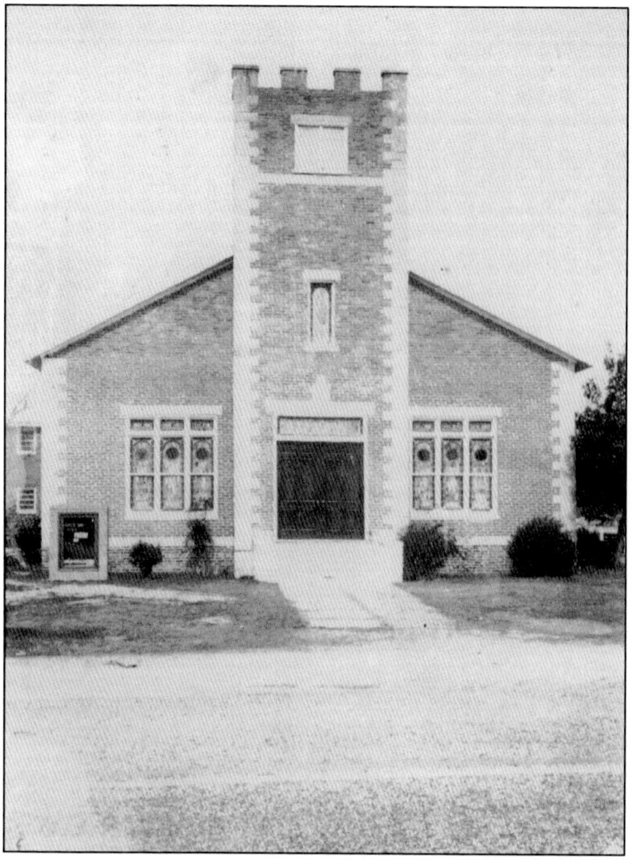

The first church building at Cootersboro was torn down by a storm, and a second structure was later constructed. Land for the current New Zion church was given by Robert Cooper, and the present-day brick sanctuary pictured at left was finished in 1949. The photograph dates from the same period. Below, Reverend Smith sits on the steps of the New Zion AME church in Wisacky. New Zion had its beginnings as a bush harbor church (sometimes called a brush arbor by historians)—an outdoor place of worship constructed from branches, sticks, and leaves held together with mud. The furniture within would have been crude and handmade. (Bernice Isaac Bradley.)

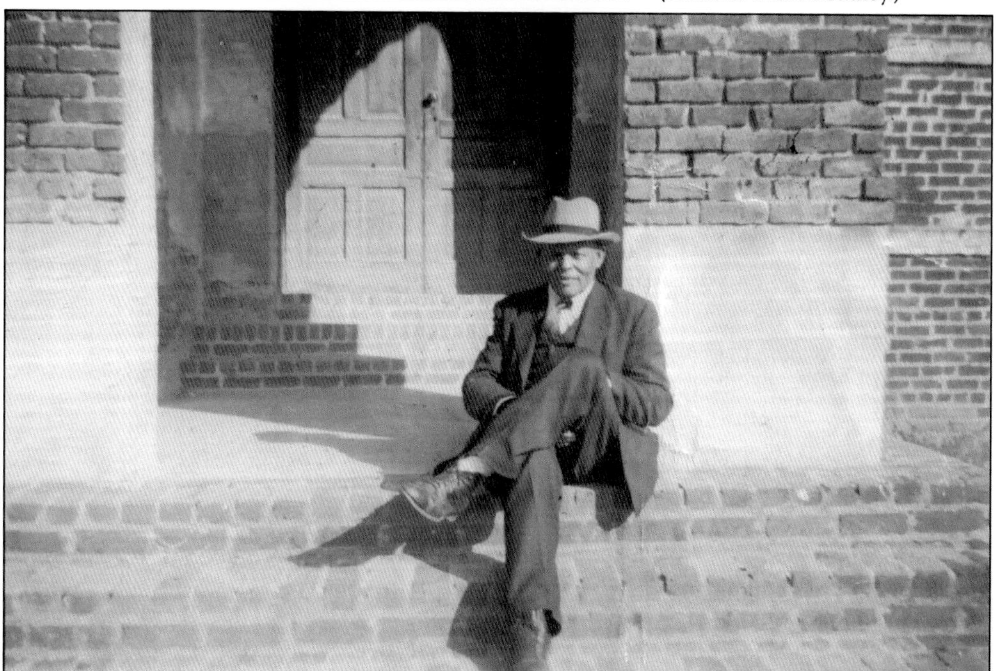

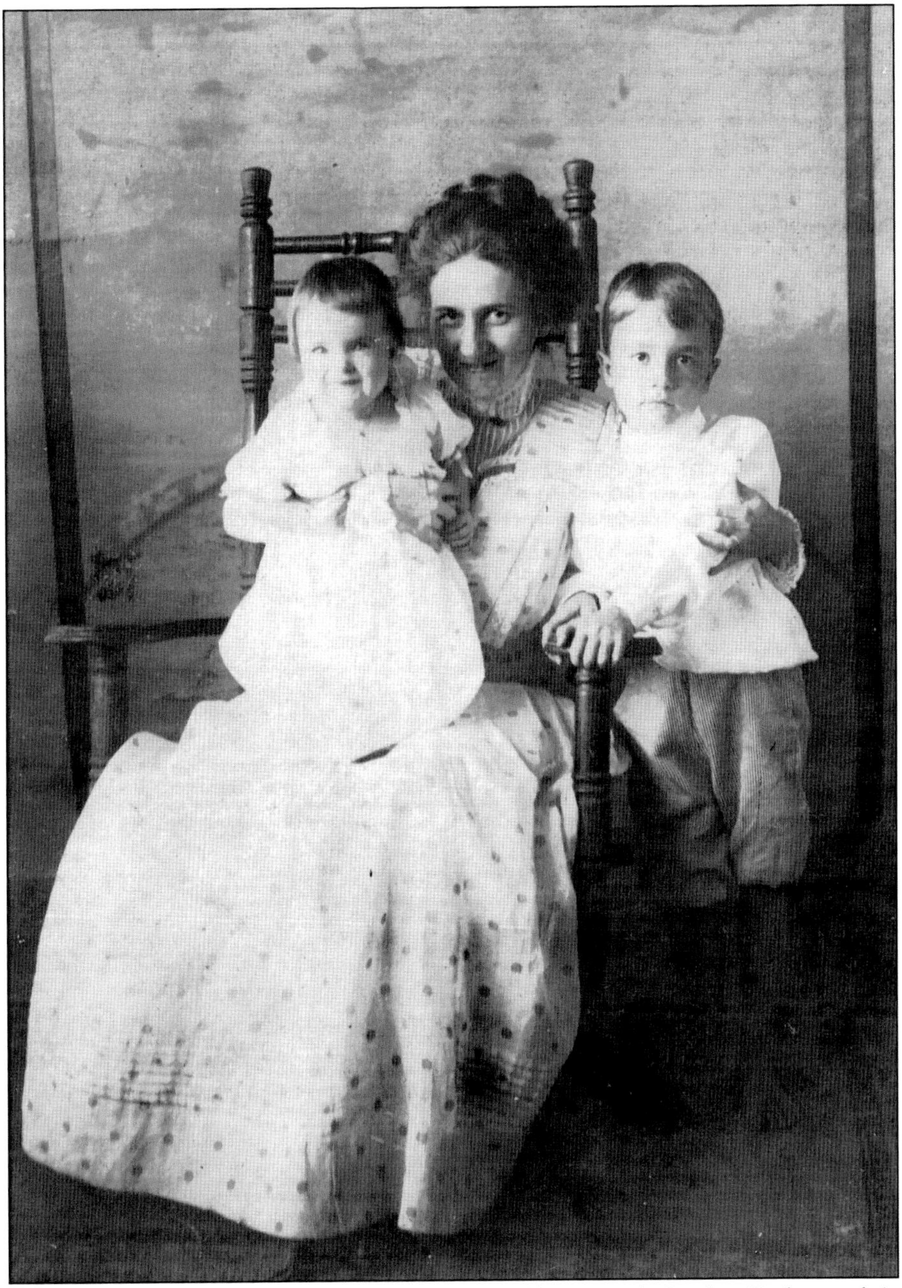

Mary Louise Walker Baskin is seen here with her children, Sarah Stuckey Baskin and Arthur Crawford Walker Baskin, about 1909. Children born later were Virginia Kirkland, Eldridge, Arthur Bayard, Louise Walker, and Marion Kirkland. After graduating from Columbia College, Mary Walker taught school in Bishopville where her father, the Reverend Arthur C. Walker, was minister of the Bethlehem Methodist Church from 1901 to 1904. Her grandfather, the Reverend H. A. C. Walker, was instrumental in the founding of Wofford College. In 1903, she married Arthur Bayard Baskin, whom she had met at church. Baskin, the son of William Peebles and Sarah Stuckey Baskin, was a farmer, and he operated a hardware store in town. The Baskins and their children lived on Ridge Street. (Louise Baskin Stevenson.)

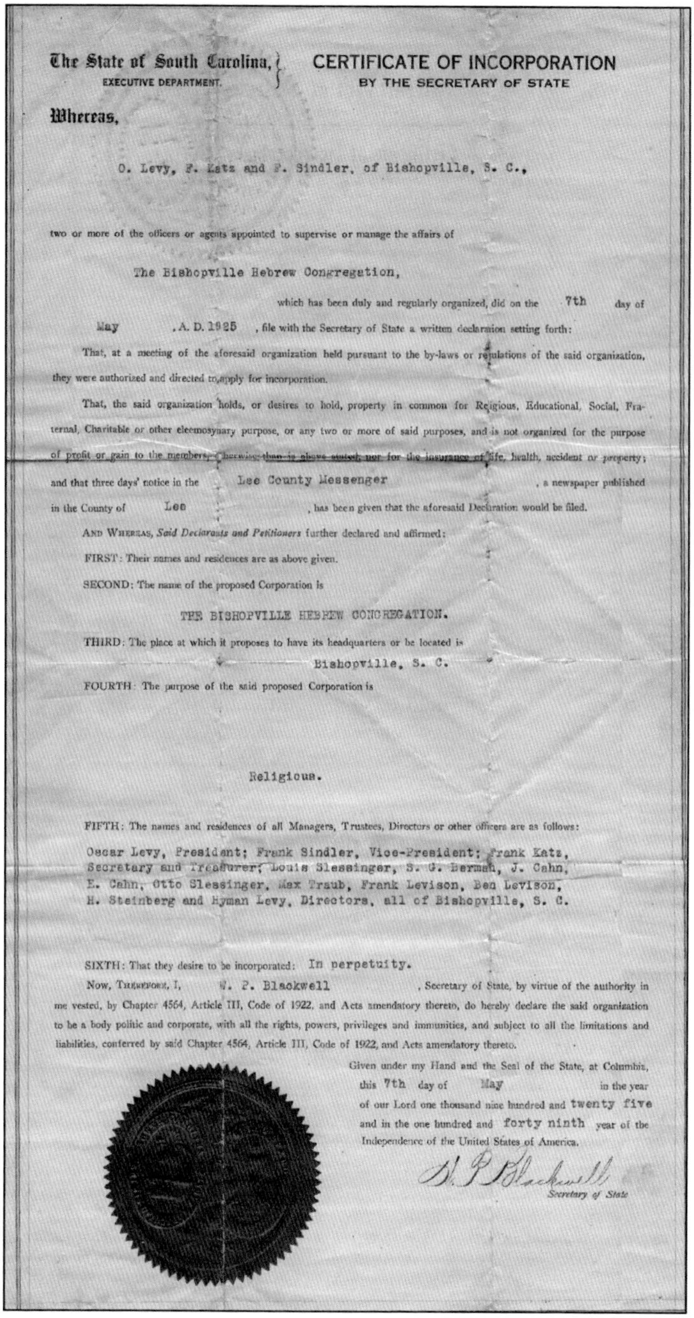

The State of South Carolina, EXECUTIVE DEPARTMENT.

CERTIFICATE OF INCORPORATION BY THE SECRETARY OF STATE

Whereas,

O. Levy, F. Katz and F. Sindler, of Bishopville, S. C.,

two or more of the officers or agents appointed to supervise or manage the affairs of

The Bishopville Hebrew Congregation,

which has been duly and regularly organized, did on the 7th day of May, A. D. 1925, file with the Secretary of State a written declaration setting forth:

That, at a meeting of the aforesaid organization held pursuant to the by-laws or regulations of the said organization, they were authorized and directed to apply for incorporation.

That, the said organization holds, or desires to hold, property in common for Religious, Educational, Social, Fraternal, Charitable or other eleemosynary purpose, or any two or more of said purposes, and is not organized for the purpose of profit or gain to the members, ~~otherwise than is above stated, nor for the insurance of~~ life, health, accident or property; and that three days' notice in the Lee County Messenger, a newspaper published in the County of Lee, has been given that the aforesaid Declaration would be filed.

And Whereas, *Said Declarants and Petitioners* further declared and affirmed:

FIRST: Their names and residences are as above given.

SECOND: The name of the proposed Corporation is

THE BISHOPVILLE HEBREW CONGREGATION.

THIRD: The place at which it proposes to have its headquarters or be located is

Bishopville, S. C.

FOURTH: The purpose of the said proposed Corporation is

Religious.

FIFTH: The names and residences of all Managers, Trustees, Directors or other officers are as follows:

Oscar Levy, President; Frank Sindler, Vice-President; Frank Katz, Secretary and Treasurer; Louis Slessinger, S. G. Berman, J. Cahn, E. Cahn, Otto Slessinger, Max Traub, Frank Levison, Ben Levison, H. Steinberg and Hyman Levy, Directors, all of Bishopville, S. C.

SIXTH: That they desire to be incorporated: In perpetuity.

Now, Therefore, I, W. P. Blackwell, Secretary of State, by virtue of the authority in me vested, by Chapter 4564, Article III, Code of 1922, and Acts amendatory thereto, do hereby declare the said organization to be a body politic and corporate, with all the rights, powers, privileges and immunities, and subject to all the limitations and liabilities, conferred by said Chapter 4564, Article III, Code of 1922, and Acts amendatory thereto.

Given under my Hand and the Seal of the State, at Columbia, this 7th day of May in the year of our Lord one thousand nine hundred and twenty five and in the one hundred and forty ninth year of the Independence of the United States of America.

W. P. Blackwell
Secretary of State

In the early 1920s, over 90 people in Bishopville identified themselves as Jewish. To meet the needs of the observant community, the Bishopville Hebrew Congregation incorporated on May 7, 1925, under Oscar Levy, Frank Katz, and Frank Sindler. The congregation did not have a synagogue but met regularly in the Masonic Hall above Frank Sindler's Main Street store. It was supplied by rabbinical students. The congregation held regular Sabbath services as well as special celebrations and observances of holy days. There was a Sunday school for religious education and Hebrew school for boys preparing for their Bar Mitzvahs. (Gift of Allan Sindler, Special Collections, College of Charleston.)

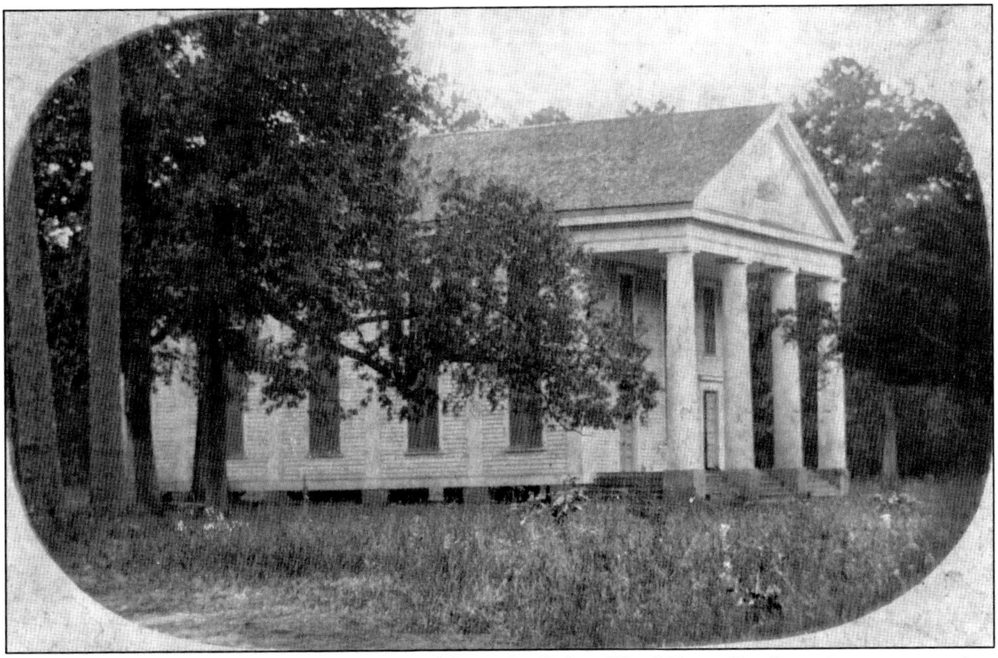

Mount Zion Presbyterian Church separated from the Salem Black River Presbyterian congregation in 1809. Built in 1855, the sanctuary pictured above was the congregation's third house of worship—but it would not be its last. The church seen here burned in 1910, and the brick building that stands today in the same location was dedicated in 1911. While the current sanctuary was under construction, the congregation met in the Session House, which was built in 1851. The Mount Zion Cemetery dates to 1830. (Mount Zion Presbyterian Church.)

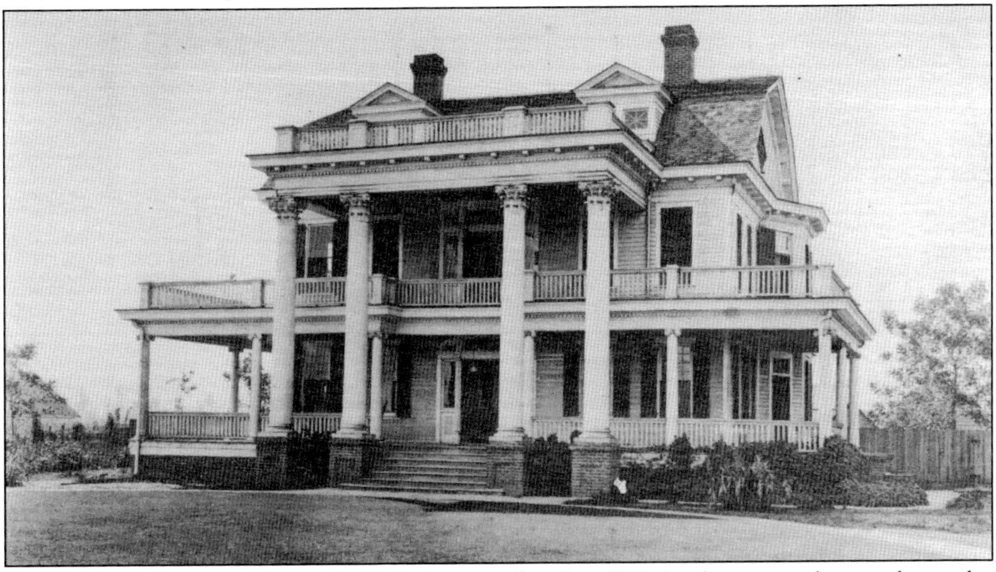

After the current Mount Zion sanctuary was completed in 1911, funds were used to purchase a lot and construct an elegant two-story parsonage in the St. Charles community. The manse was, and is, quite a showplace. Its floor plan consists of a wide central hall on both floors, flanked by rooms on each side, and porches that run across the front and sides of both stories. The most impressive feature of the home is its magnificent curved staircase. (Mount Zion Presbyterian Church.)

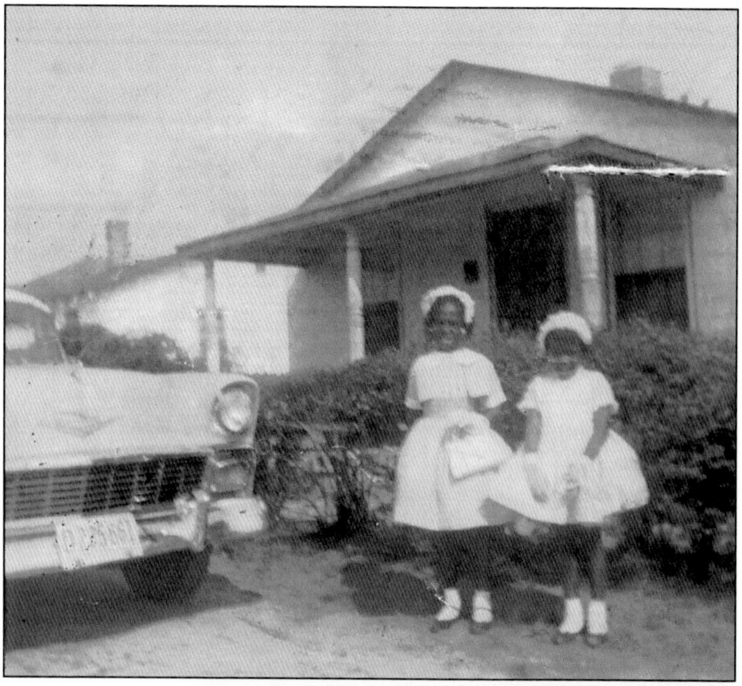

Daughters of Mr. and Mrs. Phillip Bradley, Gwendolyn (left) and Odessa Bradley head to church at Mount Zion AME in this late-1950s photograph. Two other daughters, Denise and Valerie, are not pictured. The sisters are standing in the front yard of their First Street home. Gwendolyn is now an international opera star, and Odessa is an attorney in Washington, D.C. (Bernice Isaac Bradley.)

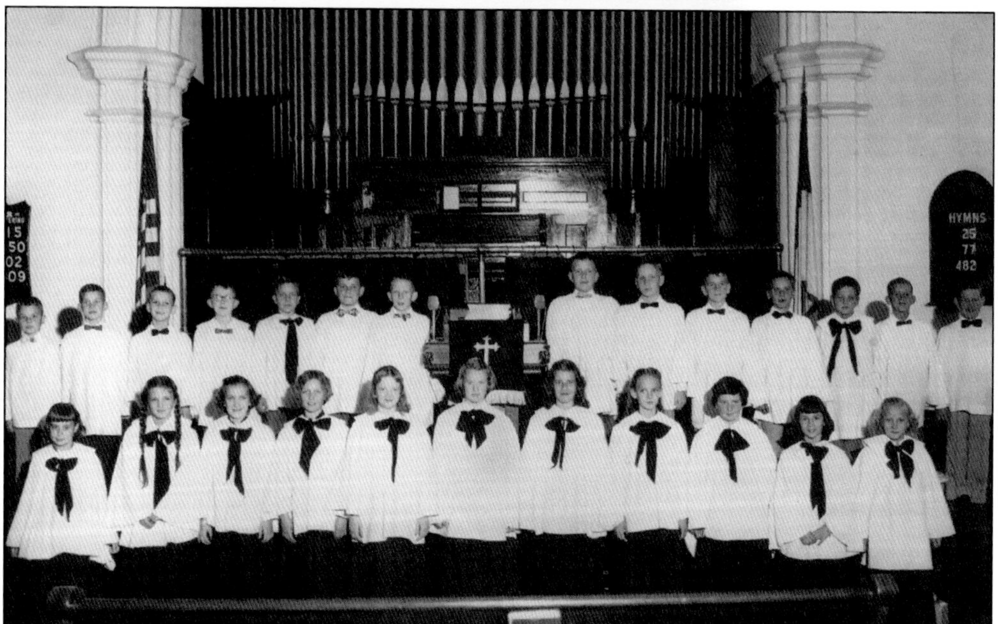

From left to right, members of the 1954 Bishopville Presbyterian Church Junior Choir are (first row) an unidentified choir member, Susan Anderson (Mathis), Nelia Eckley (Green), Martha Kay Montgomery (Hunt), Kay Hearon (Gentry), Judith Austin (Watkins), Edna McCutchen, Virginia Quattlebaum (Lacy), Harriett McCutchen (Davis), an unidentified choir member, and Manella Huggins (Calhoun); (second row) Ray Drayton, Phillip Olmert, Bobby Eckley, Buzzy Lane, Hank Martin, Allen Hobbs, Bobby Latimer, Billy Hobbs, Mike McDonald, Mike Monroe, Jess McCutchen, Mac Anderson, Ben Moses, and an unidentified choir member. (Lee County Public Library.)

Eight
COUNTY SERVICES

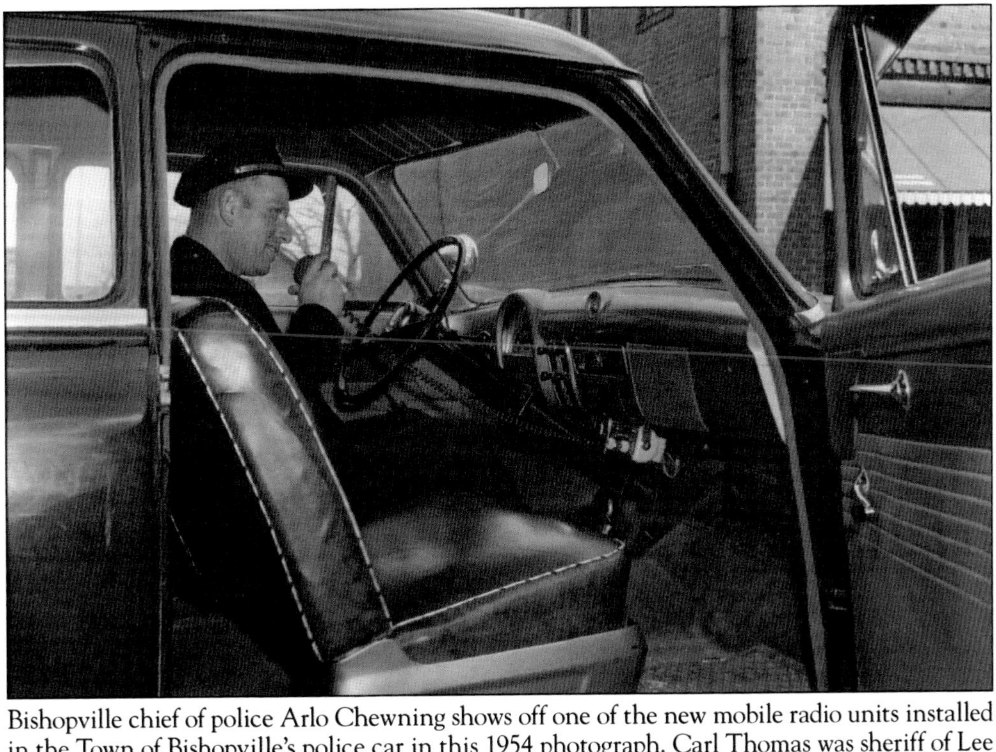

Bishopville chief of police Arlo Chewning shows off one of the new mobile radio units installed in the Town of Bishopville's police car in this 1954 photograph. Carl Thomas was sheriff of Lee County at the time, and deputy sheriff was Fred Morrell. The rural police chief was Clyde Beasley, and rural policemen were Thomas (Jut) Woodham, Cliff Hyatt, B. K. Phillips, J. Harry Smith, and Harold Capell. (Lee County Public Library.)

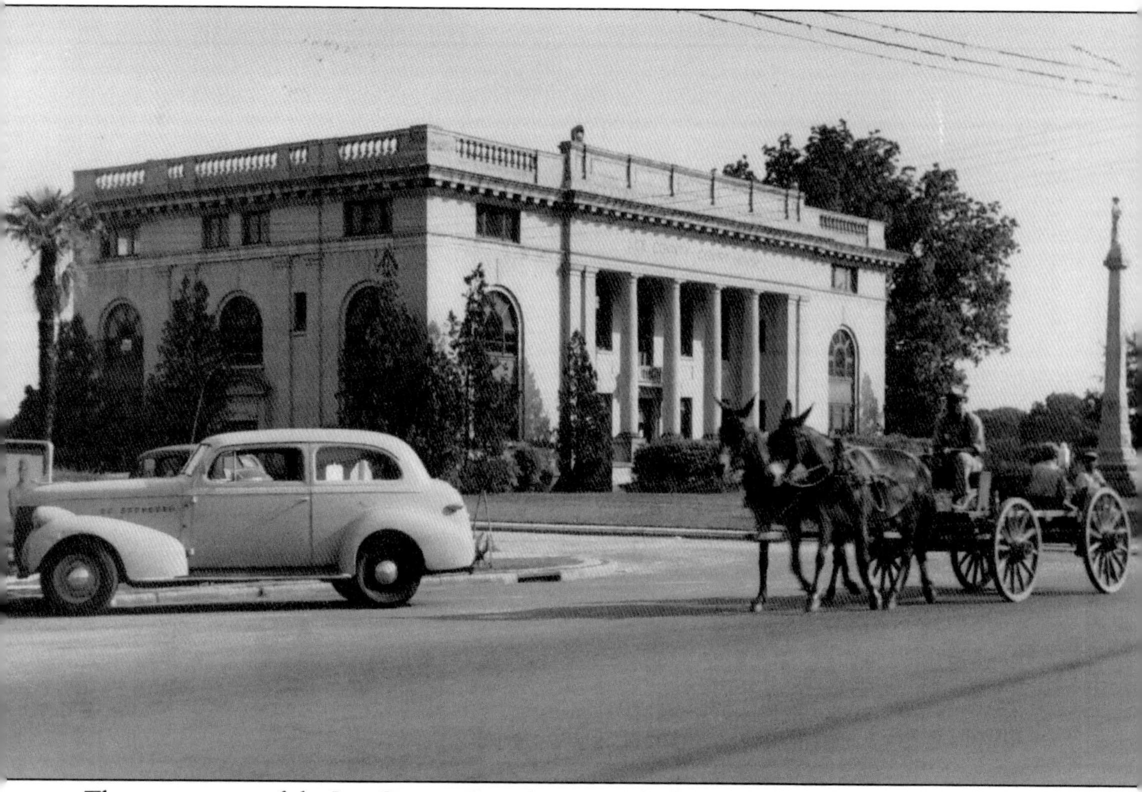

The cornerstone of the Lee County Courthouse was laid on March 22, 1909, and the building was dedicated later that year. This view is from the 1930s. Designed by the architectural firm of Edwards and Walter, total receipts for its construction came to $87,000. The first term of court had been held in 1903 on the second floor of the Bishopville Opera House. County offices had been housed in the Stuckey Building (site of William Green DesChamps's station) and in the structure that originally stood on the site of the Lee Hotel. A two-story hotel operated by R. E. Carnes originally stood on the courthouse site. (Retta Dickinson Tindal.)

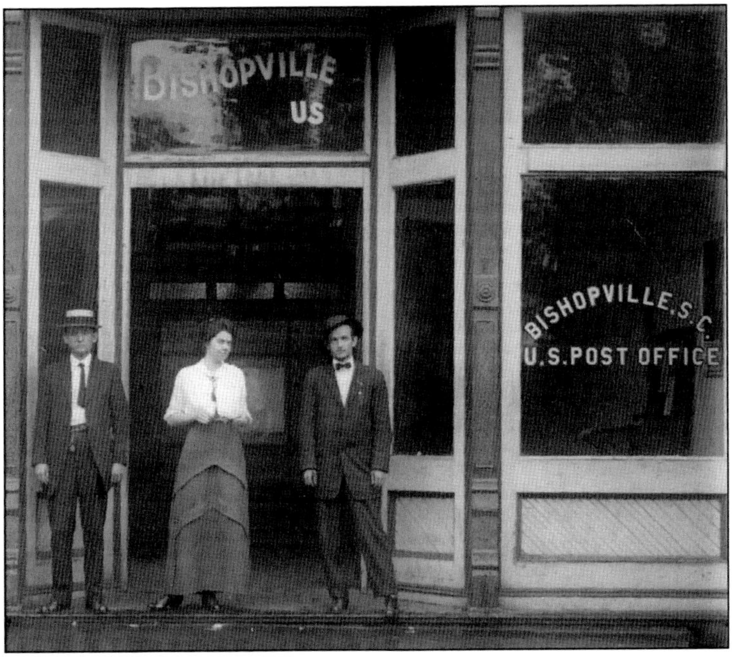

The Bishopville post office was once located on North Main Street in the former Heath-Massey-Morrow Building. In this photograph from the early 1900s are postmaster J. Edd Stuckey, Irene Weldon, and assistant postmaster Tedd Stuckey. Bishopville's first post office was established in 1824, and in 1828, William C. Bowen, business associate of Jacques Bishop, became its postmaster. (Louise Hapeshis McCutchen.)

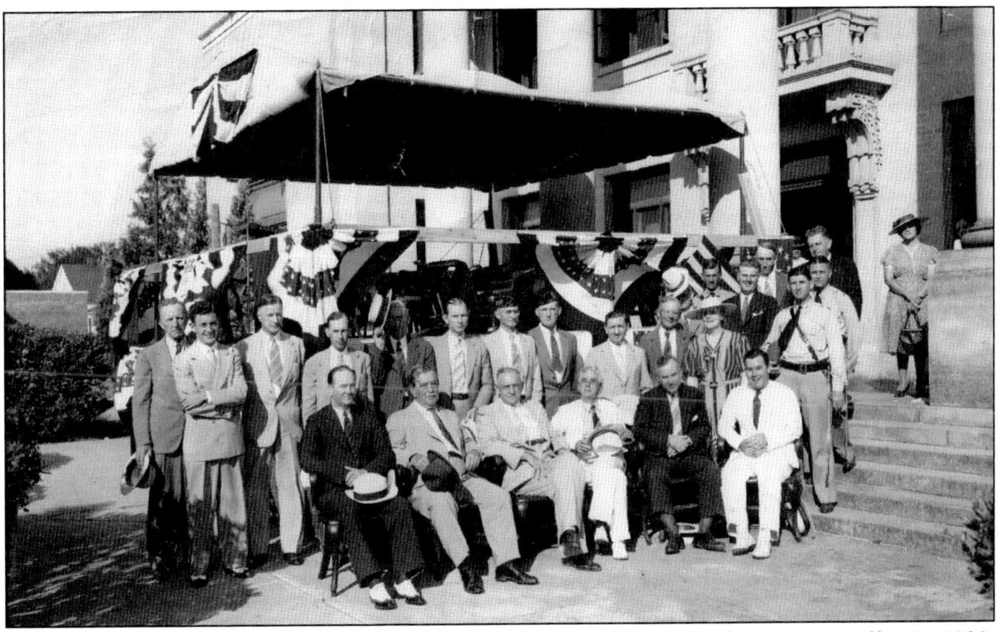

Pictured above are the attendees at the groundbreaking ceremony for the new post office in 1938. From left to right are (first row, seated) Rep. John L. McMillian, Sen. Ellison D. "Cotton Ed" Smith, postmaster R. M. Smith, Rep. Luther Moore (holding white hat), unidentified, and Rep. John Alden Munn; (second row) Dr. R. O. McCutchen, Howard Ginsberg, Bob Cooper, W. P. Baskin Jr., R. H. Singletary, Mayor Herman McElveen, F. V. Boulineau Sr. (in an American Legion cap), Rev. J. T. Littlejohn, Frank Sindler, George O. Rogers, and Mrs. C. W. Harris; (third row) unidentified (man with hat shielding his face), Lawrence M. Peebles, and unidentified; (fourth row) unidentified, Burell Tindal, and unidentified; (fifth row) Henry C. Jennings and Pauline Sindler. (*Lee County Observer*.)

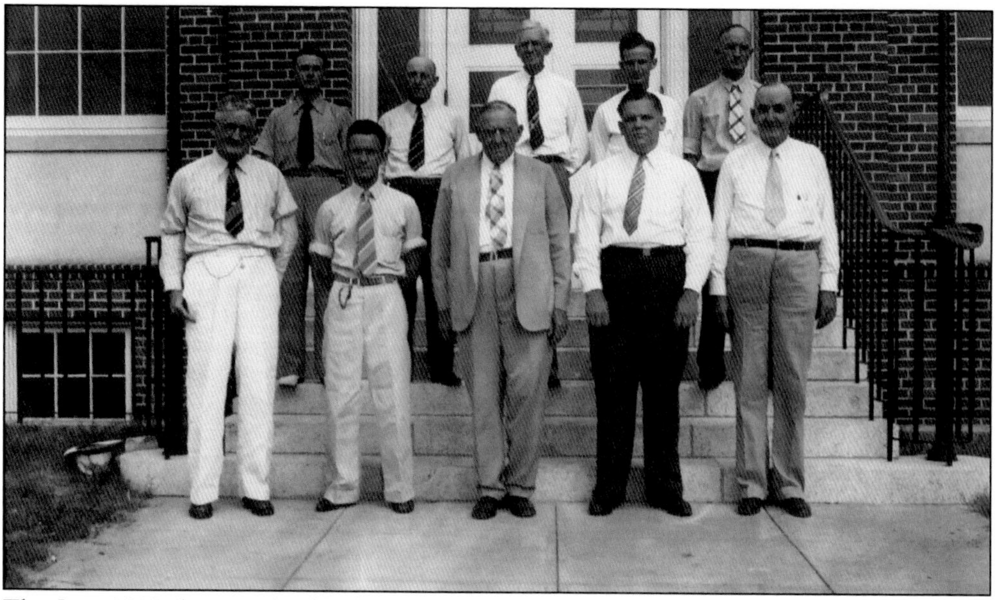

This June 1940 photograph of Bishopville Post Office employees was taken in front of the new building at its dedication. From left to right, they are (first row) rural carrier C. L. English, clerk J. B. Lane, postmaster R. M. Smith, and clerks W. C. Smith and E. L. Carnes; (second row) town carrier Robert E. Muldrow, rural carriers C. W. Stuckey and J. A. Williams, town carrier G. E. Ackerman, and rural carrier E. L. Watkins. Town carrier R. L. Jones was absent from picture. (Christine Smith Shirley.)

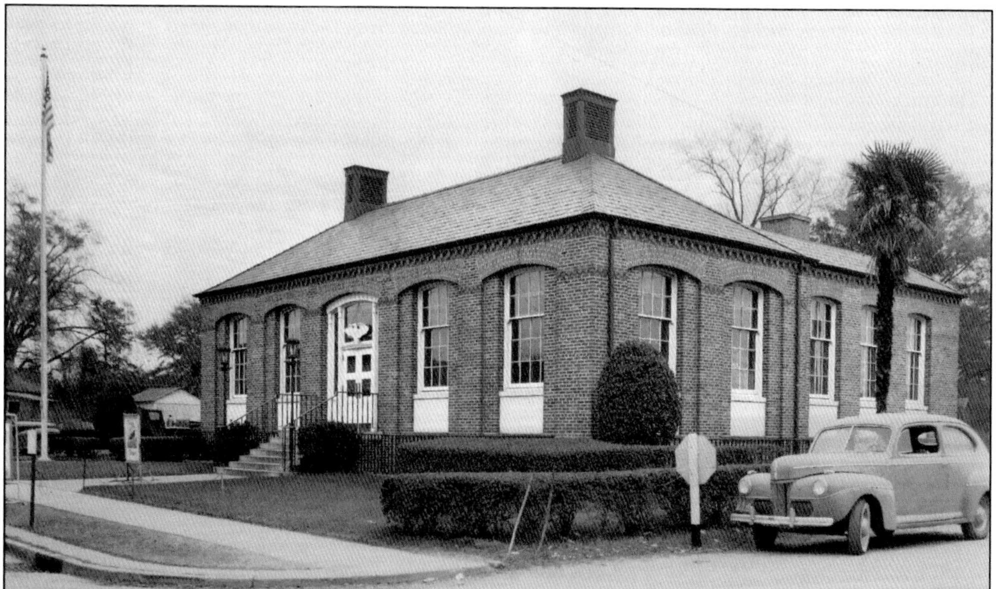

The advent of the Civilian Conservation Corps camp in Lee County increased postal receipts so drastically that, in 1935, Bishopville was placed in the $10,000-a-year income class. As a result, postmaster Gus Woodham Sr. noted that Bishopville would be in line for a stand-alone post office building for the first time in its history. The building went into service in 1940 and served the town until 2001 when a modern facility was constructed just outside of town on Highway 15 North.

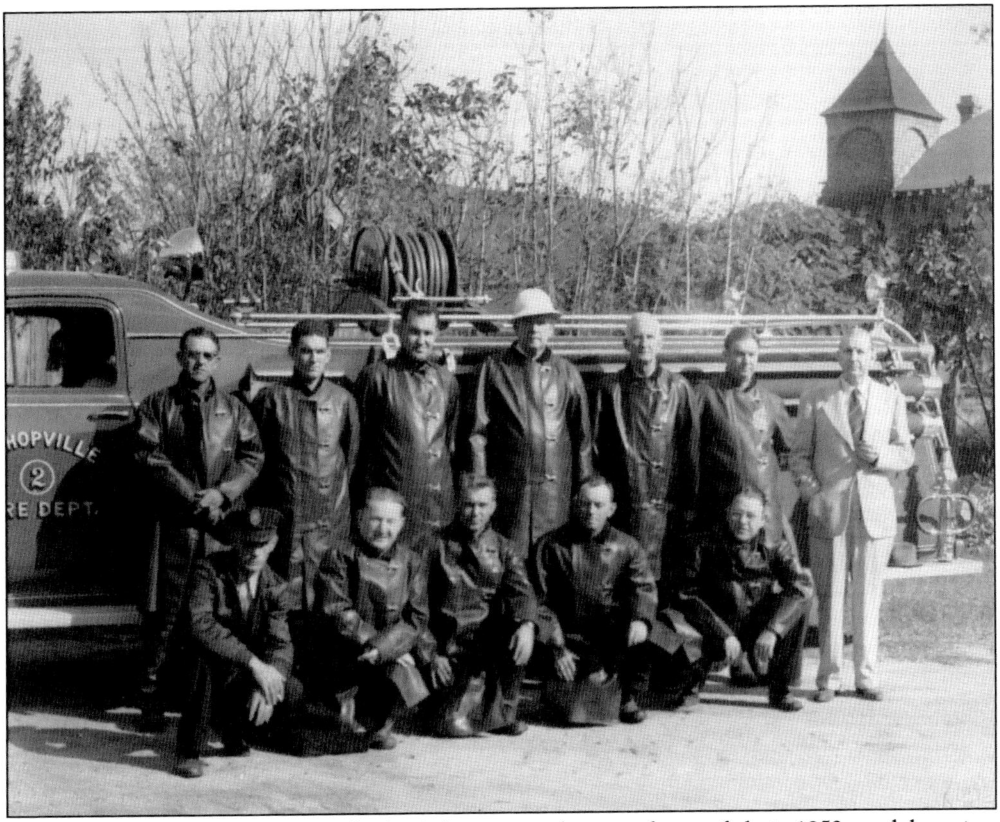

From left to right, the Bishopville firefighters seen here in front of their 1953 model engine are (kneeling) Luther Truesdale, Melisha M. Levy, Buddy Dickinson, Thurston Webb, and George O'Kelley; (standing) John O'Kelley, Edwin Wilson, Rob McCutchen Jr., Rob McCutchen Sr., Vern Hearon, Jeff Stuckey, and Mayor Herman McElveen. The old jail is visible in the background. (Bishopville Fire Department.)

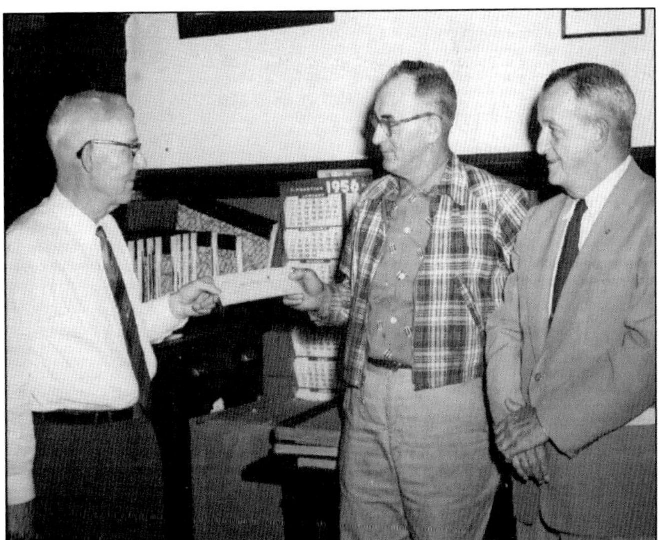

In this 1956 photograph, E. F. House (center), local manager of the Carolina Power and Light Company (CP&L), ceremoniously remits the company's tax check to Lee County treasurer Frank J. DesChamps. To House's right stands Bob Cooper. DesChamps served as treasurer of Lee County from 1942 until 1967. During much of the 1950s and 1960s, CP&L and Bishopville Finishing (Reeves Brothers) paid the highest taxes in the county. (Ralph DesChamps.)

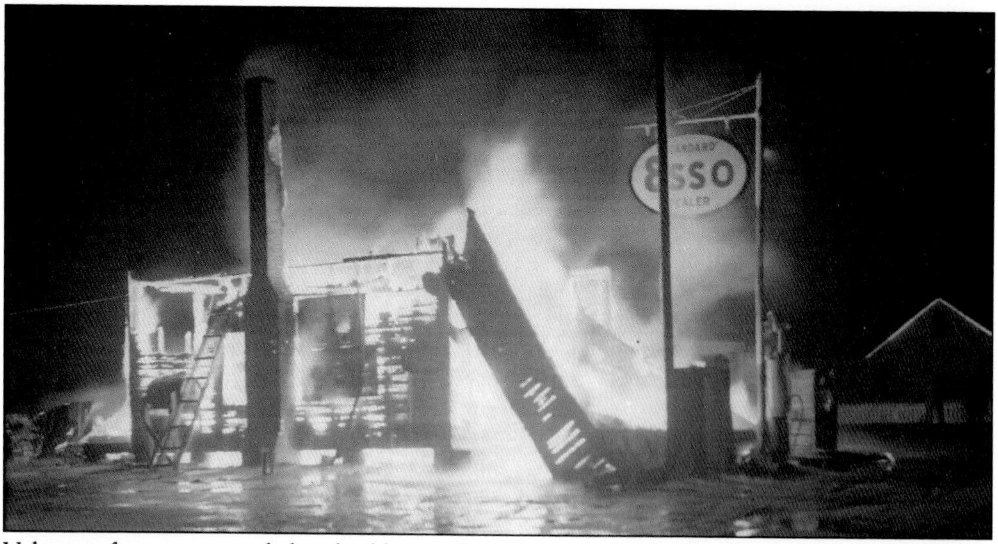

Volunteer firemen responded to this blaze at the intersection of the St. Charles Road and Highway 15, on the opposite side of the road from Doc Ackerman's store. John Blackwell originally ran the filling station, and, at the time of the fire about 1944, the owners were living on the second floor. It was virtually impossible to put out the inferno due to the hard ice on the ground, which caused the firemen to keep falling down. (Liston Truesdale.)

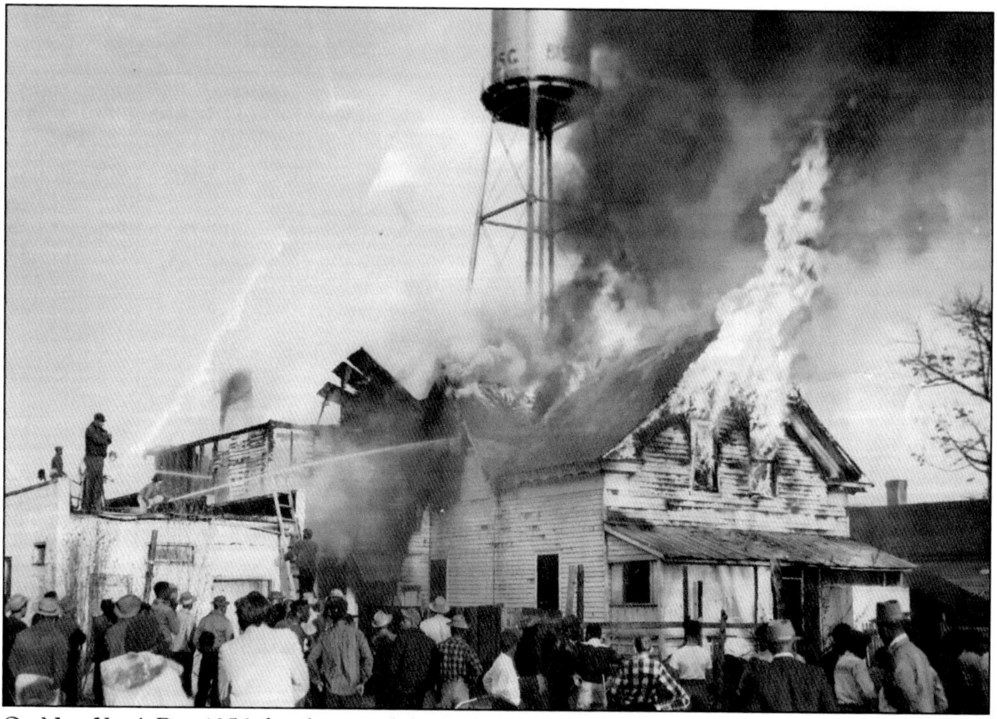

On New Year's Day 1956, fire destroyed the Wiley Hotel. The photograph was taken from the rear of what is now the Stuckey Law Office and shows the back entrance of Lewis Funeral Home and the hotel. Both buildings fronted East Council Street. The funeral home was later turned into a two-story building. The blaze killed one person. Afterwards, owner Willie Wiley built a home on the site, where his daughter, Bea Wiley Praylow, still lives today. (Bishopville Fire Department.)

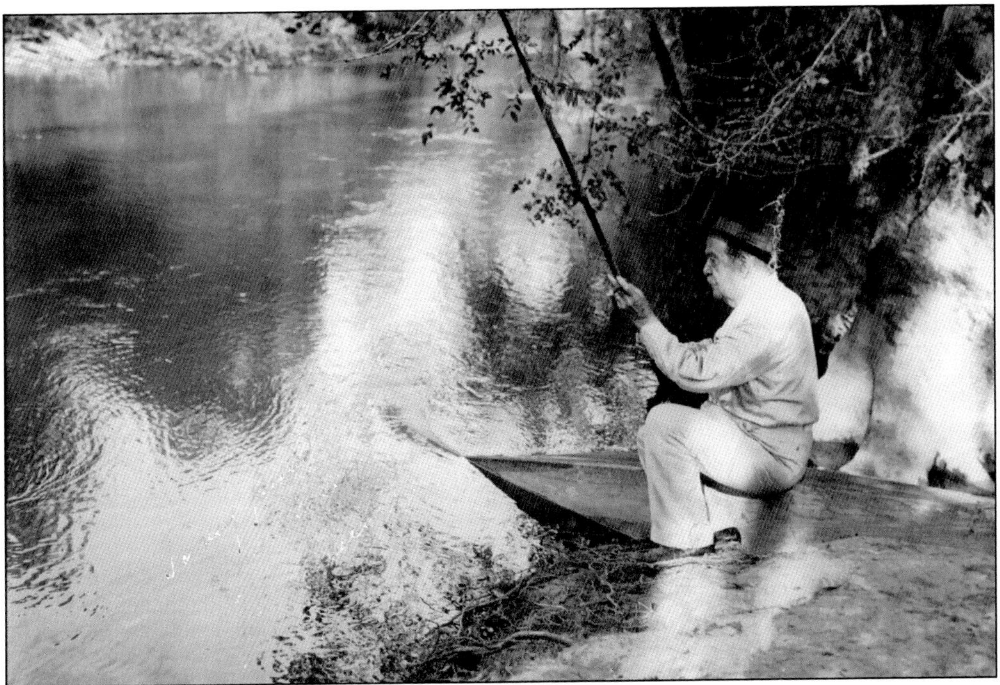

Sen. Ellison DuRant Smith was born at Lynchburg, South Carolina, in 1864. The son of a Methodist minister, his father's estate, Tanglewood, had been in the family since 1747. Smith served in the South Carolina House of Representatives from 1896 to 1900, and in the U.S. Senate from 1909 until 1944. Smith was most famously known as "Cotton Ed," a name he acquired in the early 1900s when he was known to ride into town perched atop a wagonload of cotton. (SCCM.)

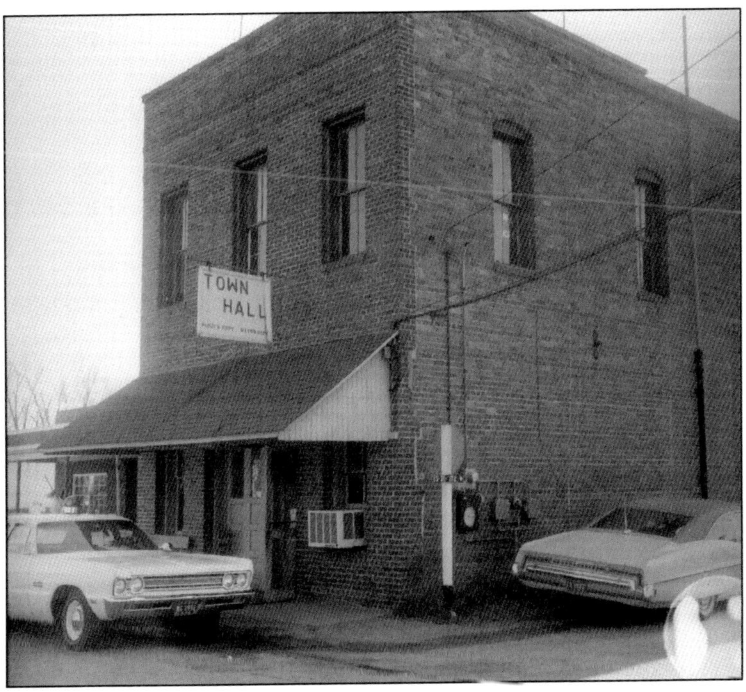

Bishopville Town Hall was once located on West Council Street directly behind the Peoples Bank building. Aside from the city offices, Bishopville's police department and jail were also located in the building. This picture dates from the late 1960s. (Liston and Betty Truesdale.)

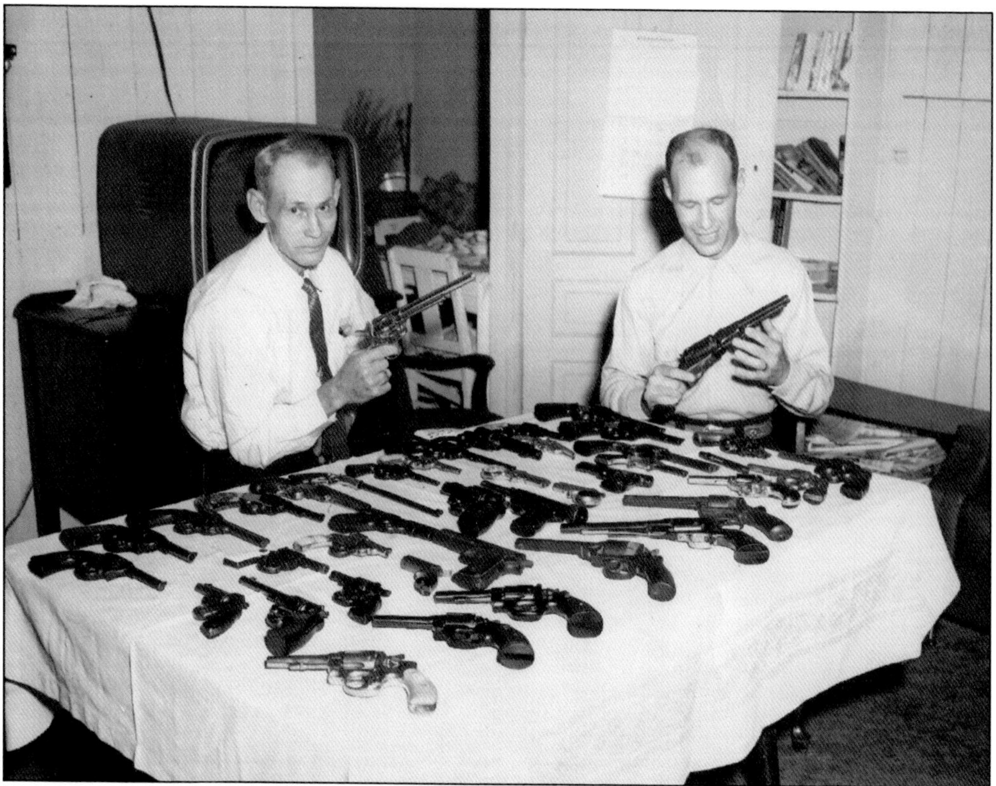

Luther Truesdale and his son, Liston, display Luther's extensive gun collection. An avid gun collector for many years, he served as engineer for the fire department from 1942 until the mid-1960s. He and his wife, Eletha, lived in a home attached to the rear of the old fire station, where this photograph was taken. In the picture below, Truesdale displays his rifle collection on a wall in his home. (Liston Truesdale.)

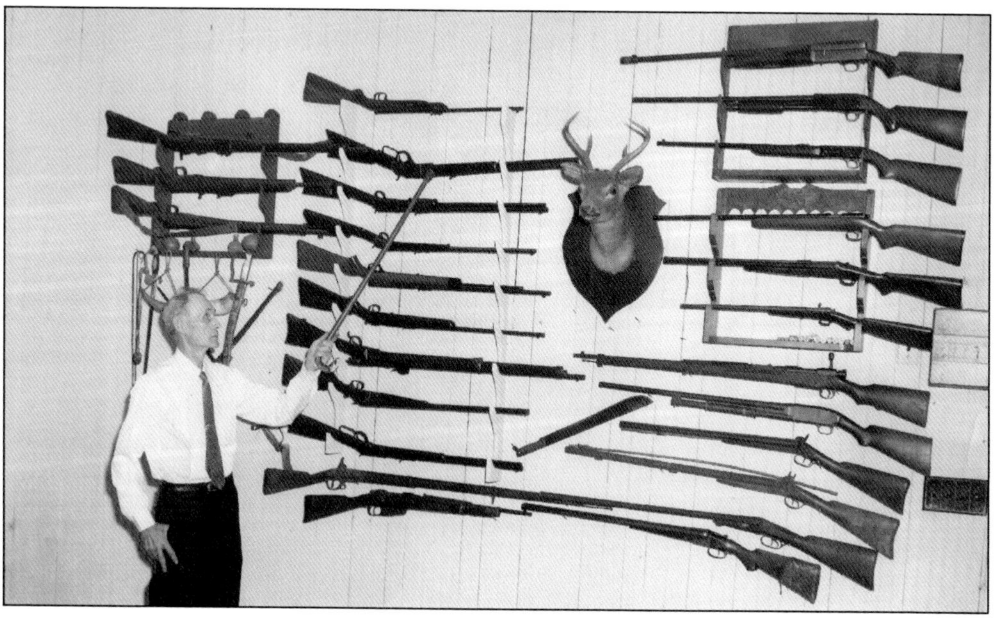

Nine
LEE STATE PARK

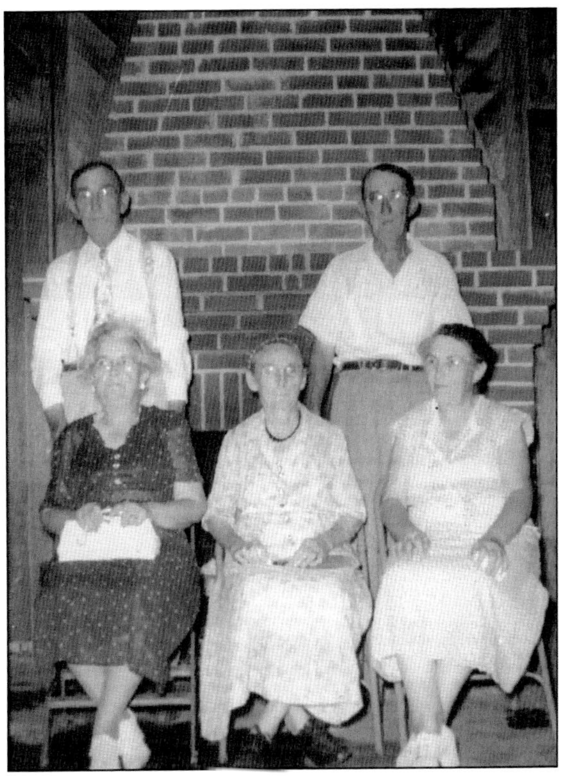

The children of Jefferson Alexander Hickson gather for the annual family reunion at Lee State Park around 1954. The photograph was taken in what was then called the community building, which consisted of a large room and kitchen that could be rented out for events. Today the building is the park office and houses an exhibit hall and an environmental lab. Seen here from left to right are (first row) Elma Hickson Tomlinson, Miona Hickson Player, and Maude Hickson McClam; (second row) Herbert Hickson and Will Hickson. Miona was the daughter of Jefferson Hickson and his first wife, Miss Gregg, but the other siblings were all the children of Hickson and Martha Elizabeth Player. Maude McClam ran a millinery store in Lynchburg and worked well into her 90s. Brothers Cliff and Henry Hickson were deceased at the time of this photograph. The family was from Lynchburg and lived in and around the area. (Betsy Redick.)

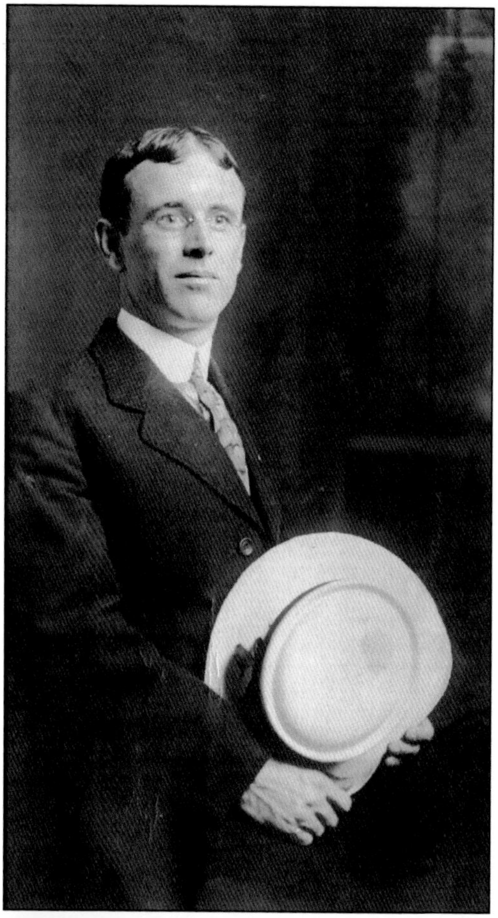

Sen. Robert Ellison Dennis, son of Dr. R. E. and Mary Green Dennis, was instrumental in bringing the CCC camp to Lee County. He was born in Bishopville in 1881, graduated from the University of South Carolina in 1902, and received his legal education from the University of Virginia. In law practice with Thomas G. McLeod, who would later become governor, Dennis served in the South Carolina Legislature from 1915 to 1916 and was reelected in 1917. He was the great-uncle of Robert and Jacob Jennings. (Robert Jennings.)

The sign over the entrance welcomes CCC enrollees to the newly opened Camp Lee. Covering approximately 1,500 acres of land, the park would soon have recreational facilities, including a bathing beach, boathouses, and fishing cabins. (Billie Steele Caldwell.)

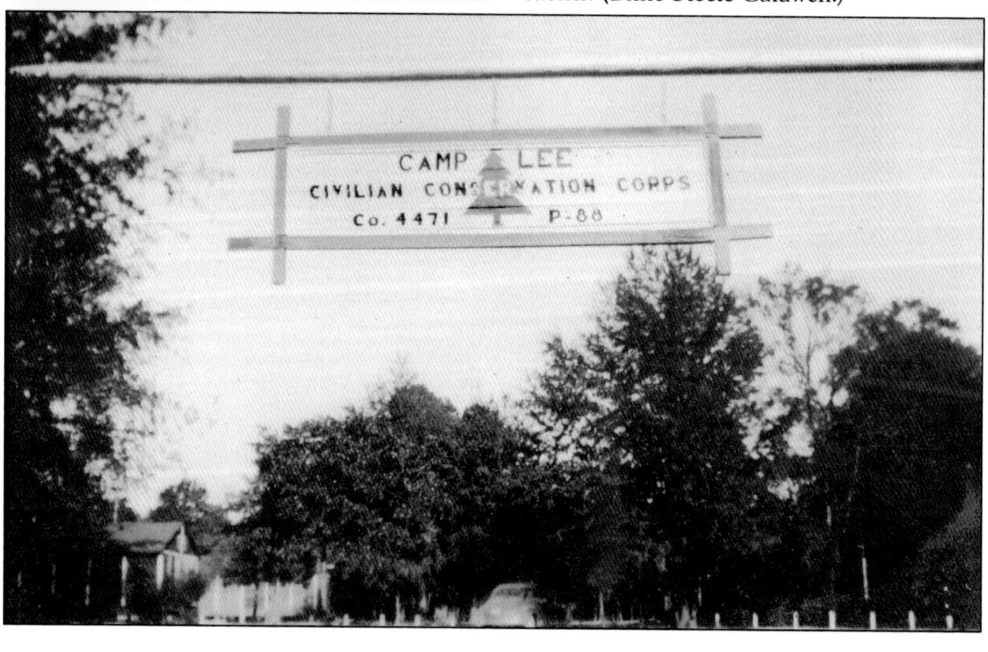

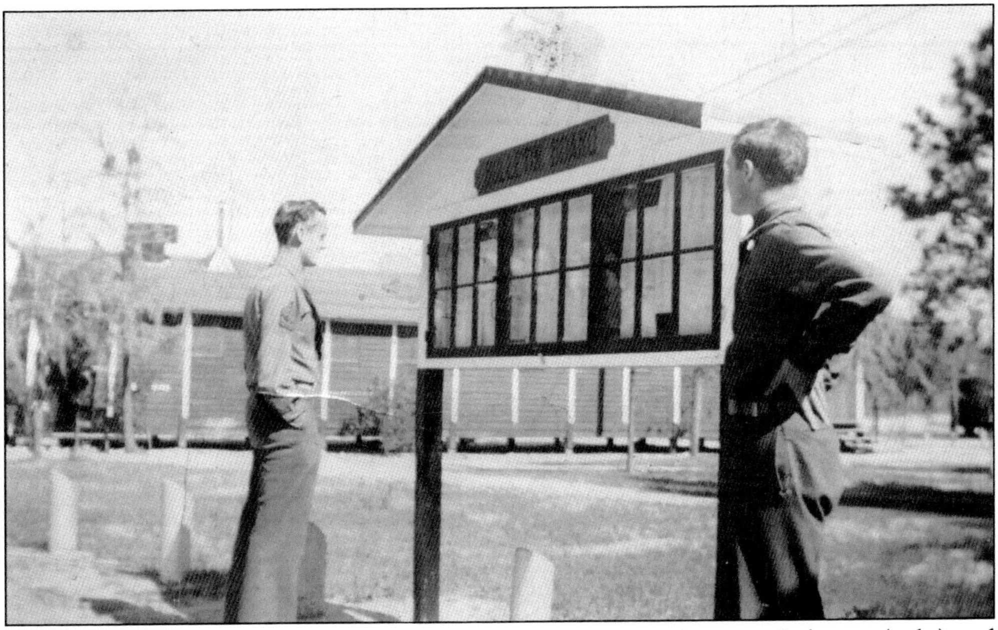

In this *c.* 1936 photograph, CCC enrollees G. C. Caldwell (left) and Spencer Robinson (right) read the latest news on the camp's bulletin board. By August 1935, the camp for the men who would create the future Lee State Park was nearly ready for occupancy. At month's end, 199 men from around the state were settled into the barracks and ready for work. (Billie Steele Caldwell.)

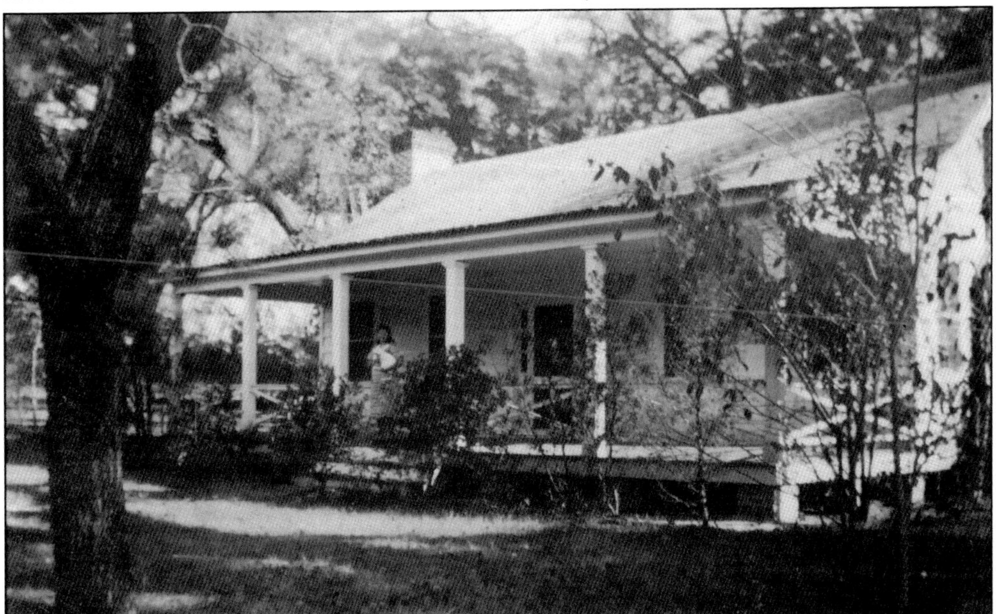

Annie Steele stands on her front porch in this late-1930s photograph. Annie, her husband, William, and their daughter, Billie, were the first residents of the caretaker's home, which had been constructed entirely by the CCC workers. The only knowledge these men had of home building had been acquired while enrolled in the corps. The house was constructed on the site of the old Josey home and was completed in 1936. It has remained a residence since its construction and is currently the home of Lee State Natural Area's interpretive ranger. (Billie Steele Caldwell.)

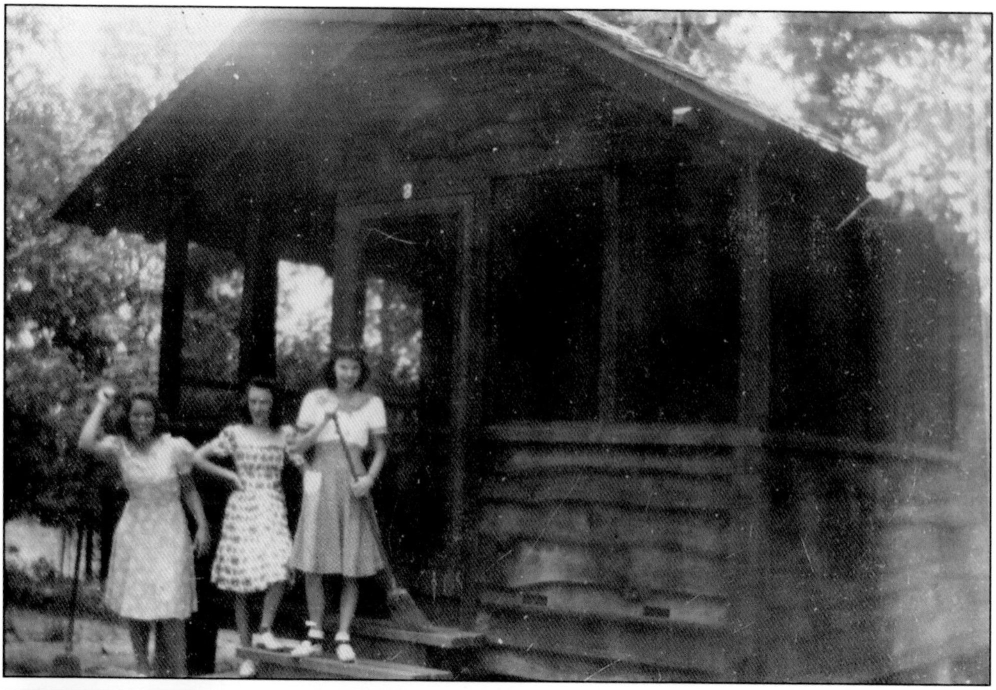

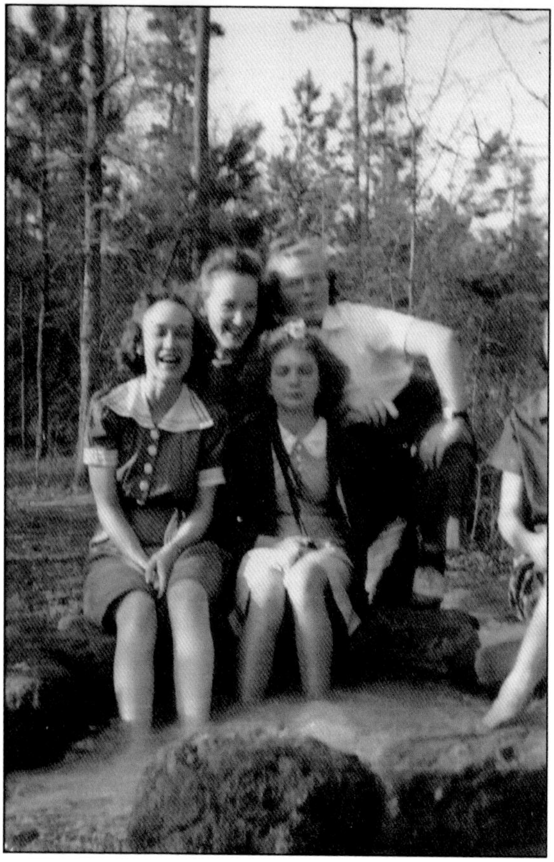

Years ago, Lee State Park had four fishing cabins. While primitive in nature (the outhouses were nearby), they provided a place for sportsmen to spend the weekend. They were also used by other groups for recreational purposes. These girls are probably using the cabin to store their belongings or take a break during the day.

Artesian wells are numerous in this part of Lee County, and the cool water was refreshing to these girls from Bishopville High on a hot day in 1941. The park was officially opened to the public in June 1941, though use of completed facilities had been allowed prior to that date. Seen here from left to right are Cile Stuckey, teacher Lib Newman (Mahaffey), Norma Alexander (Liles), and Betty Mozingo (Vaughn).

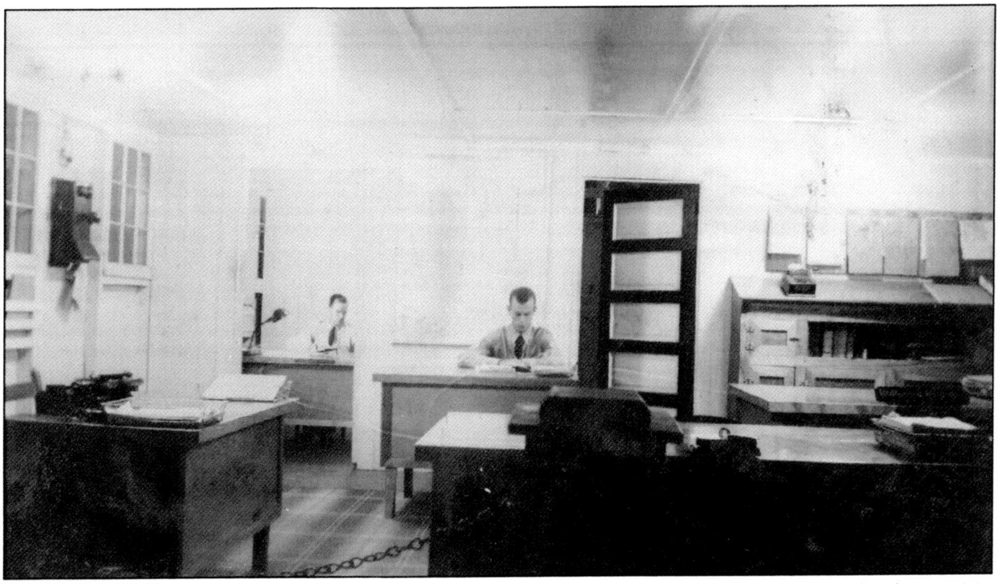

Jack Allen sits in the foreground and an unidentified man works at the back desk in this late-1930s glimpse inside one of the CCC offices. Within these rooms, plans were drawn up to build Lee State Park. Detailed outlines were made for every project and sent to Columbia and Washington, D.C., for approval. In 1938, for example, the men were engaged in building gateposts at the park entrance, increasing the size of the bathhouses and building fisherman's cabins, a dam, and more rearing pools. (Billie Steele Caldwell.)

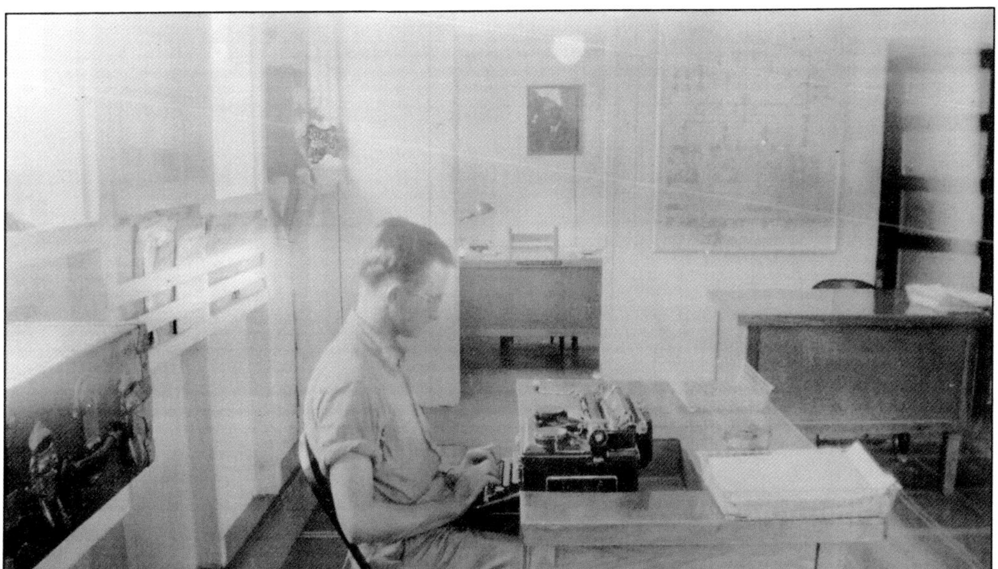

Kelly McCutcheon sits at his typewriter in this c. 1936 photograph. Kelly was editor of the CCC camp newsletter *The General*. Published on a weekly basis, the mimeographed newsletter provided information on the camp's progress as well as items of local interest to CCC enrollees. (Billie Steele Caldwell.)

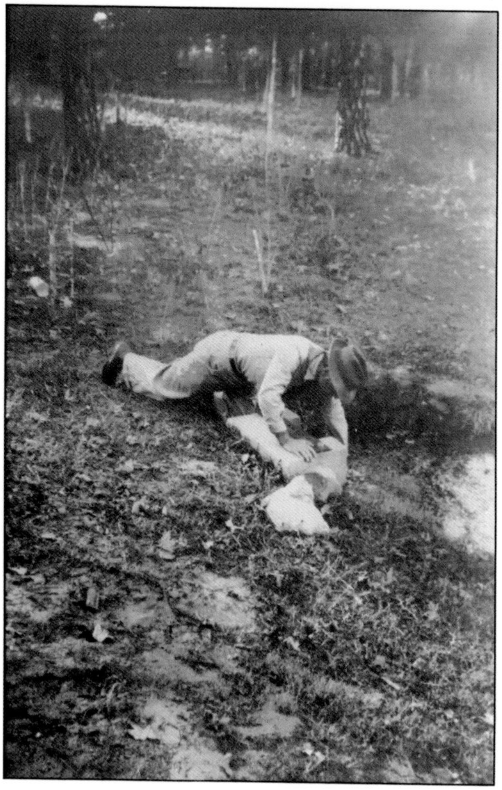

William Coleman Steele cleans out a culvert, or underground drain, on the campgrounds. W. C., a native of Montana, was living with his wife and daughter in Alabama when a work-related trip took him to the Hartsville area. He liked the region and retired with his family to a farmhouse across the road from the future state park. Hired by the CCC as a L.E.M., or Local Experienced Man, he was knowledgeable about drilling artesian wells. Steele would become the park's first superintendent. (Billie Steele Caldwell.)

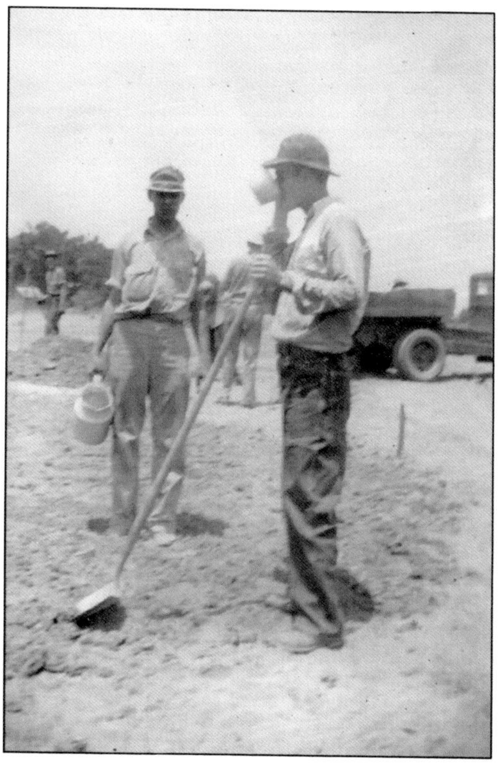

G. C. Caldwell enjoys a drink from one of the many artesian wells that supplied the water needs of the camp. On August 22, 1935, the 199 young CCC enlistees were positioned for work in Lee County. By that time, 14 buildings had already been completed on the grounds for the purpose of housing, feeding, and providing first aid to the men who built what was to become the state park. The enlistees were given the responsibility of fire protection work by cutting firebreaks in heavily forested areas throughout the area. They were also employed in reforesting the state forest that adjoined the camp. (Billie Steele Caldwell.)

Ten
Motoring Around

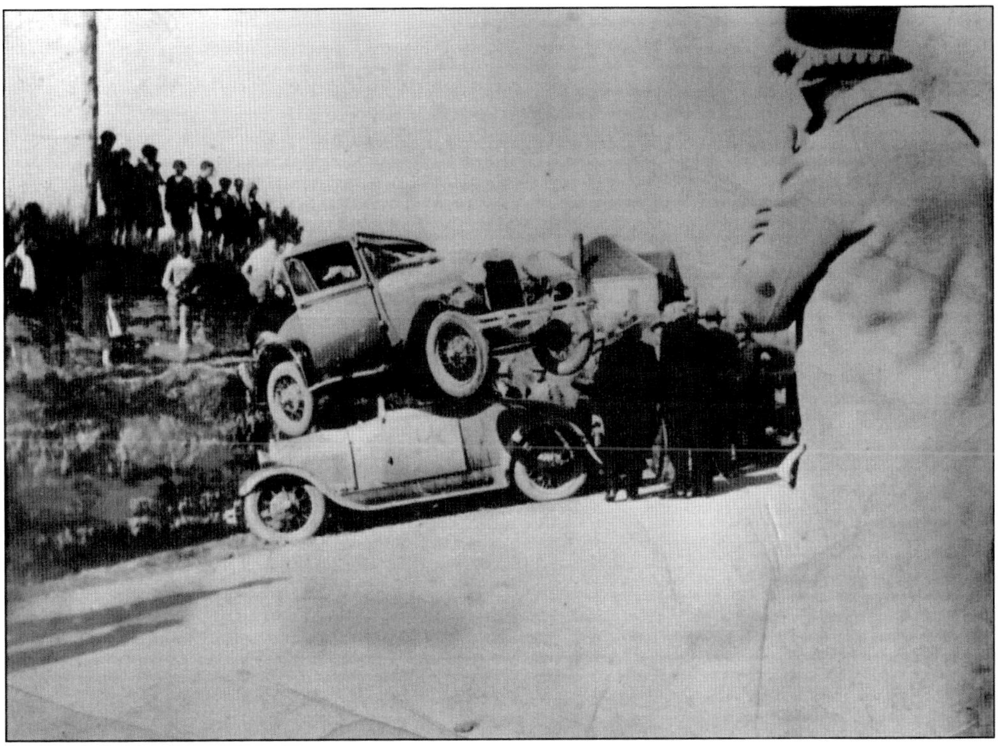

This freakish wreck occurred on Main Street in the 1920s. A new Ford Model A, occupied by Ralph McLendon, John Watkins, and Walter "Simp" Watkins, all teenagers, was heading out of town. The other vehicle, driven by C. Keys Sanders, an employee of Swift and Company Fertilizer, was coming into town. Sanders pulled over when he saw the other car coming at "a rapid rate." The cars landed in their predicament near the residence of Julian Dixon. There were no significant injuries, and the vehicles were sent to Charlotte for repairs. (Liston and Betty Brown Truesdale.)

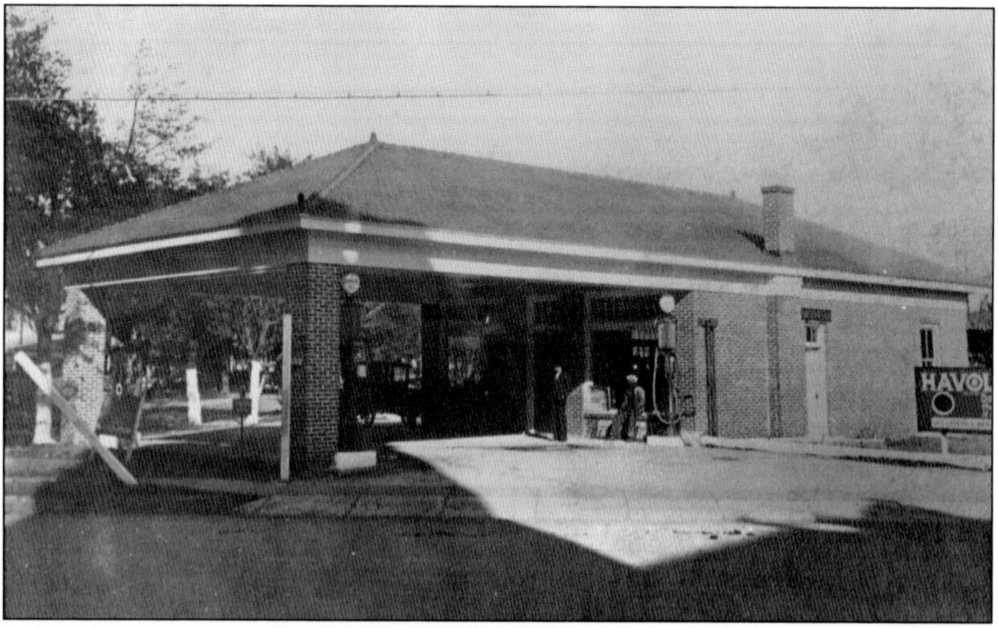

Ladson Montgomery owned and operated this filling station, which once sat at a 45-degree angle on the east corner of West Church Street and North Dennis Avenue. It was across from the Methodist church and Hancock Funeral Home. The station was operated by James Davis beginning in the early 1950s and burned down about 1960. (Ralph DesChamps.)

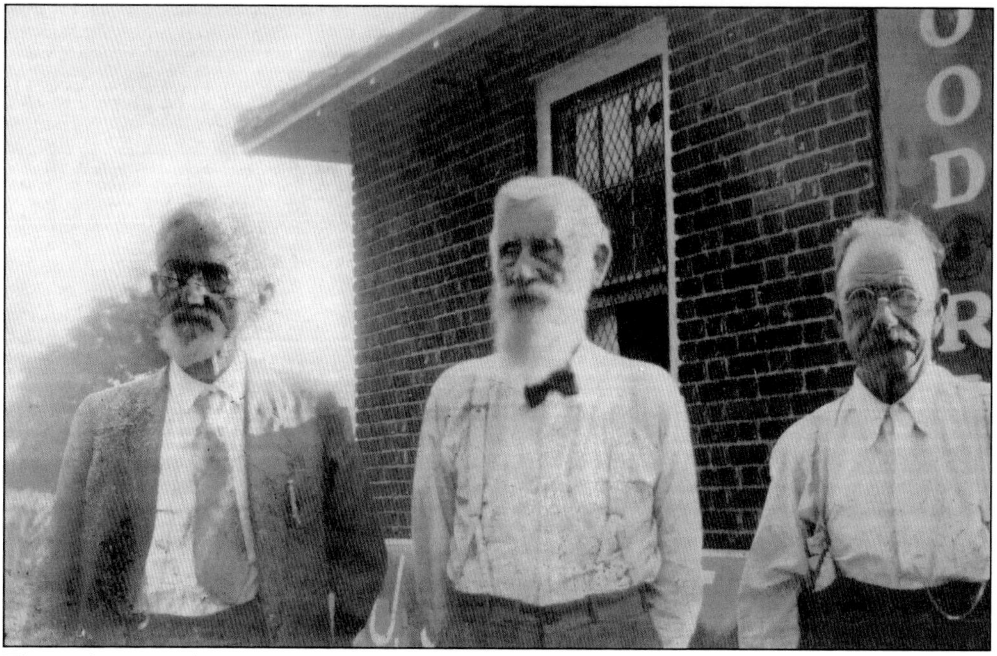

This early-1920s photograph shows, from left to right, Capt. William E. Charles, David Ashby Stuckey, and a Mr. Heriot standing outside Ladson Montgomery's filling station. Captain Charles served as commander of the Inglis Light Artillery (Company D, 2nd South Carolina Artillery) during the Civil War. Stuckey farmed cotton in the Manville section of Lee County for many years. His son, William, was married to Charles's daughter, Lucia. (Lucile Stuckey.)

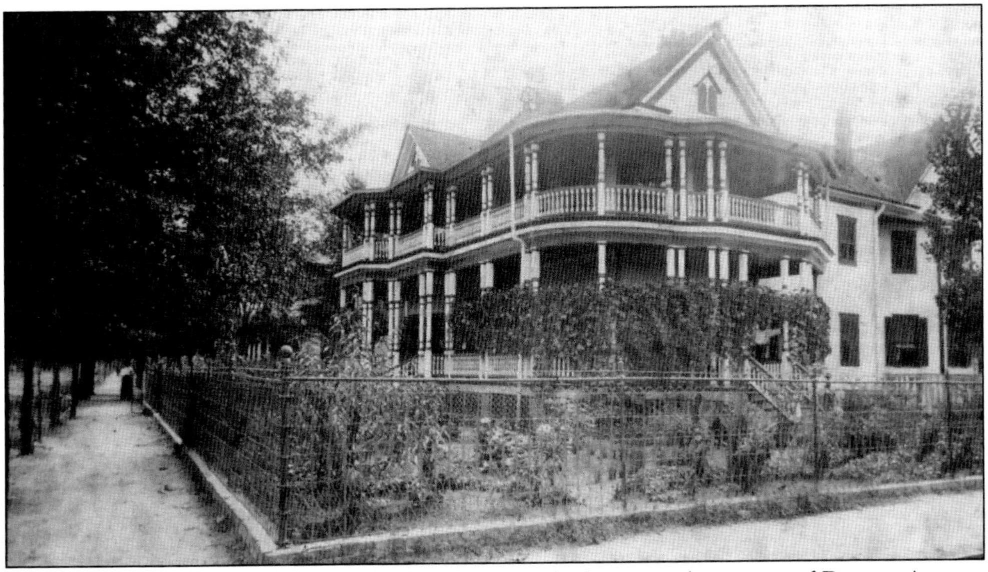

This c. 1900 photograph shows the Durant Hotel, which sat on the corner of Dennis Avenue and West Council Street. Along with the Pioneer Hotel located directly across the street, the Durant was at capacity during the cotton harvest, with buyers traveling from Wilmington (North Carolina), Charleston, and other port cities. At some point between 1910 and 1920, the Durant Hotel was destroyed, and the vacant lot was used to house the tents when the Redpath Chautauqua assembly rolled into town. The tents were hoisted by local boys, who were paid with a ticket to the show. (*Lee County Observer.*)

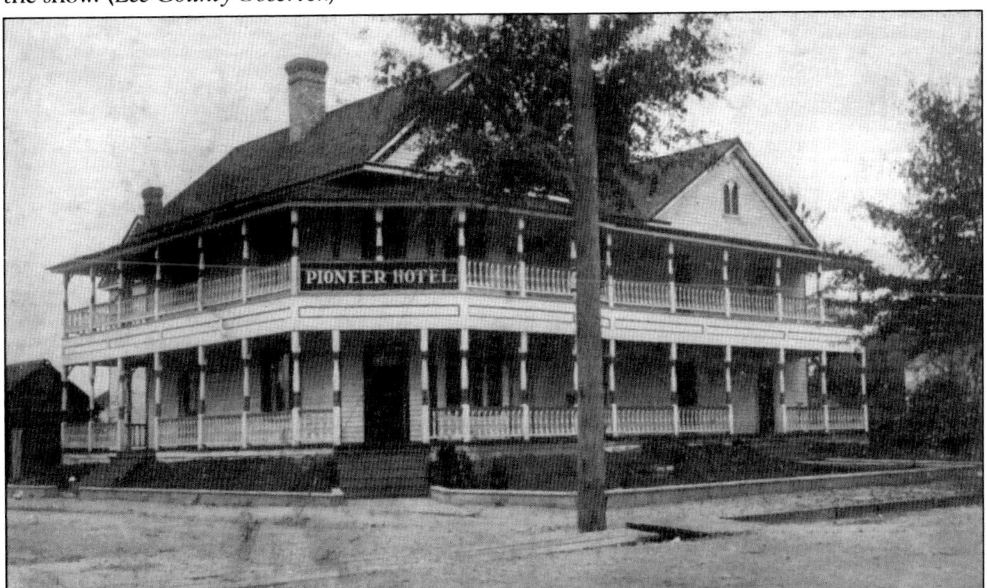

"Big hotels are said to be the 'mud sills' of the success of future towns and cities. We have the house almost completed. 'Let her roll,' gentlemen, we are going to be a city," wrote the editor of the August 15, 1888, edition of the *Bishopville Enterprise* newspaper. The Pioneer Hotel sat opposite the Durant Hotel on Dennis Avenue, and the intersection of West Council Street may be seen in the foreground. Remains of the concrete coping adjacent to the sidewalk and visible in the photograph above remain on the vacant lot that once housed the hotel. (Betty Brown Truesdale.)

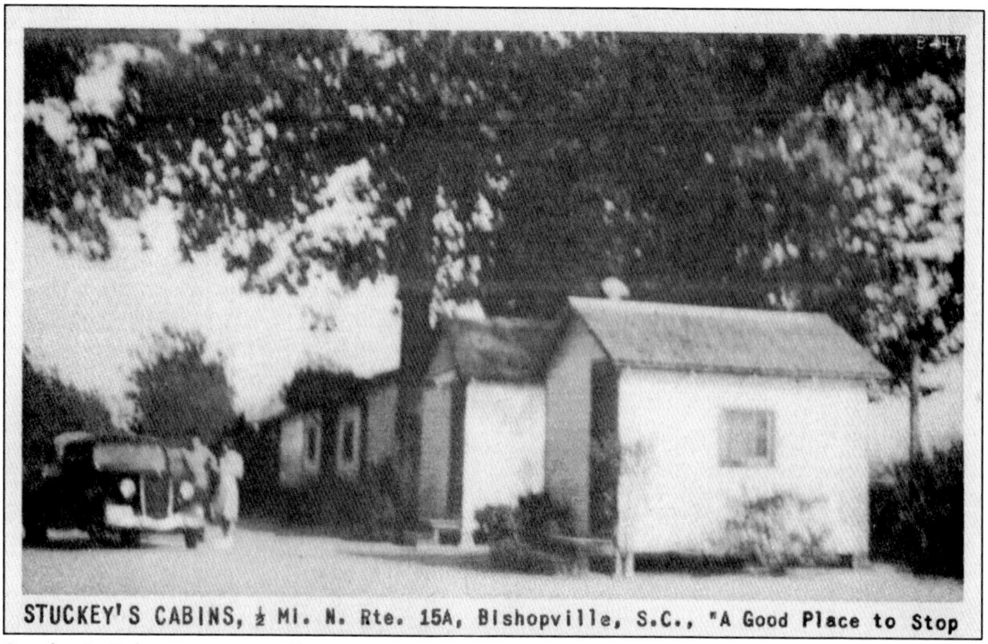

Stuckey's Cabins was a small motor court consisting of individual one-room cabins located on Highway 15 north about a half-mile past Bishopville High School. In the years before the interstate, the highway was a busy route for those traveling from New York to Florida for the winter. Many vacationers drove their trailers south and Stuckey's Cabins—owned and operated by Fred Stuckey and his wife, Maude—was a popular place to rest for the night. Guests could purchase sundries at a little store in the court and could fuel up at the Texaco pump. (SCCM.)

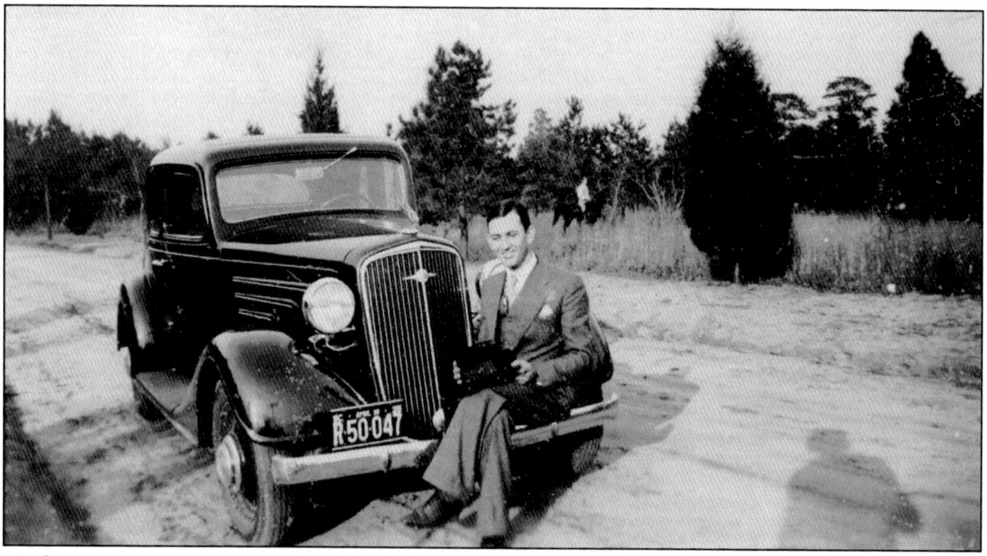

Herbert Cunningham sits on the front of his 1930s sedan in this photograph. Cunningham was a son of William Robert Cunningham. His grandfather, Herbert Shields Cunningham, was founder and editor of the *Lee County Vindicator*, which would eventually become today's *Lee County Observer*. Herbert Cunningham and the former Jewel Parrott had two daughters, Barrie and Pam. In 1976, Cunningham retired as the resident civil engineer of the Bishopville Highway Department. (Barrie Cunningham Hardwick.)

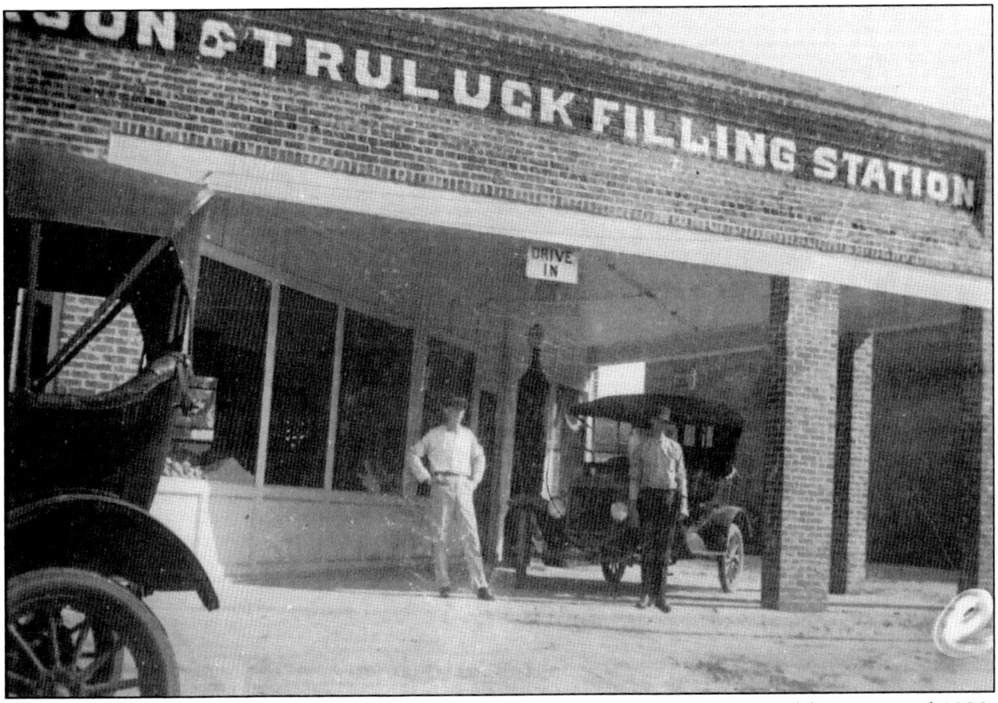

A Model T awaits service at the Hickson and Truluck filling station in Lynchburg around 1920. The increasing popularity of the motorcar presented a new business opportunity for entrepreneurs. Herbert Hickson owned the Hickson share of the business. (Betsy Redick.)

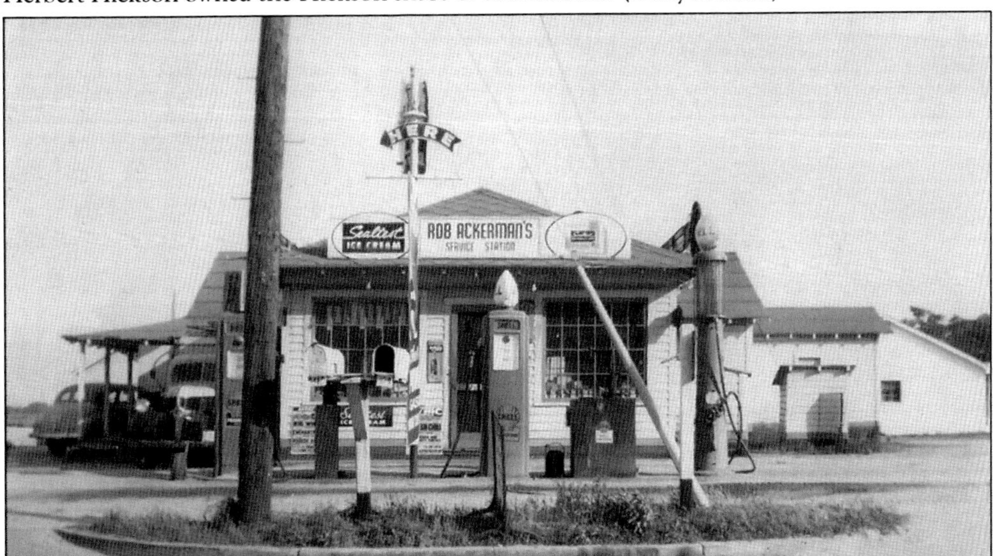

Robert "Doc" Ackerman finished medical school in Charleston and for several years ran the Ackerman Drug Company on Main Street. By the 1930s, he had gotten out of the pharmacy business and operated this service station located at the intersection of Highway 15 South and the St. Charles Road. When Doc was in a car accident in the 1940s, his son-in-law, J. W. Davis, took over the business. After Doc's death in 1954, J. W. sold the station to Darwin Elmore, who ran it for many years. (Wayne Davis.)

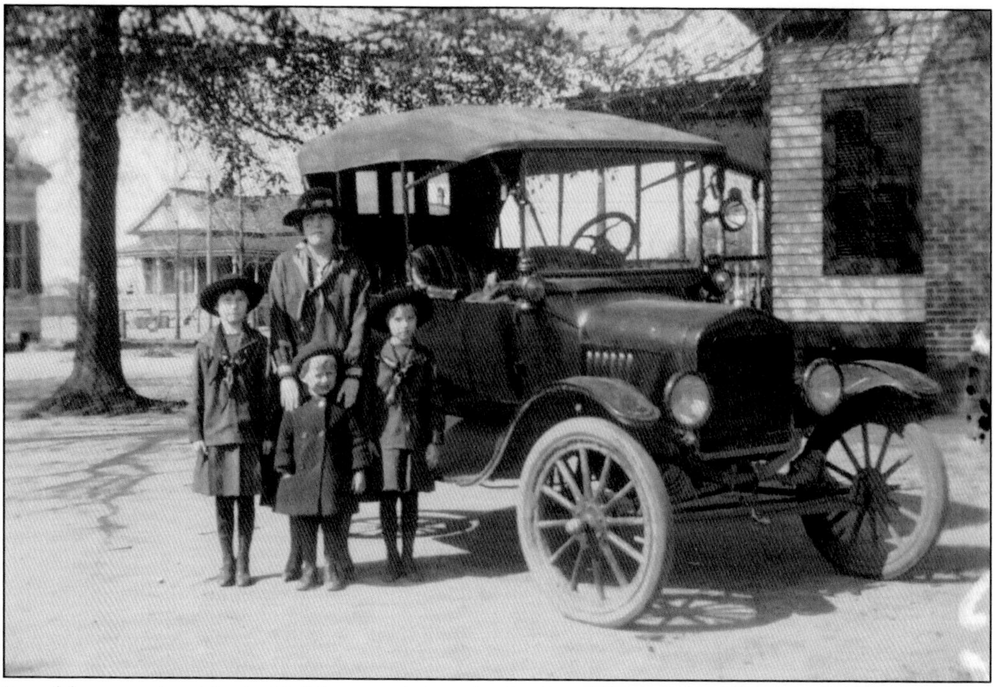

Lynchburg native Carrie Cribbs stands beside the family's Ford Model T with her young son Ashton in front of her. The young girl on the left is Caro Hickson, and the girl on the right is her sister, Annie Mae. The girls' father is businessman and store owner Herbert L. Hickson. (Betsy Redick.)

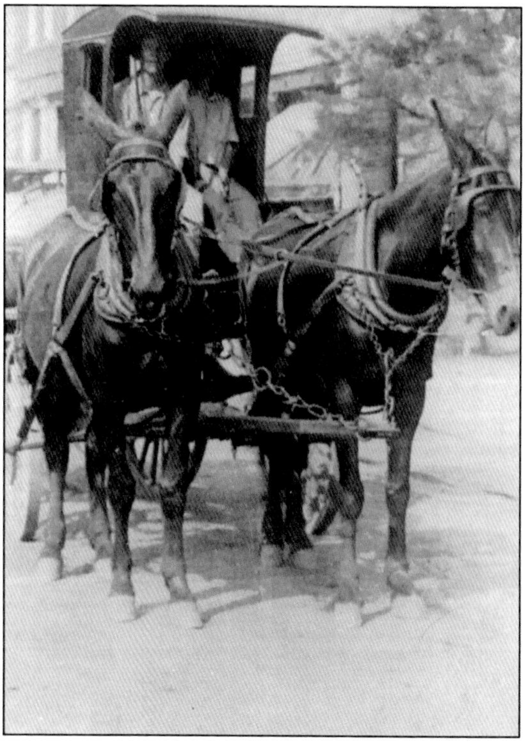

The ice and coal man was essential to the community in the days before electric refrigeration and central heat. Shown at left is Drayton's ice wagon pulling a tank of fuel down Main Street in the 1920s. The ice wagons were seen every morning in the residential district, and some of the horses were smart enough that they would automatically move from house to house while the iceman hauled 100-pound blocks of ice up the sidewalk. In the winter, the same drill would be repeated with coal or other fuel. (*Lee County Observer.*)

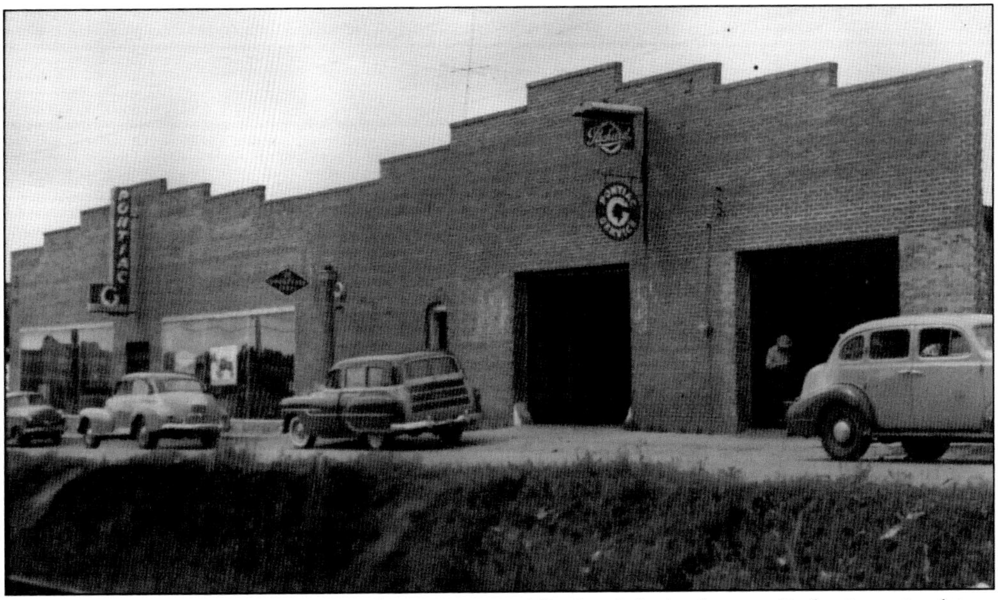

Cars wait for service outside of Traub's Pontiac and Packard dealership on Cedar Lane in this c. 1953 photograph. In 1954, the garage portion of the building with the two bays was converted into Bishopville's A&P grocery store. Over the years, the building has served as Traub's Stables and as a John Deere dealership. Today the portion of the building to the left is recognizable as the South Carolina Cotton Museum. The photograph was taken from the bottom of the railroad bed that used to run to the train depot and stood about one block north of Traub's. (Lee County Public Library.)

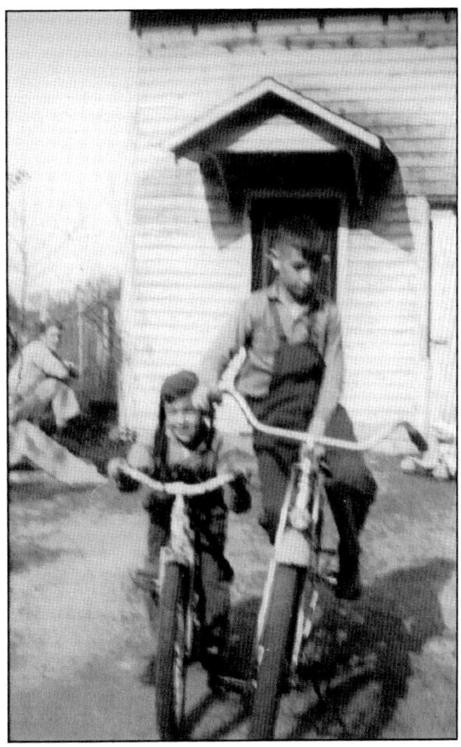

Leo DuBose Jr. and his younger brother, Burnett, ride their bikes behind their home on Harris Street in this 1944 photograph. At the time, their father, Leo DuBose Sr., was owner and pharmacist at McLeod's Pharmacy. Burnett is wearing his aviator cap, which, along with knickers and dungarees, was typical dress for students at the Bishopville Grammar School. In the background sits Buddy Stevenson, whose brother and sister-in-law, David and Martin (Stuckey) Stevenson, were living in the DuBose's garage apartment.

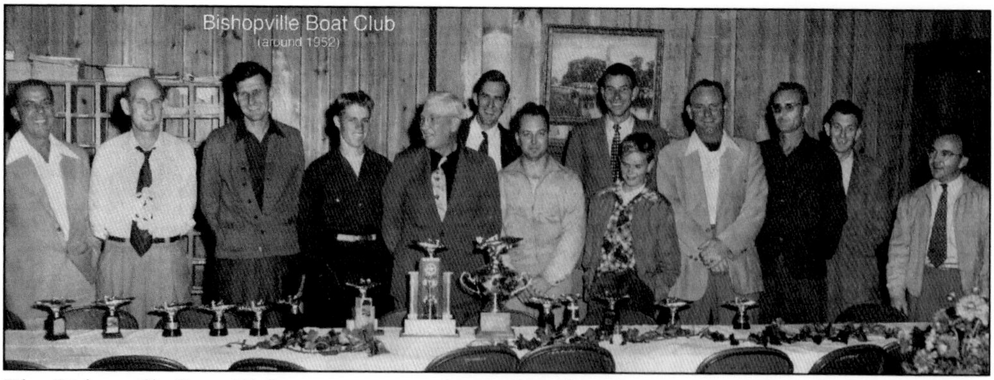

The Bishopville Boat Club was quite popular within the community, and members raced their watercraft all over the state. Many members, like Hal Austin and his brother, Roy, built their own boats. Locally, the men raced at Ashwood Lake, which was a popular spot for swimming and picnics as well. This photograph shows the boat club members in 1952. From left to right, they are (first row) an unidentified member, ? Holloman, and Yah Yah Segars, the youngest member of the club; (second row) an unidentified member, Hal Austin, Roy Austin, an unidentified member, Toby Carnes, Mocus Moore, B. J. Barnett, Jack Berry, Howard Ginsberg, and ? Woodham. (Judith Austin Watkins.)

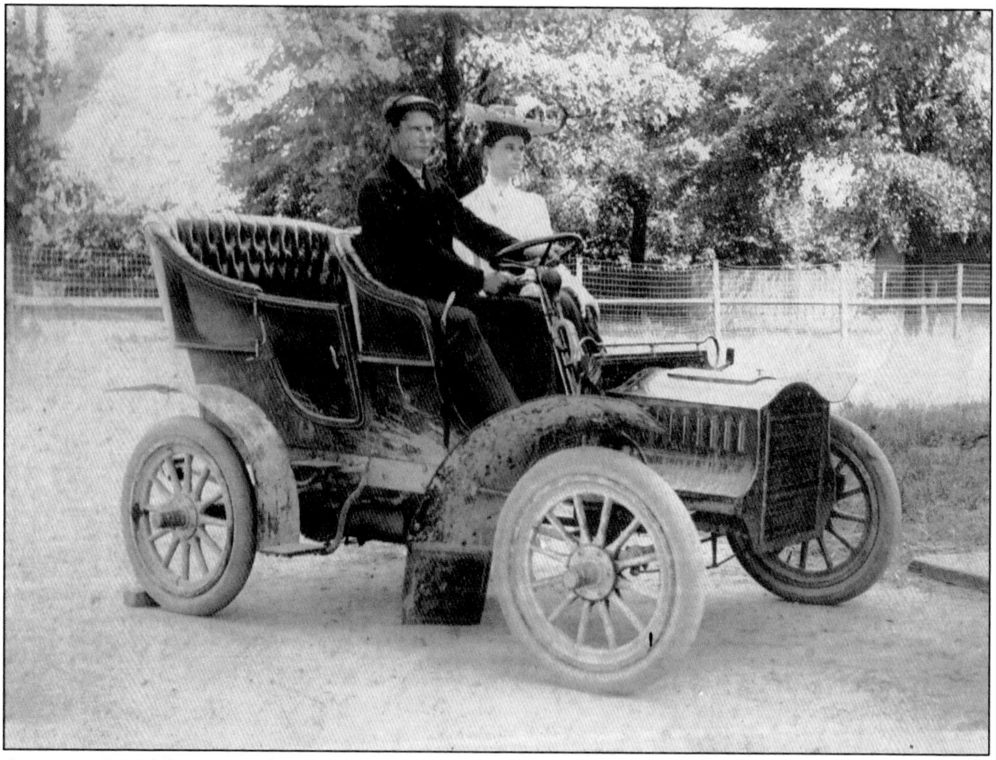

A young Lynchburg couple prepares to go motoring in what appears to be a 1905 Ford Model F. The mud splatters on the side illustrate the need for what were known as dusters, full-length overcoats to protect the rider's clothing from the mud and dust kicked up from the unpaved roads. The parking brake was a mere brick under the rear tire. Nonetheless, the average price of a new Model F was $2,000, roughly $40,000 in today's money, so this gentleman and his friend are unquestionably riding in style. (Betsy Redick.)

BIBLIOGRAPHY

While this list is not exhaustive, much of the information in this book was gathered from the archives of the *Bishopville Mirror, Bishopville Eagle,* and *Lee County Vindicator* and from the following sources:

Austin Jr., Mrs. Hal., et al, eds. *Legends, Superstitions, and Home Remedies by the Good Folks of Lee County.* Lee County Schools and Lee County Arts Council joint project, 1989.

Campbell, Rev. John P. *The Southern Business Directory and General Commercial Advertiser.* Volume I. Charleston: Steam Power Press of Walker and James, 1854.

Hemphill, J. C., ed. *Men of Mark in South Carolina.* Volume Two. Men of Mark Publishing Company, Washington, D.C., 1908.

Lee County Chamber of Commerce. *Lee County, South Carolina, Past and Present.* Volume II. Fine Books Publishing Company, LLC, St. Augustine, Florida, 2002.

Lee County Messenger. August 6, 1970. Volume 69, no. 32.

Lockwood, Thomas P. A *Geography of South Carolina.* Charleston: J. S. Burges, 1832.

Neuffer, Claude Henry, ed. *Names in South Carolina.* Volume 12, no. 10. Winter, 1965.

Rice, William. *Reports of Cases at Law Argued and Determined in the Court of Appeals.* Volume I. From December 1838 to May, 1839, inclusive. Charleston, Burges and James, 1839.

"Seventy-Six-Year-Old Frank Levenson: He Claims Bishopville Merchant 'Deanship.'" The *State.* September 7, 1962. Page 2D.

Simms, William Gilmore. *The Geography of South Carolina.* Babcock and Company, Charleston. 1843.

Snowden, Yates, ed. *History of South Carolina.* Volume Four. The Lewis Publishing Company, Chicago and New York, 1920.